Alive to the Word

Alive to the Word

*A Practical Theology of Preaching for the
Whole Church*

Stephen Wright

scm press

Published in 2010 by SCM Press
Editorial office
13–17 Long Lane,
London, EC1A 9PN, UK

SCM Press is an imprint of Hymns Ancient and Modern Ltd
(a registered charity)
13A Hellesdon Park Road
Norwich NR6 5DR, UK
www.scm-canterburypress.co.uk

British Library Cataloguing in Publication data

A catalogue record for this book is available
from the British Library

978-0-334-04201-3

Originated by The Manila Typesetting Company
Printed and bound by
CPI Antony Rowe, Chippenham SN14 6LH

Contents

Acknowledgements

I was honoured to be approached by Natalie Watson on behalf of SCM Press to write this book. I am most grateful to them for the opportunity, and thank Natalie especially for her encouragement, advice and patience.

I could not have written this book without the wonderfully supportive atmosphere I have enjoyed in what have been the three main dimensions of my life over the last couple of years.

First, in my place of work, Spurgeon's College, London, which has been an environment of rich Christian fellowship and intellectual stimulation. I am grateful for the continued encouragement of the Principal, Nigel Wright, and all my colleagues. I would like especially to mention Peter Stevenson, Roger Standing, Chris Voke, Richard Littledale and John Woods, with whom I have been privileged to share in the teaching and discussion of preaching. In addition, Tim Grass read a draft of Chapter 1 and Pieter Lalleman a draft of Chapter 5, and I am indebted to them for their willingness, care and correction, while of course retaining full responsibility for the chapters as they now stand.

It has been a great privilege to work with a number of postgraduate students on dissertations and theses in the area of preaching over the last decade. They have stimulated my thinking in many areas. Although I have only been able to refer by name to a few in the footnotes, I acknowledge my debt to them all.

It has been a joy to get to know groups of undergraduate students as well, and I am continually refreshed by their love for Christ and for others. I would like especially to mention the two pastoral groups which I have been privileged to lead over the last year or more. I have greatly appreciated their friendship and support, not least as 'the book' has regularly featured in my personal prayer requests.

Second, in my local church, St John the Divine, Selsdon, where I have been continually grounded in the great tradition of faith and spiritually nurtured through regular worship and fellowship. I would like to thank particularly the Rector, Ian Brothwood, for his supportive friendship and thoughtful, biblical, imaginative preaching.

Third, in my family, both immediate and wider, which continues to offer such a secure framework for life and work, which I hope never to take for granted. As always my wife, Linda, has been exemplary in her love and longsuffering.

I write this on Good Friday. Pragmatically, the reason for that is that I have stretched my 'deadline' to breaking point. But as a preacher, I cannot help thinking of Paul's words: 'We preach Christ crucified' (1 Cor. 1.23). Far be it from me to boast except in the Cross of our Lord Jesus Christ, by which the world has been crucified to me, and I to the world (Gal. 6.14). Thanks be to Him.

Lord, how can man preach thy eternall word?
He is a brittle crazie glasse:
Yet in thy temple thou dost him afford
This glorious and transcendent place,
To be a window, through thy grace.

But when thou dost anneal in glasse thy storie,
Making thy life to shine within
The holy Preachers; then the light and glorie
More rev'rend grows, & more doth win:
Which else shows watrish, bleak, & thin.

Doctrine and life, colours and light, in one
When they combine and mingle, bring
A strong regard and aw: but speech alone
Doth vanish like a flaring thing,
And in the eare, not conscience ring.

George Herbert, 'The Windows'

Introduction

My aim in this book is to develop a theological understanding of the Christian ministry of preaching, with a view to encouraging a mature and reflective approach to this historic and contemporary practice of the Church.

The book follows a process of 'practical theology'. In one sense, of course, all theology should be 'practical'. Yet 'practical theology' has become a distinct and important discipline in its own right, which consciously and explicitly reflects on the practices of the Church, or indeed phenomena of the world, seeking to understand them in the light of God's revelation in Christ, and to allow that understanding to inform proposals for more adequate forms of practice. My hope is that the book will be helpful on two levels: first, for the Church as a whole as it continues the debate about what forms of preaching are most adequate to its mission today; but second, for individual churches and preachers who wish to review their own preaching ministry. Pointers as to how the general discussion might be brought to earth in a specific and local review of preaching, or indeed of particular sermons, are included at the end of each chapter.

Each part of the book follows one stage of this practical theological process. For these stages I am indebted to the terminology and descriptions in Richard Osmer's book *Practical Theology* (2008).[1] The first stage is to *describe* the practice of preaching as it has been carried on over two millennia, and as it fulfils particular functions today. This is the 'descriptive–empirical' task, in which the practice or phenomenon to be studied is laid bare as clearly as possible. The second stage is the 'interpretive' one, in which we analyse preaching from the point of view

---

1 Richard R. Osmer, 2008, *Practical Theology: An Introduction*, Grand Rapids: Eerdmans. On the significance of the development of the discipline of practical theology for preaching, see Thomas G. Long, 2005, *The Witness of Preaching*, 2nd edn, Louisville: Westminster John Knox, pp. ix–xi. For preaching as a Christian 'practice' see Thomas G. Long and Leonora Tubbs Tisdale (eds), 2008, *Teaching Preaching as a Christian Practice*, Louisville: Westminster John Knox.

of the human sciences, especially those concerning communication within society. The third stage entails the task of 'prophetic discernment', in which the understanding developed in the previous stage is placed within a theological matrix, with the purpose of discovering how it is that God is involved in this human activity and what norms might follow from this to guide our practice. The fourth and final stage is called the 'pragmatic' one, in which we draw conclusions from this theological discernment for the way in which preaching is to be carried out.

It will become clear that in each stage I can only outline a sample of the questions that are naturally raised by the discussion. As an additional feature at the end of each chapter, I will suggest some possible lines of research on that topic. Research in the area of preaching continues to be much sparser in Britain than it is in North America, and there are many avenues which could be pursued.

Let me highlight three features of the book which are entailed in this attempt to provide a 'practical theology of preaching'.

First, this is a *reflective* book rather than a prescriptive one. The principle here is familiar. A child needs basic boundaries and rules, but as she grows into adulthood, she needs to develop the art of making moral and practical judgements for herself. Everyday life demands that we go on making decisions for which no simple guidelines are sufficient. So it is with learning to hear and speak God's word. There comes a point where we must move beyond the safety of maxims and structures which served us so well as a foundation, into the less charted territory of taking responsibility for our own listening and voicing. Important as it is to have basic instruction and guidelines in preaching (for which a number of excellent books are available),[2] not least for those just setting out on the journey, it is even more vital that we should grow in the ability to consider our task maturely and creatively for ourselves.

In fact there is a great practical difficulty for anyone who does try to offer prescriptive advice about preaching today, which is simply that the Christian 'community' and its practices (not to mention the individuals who inhabit them) are so diverse. Many books on preaching run the risk of addressing one particular segment of that 'community' but leave others feeling 'this isn't me' or, especially, 'this isn't us'. They may thus serve a particular denomination or tradition well, but reinforce a sense that each stream of church life must course through its own well-formed channel without being allowed to feed into the others, and form larger rivers that do a better job of irrigating the land

---

2 For example, David Day, 1998, *A Preaching Workbook*, London: SPCK.

or empowering its people. This is unfortunate at a time when there is, in fact, a good deal of 'breaking the banks', of merging of streams. For example, many Anglican services would be quite unrecognizable as 'Anglican' to many of that denomination thirty or fifty years ago (and indeed today!), so much have they adopted styles, patterns and moods that would previously have been associated with the less formal end of 'Free Church' life. At the same time, fascinatingly, many of those in the Free Churches are rediscovering the wealth of 'catholic' tradition, for instance in liturgical structures, the use of symbol in worship, and sacramental understandings of word and ministry.[3] A part of what is indicated by terms such as 'emerging church', 'deep church' or 'ancient–future church' is impatience with old distinctions and a readiness to be eclectic in the communal expressions of Christian life.[4] I want this book to serve precisely this fascinating contemporary reality of a Church whose contours are not as familiar as once they were. That means, now like perhaps never before, that serious guidance cannot mean prescriptive guidance; listening for and uttering the word of God is bound to take different and often unexpected forms in different places.

Second, this aims to be a *theological* book, not a merely pragmatic one. It recognizes that the fundamental meaning of our life, out of which all our practices and behaviour emerge, is a meaning shaped by God our Creator and Redeemer. All we do is to be understood *theologically*, and our lives are a perpetual ebb and flow between God-inspired action and God-directed reflection. Above all, surely, this must be so when we consider the very activities through which we seek most visibly and specifically to pay attention to what God has said and is saying. Without understanding the event of preaching *theologically*, our 'wisdom' descends to mere 'communication skills' or even advertising techniques, and we have no way in which to grapple with either the meaning or the practical implications of an activity through which we hope and pray that *God himself* will speak.

---

3 See for example Ian G. Stackhouse, 2004, *The Gospel-Driven Church: Retrieving Classical Ministry for Contemporary Revivalism*, Milton Keynes: Paternoster; John E. Colwell, 2005, *Promise and Presence: An Exploration of Sacramental Theology*, Milton Keynes: Paternoster.

4 On these developments see, for instance, Eddie Gibbs and Ryan Bolger, 2006, *Emerging Churches: Creating Christian Communities in Postmodern Cultures*, London: SPCK; Andrew Walker and Luke Bretherton (eds), 2007, *Remembering Our Future: Explorations in Deep Church*, Milton Keynes: Paternoster; Robert E. Webber, 2008, *Ancient-Future Worship: Proclaiming and Enacting God's Narrative*, Grand Rapids: Baker.

This does not mean that the insights of 'the world' concerning communication are to be rejected or ignored. On the contrary, they are taken very seriously, since the world is created by God and despite its fallenness, continues to reflect something of his wisdom. The wisdom literature of the Old Testament displays this readiness to draw on observation of 'the way the world works' in order to instruct people in the wisdom of Yahweh, the Creator. Thus in Part 2 we seek 'wisdom' related to preaching in a variety of disciplines of thought, while in Part 3 we seek to evaluate what we have found in the light of an explicit theological framework.

Third, this book is for the *Church* and not only for preachers. The task of discerning how God may be directing us within and through the community of Christian faith, so that we live out our lives with God-shaped meaning and focus, surely belongs to the Church as a whole. Certainly I envisage that many readers will be either experienced preachers, who want to review their ministry in some depth, or students of preaching who have moved beyond the foundational stage to a position of greater critical reflection on the practice. However, a noticeable and welcome feature of church life across the spectrum today is a readiness to widen responsibility for the Church's fundamental task of attending to the word of God. More people are being given opportunity to voice that word in public – with or without some official authorization. There is a hunger, in some quarters at least, for smaller, more informal gatherings in which the Scriptures may be studied, insights shared, God's will sought, and some serious theological learning may take place. 'Believers' learn to be honest about their doubts and questions and 'non-believers' feel safe acknowledging theirs. In such an atmosphere, there is no place for a 'preacher' in the familiar sense, yet the word of God has not been silenced. Some would say it has been liberated. It does not, therefore, make sense to me to design a book such as this for 'preachers' in a narrowly defined way. There is a rediscovery in all sorts of churches that it is God's people as a whole who have responsibility for discerning God's word, in all sorts of ways.

Even when we consider the activity of preaching as traditionally understood, it is vital for others *as well as* preachers to think through what it means and how it is to be done. On the one hand, there are those who regularly listen to sermons. In vital ways, the meaningfulness of the event depends on them as much as on the preacher.[5] A renewal of

---

5 See David J. Schlafer, 1992, *Surviving the Sermon: A Guide for those who have to Listen*, Cambridge, MA: Cowley; 2004, *Playing with Fire: Preaching Work as Kindling Art*,

the preaching ministry in forms appropriate to today's cultures will surely entail a much fuller 'owning' of the event by churches than has often been the case. On the other hand, there are those responsible for the selection, training, oversight, mentoring and support of those exercising a preaching ministry. Many of these people will of course be preachers themselves, but many will not, nor need they be. They do, however, need sufficient theological equipping to carry out their task with diligence and effectiveness. I hope, then, that this book will be of interest to a range of people within the churches – and even to some who would not consider themselves part of any 'church', but take a sincere interest in its role within society, and may, perhaps, be among the prophets through whom the Church may hear God's voice.

At the outset of the book I want to acknowledge that I bring my own experiences of preaching and listening, of learning and teaching, of encouraging and being encouraged, to the task. I bring also the channels of spiritual and intellectual life which have formed both my perspectives and, no doubt, my prejudices: I am involved, not detached. As I reflect on some of these channels, I smile at God's sense of humour and those surprise reversals which are so characteristic a feature of how he reminds us of his sovereignty and of our dependence on his grace. I will mention three such paradoxes.

First, there has been the surprise of call. I still remember the terror of my first public speaking engagement: when I was asked by my teacher, aged eight or nine, to say a word of thanks to a visiting speaker in front of my classmates. It was at short notice, and I had no idea what was expected. As I recall, the teacher relented (perhaps having noticed my confusion), and I was allowed to go up to the visitor and convey the thanks in private. I thank God for the amazing privilege of being called to preach, and for building my confidence, but also for constantly reminding me that I could never do it apart from dependence on him.

Second, there has been the surprise of denomination. An Anglican born and bred, as an adult I have always deeply valued this heritage as a home in which evangelical faith, biblical spirituality, catholic sensibility and intellectual freedom may flourish. Yet for the longest period of my working life I have been based in a Baptist community, which I have discovered to be most conducive to the very same things, with – of course – a distinctive twist. Such is the twinkling of the kaleidoscope of God's people.

Cambridge, MA: Cowley; Roger E. Van Harn, 2005, *Preacher, Can You Hear Us Listening?*, Grand Rapids: Eerdmans.

Third, there has been the surprise of academic specialism. After three years' intensive research in New Testament studies, I found myself in a job which entailed the teaching and training of preachers. Now that I have the special joy of teaching *both* preaching and New Testament, I can look back and see what an unexpected, gracious enrichment by God it has been to have spent over a decade focused on the strange and oft-despised vocation and event of preaching. I truly feel as if nothing has been lost in that time, and much has been gained.

This is something of the particular mixture of experience I bring to this book, but I am very conscious that it owes far more to the giants, past and present, on whose shoulders I stand. Although there will certainly be serious explorers of preaching to whom I do not attend as they deserve, I trust that the process which follows will act at least as a map of the territory, and that preachers and others will be helped and refreshed as they explore the land it seeks to open up.

Stephen I. Wright

Spurgeon's College, London
Holy Week 2010

PART I

Introduction

In the first part of the book, we will examine the variety of events which we call 'preaching'. We cannot begin the task of analysing preaching, discussing its theological foundations, or exploring how it should be practised in the Church today, without some overview of *what* it is exactly that we are talking about.

Osmer describes this stage of the reflection process as 'The Descriptive-Empirical Task: Priestly Listening'.[1] Having 'listened' not just to sermons, but (as it were) to the preaching ministry as a whole for a number of years, I offer in this part a framework in which preachers, and others, can themselves *listen* to what is occurring in the event of preaching, so that they may then go on to interpret it, evaluate it through a theological matrix, and allow this to lead into practical steps of development.

In the following two chapters, then, I attempt a description of preaching which is broad enough to 'catch' the full range of activities which may helpfully bear that label, yet focused enough to exclude activities which are best regarded as 'preaching' in only a metaphorical or extended sense. This is more difficult than it may sound! *Defining* 'preaching' is notoriously tricky, and rather than offering a definition that is bound to include too much or too little, it is better to offer a 'thick' *description* which at least does some justice to the variety of actual practice. Any study, however, must have boundaries: these are the four I have set myself.

First, I focus on *Christian* preaching. In a multi-religious culture, this should not be taken for granted, and the fact that others also 'preach' will be part of the cultural context to be noted in Chapter 2. It is beyond my scope, however, to offer any analysis or evaluation (still less, advice!) concerning the preaching of other great world faiths.

Second, I focus on preaching as Christian *speech*. This needs to be said, because in any discussion of preaching, sooner or later someone

---

1 Osmer, *Practical Theology*, pp. 31–78.

I

will quote the (supposed) words of Francis of Assisi: 'Preach the gospel at all times. If necessary, use words.' Regarding this saying, I share the sentiments of Leanne Van Dyk in a discussion of the Trinitarian basis of preaching:

> I have always reacted negatively at some visceral level to that little maxim for theological reasons connected with this topic of Trinity and proclamation. Although the saying affirms the proclamation of visible actions, it diminishes the proclamation of speech and completely misses the integration and common Trinitarian basis of both.[2]

As will become clear, I too regard the integration of word and action in Christian mission as absolutely fundamental. But with Van Dyk, I regard it as completely proper to focus at times on Christian *speech*, provided one makes this necessary integration clear. Indeed, without such a focus, there is a great danger that we will not think adequately or Christianly about a vital aspect not only of our Christian mission but also of our human calling. And without such a focus, this would have to be a book on mission, not on preaching, and the attempt to do some 'adequate and Christian thinking' on Christian *speech* would be aborted.

Third, I focus on *public* Christian speech. The word 'preaching' is sometimes used loosely to describe (often pejoratively) one-to-one address, whether this be Christian evangelism or some more general kind of (usually unwelcome) exhortation. Again, to encompass such 'preaching' in this book would simply cast the net too wide; it would become a book on evangelism in general. On the other hand, I do not want to foreclose debate about what 'public' might mean today – when, some might argue, the airwaves and internet are more genuinely 'public' space than a church building or even an open square.

Fourth, I focus on public Christian speech *on behalf of the Church*. My first three boundaries would still allow the inclusion of (say) a Christian politician arguing a case in Parliament, shaped by Christian principles. Such events, like embodied mission and one-to-one evangelism, are important expressions of Christian witness. Their exclusion

---

2 Leanne Van Dyk, 2009, 'The Church's Proclamation as a Participation in God's Mission', in Daniel J. Treier and David Lauber (eds), *Trinitarian Theology for the Church: Scripture, Community, Worship*, Downers Grove, IL Nottingham: InterVarsity Press VP Academic/Apollos, pp. 225–36, here p. 232. Fans of Francis can be reassured that according to Van Dyk, he almost certainly never made the famous comment!

from attention here is by no means a denial of that importance, simply a recognition that any subject can get too big for helpful practical learning. By saying 'on behalf of the Church' I am not presupposing that the preaching I discuss is necessarily 'official', or that it takes place in a church building, or that a specific local congregation or wider Church body is somehow directly engaged with or supportive of it. In view of the rise in electronic media, I am not presupposing, either, that it is always a face-to-face event. This fourth boundary simply indicates that (unlike the case of the Christian politician in Parliament, or the general blogger offering opinions on a range of topics) its purpose is to advance and advocate, in some sense, the knowledge and practice of the faith to which mainstream Christianity bears witness.

Within these boundaries, however, a rich and broad spread of preaching has been and continues to be embraced. In this part of the book I offer a description that encompasses three central social dynamics of preaching in the past (Chapter 1) and four key functions that it fulfils in the present (Chapter 2). This will be an important prelude to the subsequent Parts in which we will seek to interpret what is going on in preaching, assess its theological significance, and ponder the implications for how we do it.

I

The Historical Phenomenon of Preaching

Preaching has a rich and varied history. This cannot be recounted here, but in this chapter I want to describe three social settings of preaching which seem together to gather up a very wide range of practices within the boundaries I identified in the introduction to this part of the book. Here and in the next chapter I am considering external phenomena of preaching, the way in which it connects to the world both of Christian activity and secular activity; an 'internal' account of how the style and content of preaching have varied and continue to vary is beyond my scope.[1]

None of these social settings is limited to a particular time or place, but each brings together (with inevitable blurring of differences) movements in preaching that are held together by a common dynamic in relation to the wider society where they are found. History is always a lot messier than our analysis of it, and I am well aware that in presenting these three models I am oversimplifying considerably. Nevertheless, as a broad-brush way of describing the phenomenon of preaching, I find this categorization helpful.

The first setting is a Christian community, maybe marginal and often small, gathered together in celebration and reinforcement of their identity, while someone – the 'preacher' – leads them in the recollection of their story, teaching and encouraging them on the basis of their Scriptures. This setting encompasses groups as diverse as the early Christian house churches, fellowships emerging from the radical Reformation,

---

1 For a recent account of older approaches to preaching style, see Jonathan Hustler, 2009, *Making the Words Acceptable: the Shape of the Sermon in Christian History*, London: Epworth. See also the classic account of Charles Smyth, 1940, *The Art of Preaching: Preaching in the Church of England 747–1939*, London: SPCK. Smyth's account is of relevance to the Church much wider than Anglicanism, especially in that nearly the first half of the book is devoted to the pre-Reformation period. My main historiographical reference-point in this chapter is O. C. Edwards Jr, 2004, *A History of Preaching*, Nashville: Abingdon. References below are to vol. 1. Vol. 2 consists of extracts from sermons and writings on homiletics, and is contained on a CD ROM within vol. 1.

and the liturgical assemblies of modern Catholicism. The second setting is that of the officially recognized (or at least socially acceptable) Christian church in which a spokesperson has a platform to address not only the congregation immediately gathered but also, to some extent, the wider populace, and in some cases their rulers. Under this umbrella comes the preaching of the Christendom era, whether Catholic, Orthodox or Protestant: an era now on the wane, yet still offering such a platform in many places. The third setting is beyond the physical walls enclosing a gathered community, whether marginal or central. Here are included sometimes unlikely bedfellows such as medieval friars, eighteenth- and nineteenth-century revivalists, and twentieth-century 'crusade' evangelists such as Billy Graham or 'social gospel' figures such as Donald Soper.

Community interpretation

The first setting is that of *community interpretation*. This is preaching in which the Church is reminded of its identity, taught in the truths of its faith, instructed in discipleship and encouraged in witness. It is focused on those who identify themselves as part of the covenant people of God as he is known in Jesus Christ.

The distinguishing mark of this setting for preaching, which I argue gives it unity despite the diversity of its representatives, is this essential focus on a gathered community of believers. The early examples are the preaching which took place within the worship of the pre-Constantinian Church, when the distinction between 'Church' and 'State' remained sharp. Congregations might have been small or large, but they were recognizably set apart from the population as a whole. Their need was for teaching which strengthened this sense of a shared story and a distinct calling. Surviving homilies from this period include the striking Passover sermon of Melito of Sardis, underlining (to the extent of some unfortunate anti-Judaism) the separation of Christian identity from Jewish,[2] and the learned exegeses of Origen.[3]

The dawn of 'Christendom' with Constantine's establishment of Christianity as the official religion of the Roman Empire produced an inevitable change in the focus of preaching. The words spoken in the Christian gathering were immediately more 'public' in the sense that

---

2 Edwards, *History*, pp. 17–21.
3 Edwards, *History*, pp. 32–46.

their challenge and implications applied not only to a gathered community, but also to the wider polity now being oriented (in theory at least) on Christian lines. Not everyone might in fact be gathered in the basilicas to hear them, but everyone lived under a regime in which these words now represented reigning orthodoxy rather than minority testimony. We will consider the dynamics of such preaching in the next section. I mention the shift here because it explains the interesting differences in time, place and style among the other examples of the 'community interpretation' model which I will mention.

First we might cite preaching in a monastic community, such as that which has survived from Bede.[4] Speaking broadly, one might say that as the Church in 'Christendom' became more 'public', and as its borders became more fuzzy, the option of a monastic life in which one could, while remaining part of this Church, lead a life of serious holy separation to God became more attractive for the committed believer. This was not self-indulgent reclusiveness, but a genuine quest for God. That quest is reflected in the devotional emphasis of medieval monastic sermons such as those of Bernard of Clairvaux on the Song of Songs.[5] In the seventeenth and eighteenth centuries, there is a parallel to monastic preaching in Pietist preaching, especially in that, like the monks, Pietists 'often functioned as an order within the church'.[6]

A more radical manifestation of a strong community orientation to preaching is found in the groups of the radical reformation such as the Anabaptists. Here again is the key mark of a desire for separation and holiness, not for its own sake but as an authentic expression of the way of Christ in the world. If monastic preaching could be seen as an expression of the desire to gather a community for serious teaching out of the widening number of the baptized, some of the radical reformers seem to have practised a 'congregational hermeneutic' in which the role of the appointed leader or preacher was itself considerably diminished in favour of discussion, discernment and mutual correction by the congregation.[7] This may be seen as a rejection of the autonomous

4 Edwards, *History*, pp. 147–8.

5 I am indebted to Tim Grass for his comments on this point: private communication, 5 January 2010. See also Edwards, *History*, pp. 191–2.

6 Tim Grass, private communication, 5 January 2010.

7 Stuart Murray, 2000, *Biblical Interpretation in the Anabaptist Tradition*, Kitchener, Ontario: Pandora Press, pp. 157–85. Edwards writes: 'Anabaptist gatherings probably consisted of informal teaching, prayer, and mutual exhortation in which many participated. Holy Communion was also held frequently. The centrality of preaching in Reformation worship grows out of an assumption that many church members were unconverted, an assumption the Anabaptists did not make.' Edwards, *History*, p. 323 n. 15.

individualism of the so-called 'Spiritualist' groups, of submission to ecclesiastical tradition in Catholicism, and also of the mainstream Reformers' continued dependence on doctrinal formulae and theological scholarship.[8] Stuart Murray comments interestingly on the absence of pulpits in places of Anabaptist worship:

> Church architecture plays a large role in how congregations operate. Typical state churches were designed to allow the speaker to be seen and heard clearly. Anabaptist meetings, in woods, caves, boats, homes, and open fields, lacked such influential symbolic restrictions. Multiple participation is much more likely in such settings, especially when ecclesiological perspectives support it. Indeed, these widely held convictions make it hard to imagine communal hermeneutics being marginal.[9]

Heirs to this tradition of 'preaching' (better, perhaps, 'non-preaching') remain to this day and have an important testimony in an age suspicious of authority.[10]

This 'community interpretation' approach of the early Christians, monks, Pietists and radical reformers also joins hands with some more familiar and 'mainstream' settings of preaching today. While monasticism, notwithstanding its 'separated' character, had often been a pillar of Christendom, more contemporary 'community interpretation' approaches are marked by a sense that to some degree Christendom is to be resisted.[11] Thus the preaching of many Free Churches is clearly focused on the needs of that particular gathered community. It may take a range of forms – from detailed exegesis of Scripture, to inspiring exhortation and encouragement, to the exercise of strategic pastoral leadership – but it has this in common, that it is addressed to the needs and calling of the Church as a specific called-out group of God's people in the world.[12] Strikingly, however, the Roman Catholic Church in Britain (as well as the smaller Orthodox Churches) can also be included under this model, as groups seeking to maintain their identity over against the reigning establishment. An important historical antecedent here is the loss of temporal power by the Roman Catholic Church in

---

8 Murray, *Biblical Hermeneutics*, pp. 157–9.
9 Murray, *Biblical Hermeneutics*, p. 172.
10 See for instance the material on the website http://www.anabaptistnetwork.com
11 My thanks to Tim Grass, private communication, 5 January 2010, for this distinction.
12 See Christopher J. Ellis, 2004, *Gathering: A Theology and Spirituality of Worship in Free Church Tradition*, London: SCM.

the nineteenth century, leading to the centralization of authority in the Papacy and the conception of the Church as an alternative society.[13] No less than in Baptist churches or Brethren assemblies, Roman Catholic preaching seeks to nurture the faithful in their particular calling as members of the Church, whether through liturgical preaching linked to the regular celebration of the sacrament, or the catechetical preaching which prepares and instructs new communicants or converts.[14]

Speaking to the nations

The dawn, dominance and decline of 'Christendom' remain controversial subjects, and analysis of this phenomenon remains (fortunately!) outside the scope of this book. It is vital, however, to underline its crucial importance for understanding the function and setting of preaching through many of the centuries and locations of Christian history. For the central impulse of Christian preaching has always been to communicate the faith *now*, in the social contexts of the particular time and place, for the people who participate in them. Thus whatever we think of Christendom, this has been the social setting in which many Christian preachers have been called to work.

When Christianity is seen as a publicly acceptable faith, those who preach it have both wider scope and a more delicate and dangerous responsibility than those who operate within the walls of a settled, gathered community. On the one hand, there is the opportunity to address not only individuals and Christian communities, but also the societies of which they are a part and whose structures deeply shape those individuals' and communities' lives. There is the opportunity to work towards the transformation of those societies.[15] There is the opportunity to speak to rulers as well as the ruled, indeed to call those rulers to account. Testimony

---

13 On this latter point, I am indebted to Tim Grass, private communication, 5 January 2010. See 'Ultramontanism', in F. L. Cross (ed.), 1958, *The Oxford Dictionary of the Christian Church*, London: Oxford University Press, p. 1387.

14 See Duncan Macpherson, 'Preaching in the Roman Catholic Ecclesial Context', in Geoffrey Stevenson (ed.), 2010, *The Future of Preaching*, London: SCM, pp. 27–33. Interestingly, on the day I was writing this (27 February 2009) it was mooted publicly that the retiring head of the Roman Catholic Church in England and Wales, Cardinal Cormac Murphy O'Connor, might enter the House of Lords. He has since done so, as the first Catholic bishop to become an 'establishment' representative of this kind since the Reformation. Free Church leaders such as Leslie Griffiths have already been honoured in this way.

15 'Christ the transformer of culture' was the fifth model of the relationship of Church to culture outlined by Niebuhr in his classic study: H. Richard Niebuhr, 1951, *Christ and Culture*, New York: Harper & Row, pp. 190–229.

to all this is borne by the sheer size of the basilicas built to accommodate the newly enlarged congregations. Even those who were not present would have felt the influence of what was taught there as it shaped, in various ways, the ideology and practice of the empire. The preaching giants of the early Christendom era, Chrysostom and Augustine, exemplify the enormous influence such preaching may exercise.[16]

Edwards summarizes well the nature of preaching under such a régime, referring to the major religious and social reforms across Europe instigated by the Emperor Charlemagne in the ninth century: 'A major goal of promoting preaching in the Carolingian reform was socializing new peoples into the Christian faith.'[17] Later, a quintessential example of this kind of preaching was that which became central to the life of Geneva under the leadership of John Calvin.[18] The fact that converted and unconverted were gathered in churches presented a huge opportunity. 'Those to whom [Calvin] preached were, he believed, either in a fearful plight under the wrath of God for their sin, or they were believers who needed to be encouraged and urged to strain every effort to arrive at the salvation which was theirs in heaven.'[19] The Evangelical preaching of the eighteenth century and later also owed much to the 'Christendom' context in which it was born.[20]

An adjustment in the focus and tone of preaching is natural when its setting moves from 'community interpretation' to the 'public speech' of Christendom. With a much larger group of people, one can probably assume much less in prior knowledge of the faith and the Scriptures. When, by and large, baptism as a mark of 'belonging' to Christ and his people precedes an articulate understanding of the elements of Christian 'belief' or deliberate Christian 'behaviour', there will be a lot of groundwork to lay and go on laying as new generations enter the Church's life. Thus in early medieval Britain, for a populace which had been 'Christianized' yet remained largely untaught, Aelfric led the way in a revival of catechetical preaching – not simply for 'catechumens', for that group was now largely non-existent since the rise of infant baptism, but rather for all the people.[21] It became all the more crucial

16 See Edwards, *History*, pp. 72–87 (Chrysostom), 100–16 (Augustine).

17 Edwards, *History*, p. 166.

18 Edwards, *History*, pp. 312–13.

19 T. H. L. Parker, 1947, *The Oracles of God: An Introduction to the Preaching of John Calvin*, London and Redhill: Lutterworth, pp. 75–6, cited in Edwards, *History*, p. 319.

20 Tim Grass, private communication, 5 January 2010; he also points out that Orthodoxy also has noted exponents of such 'renewal' preaching within Christendom, for example St Symeon the New Theologian or St John of Kronstadt.

21 Edwards, *History*, pp. 166–7.

that such instruction should take place, lest the very notion of what it means to be 'Christian' should get so watered down as to be meaningless. This, of course, is exactly what the critics of Christendom, with a degree of justification, say has happened over the centuries. However, this does not mean that we can write off the preachers, famous and unknown, who over the Christendom years have faithfully striven to explain and expound the Gospel to crowds great and small. There have been many preachers, from Augustine and Chrysostom via Luther and Calvin down to the distinguished representatives of 'established' churches in our own day, such as Rowan Williams, Archbishop of Canterbury, who have put heart and soul into the task of proclaiming and teaching Christ not only for a gathered community, but for the wider population.

The huge advantage of preaching within a 'Christendom' situation is that it can encourage one to give full voice to the hopeful and inclusive nature of the gospel. When Christians do not have their backs to the wall, when they have not been pressed into an 'us and them' mentality (as, sadly, they often have been, especially by each other), their words can be outgoing, as water to the thirsty in heart, as well as fibre for the weak in body, mind or morals. They can use the favourable position of their faith within society as a sign and means of the progressive transformation of that society by God, who in Christ has begun a new creation. They can welcome hearers of all kinds as those within the scope of God's gracious purposes, rather than dividing them mentally (if not actually verbally) into those who are 'in' and those who are automatically excluded by belief, lifestyle, background or family identity.

In Britain, this is an opportunity afforded not only in that last vestige of Christendom, the Church of England, but also in most of the other churches too. Though some may indeed, on many occasions (and with perfectly good reason) focus on interpreting the faith for the gathered community, most benefit from the fact that Christendom is at once dying and yet still hugely influential. There is little detectable nationwide predisposition in favour of the established church rather than any other, yet the fact that Christianity has been central to the life of our islands for so long makes 'church' – of whatever kind – still a safe and attractive place for many, at least on some occasions. This gives the preacher the challenge and opportunity of making every preaching occasion one where the 'outsider' who chooses to come in will hear genuine good news.

In the USA the situation is subtly but markedly different (a difference which perhaps largely accounts, more than linguistic reasons, for the necessity of some 'translation' when some American books on preaching are applied to the British context). No US church is 'established'; thus the American churches remain more distanced from the centres of state power than those in Britain.[22] However, churchgoing is far more popular and socially acceptable in the USA than in Britain.

This highlights twin advantages and disadvantages. The advantage of the British situation is that in principle the channels remain open from the Church and its preachers into society as a whole. The disadvantage is that the Church may still be perceived as over-entwined with official structures (structures which maybe, like the House of Lords, enjoy questionable status in the nation at large), or indeed with 'authority' as such. The advantage of the American situation is that it is probably much easier to go to church or invite others to do so; attending a church of one's free choice is, after all, the original expression of that freedom which is foundational to the American ideal. The disadvantage is that it is perhaps less 'instinctive' for preachers to address directly the structures of their society, or their congregations as potential transformers of that society; it is too easy to retreat into a 'safe' community of like-minded believers, and effectively to 'baptize' the existing social order.[23]

Of course huge generalizations are at work here. On the last point, for example, great exceptions can be named. The 'black' preaching tradition, of which the best-known representative was Martin Luther King, stands out in its refusal to separate a 'private' church from the 'public' ordering of the nation – to separate spiritual from physical freedom. Today also, white preaching voices such as that of Walter Brueggemann speak out powerfully and subversively against prevailing cultural mores. Nonetheless, highlighting the basic differences between Britain and the USA in this respect helps to sharpen the sense of the preacher's situation in both places.

The great risk of any 'Christendom' or 'Christendom-like' situation for preaching is that the openness, welcome and outgoing spirit which

---

22 Partly through ecumenical bodies, representatives of the Free Churches and the Roman Catholic Church are now involved in State affairs to a much greater extent in the UK than was the case until quite recently (see n. 14 above). It would be unthinkable, for example, to have a large state occasion like the annual Act of Remembrance or a royal funeral without the presence of leaders from all the main denominations and, indeed, the major faiths. This means that 'Church' as a whole – indeed 'religion' as a whole – not just the Church of England, continues to have a visible role within the State which may give it considerable opportunities when it comes to preaching.

23 On this last point I am indebted to Tim Grass, private communication, 5 January 2010, and see also John W. Wright, 2007, *Telling God's Story: Narrative Preaching for Christian Formation*, Downers Grove, IL: InterVarsity Press Academic, especially pp. 47–76.

I have been emphasizing as a great potential strength is replaced by authoritarian domineering, exclusion and, at worst, collusion in naked and worldly power-play. Thus, we must recognize, particularly, the appalling anti-Jewish rhetoric of some 'Christendom' preachers – so much more damaging and destructive from the mouth of Chrysostom and Luther than from Melito of Sardis, not because of the words they used but because of the public platform they enjoyed.[24] Worst of all in the annals of preaching, perhaps, were the sermons in support of the Crusades.[25] More commonplace has been lower-key but nonetheless dangerously uncritical validation of the contemporary order, seen for instance in the way that Eusebius eulogized Constantine in almost Messianic terms.[26] In the case of Christian power-play against other Christians, the sometimes poisonous preaching voices of 'establishment' lead easily and naturally to the equally poisonous preaching voices of 'anti-establishment' (one could substitute here various other oppositions, such as 'Protestant' and 'Catholic'). Public preaching carries power, and that power is the more dangerous when the Church itself, or individual churches, carry power.

The word beyond walls

The third setting of preaching encompasses those movements in which the gospel has been taken, publicly, beyond the confines of the Christian gathering altogether. At no time, of course, has the gospel itself been confined to that gathering, for Christian people live and speak it day by day. But only at certain times has it been *publicly* proclaimed outside the Church. The first two models had this in common, that they were addressed to a Christian gathering – whether demarcated from the wider society, in the first, or open to influencing it and being influenced by it, in the second. But throughout the last two thousand years there have been times and places where the gospel has burst out in public beyond the limitations of any Christian gathering and any physical walls in which it might be enclosed.

---

24 On Chrysostom's anti-Jewish preaching see Aaron A. Milavec, 1989, 'A Fresh Analysis of the Parable of the Wicked Husbandmen in the Light of Jewish-Catholic Dialogue', in Clemens Thoma and Michael Wyschogrod (eds), *Parable and Story in Judaism and Christianity*, New York: Paulist Press, pp. 81–117, here p. 83.

25 See Edwards, *History*, pp. 181, 195.

26 'Oration in Honour of Constantine on the Thirtieth Anniversary of his Reign', in Maurice Wiles and Mark Santer (eds), 1975, *Documents in Early Christian Thought*, Cambridge: Cambridge University Press, pp. 230–4.

It is hardly surprising if not as much of this kind of preaching survives today as of the other kind; in the nature of the case it may often be more spontaneous, less thoroughly prepared beforehand, and with fewer hearers taking notes! However, it has surely existed in all periods. One may assume that it continued to take place in the early period alongside the in-church 'community interpretation' that we have identified – in the kind of debating fora where Paul and the apostles found a hearing, if not always a response. After the Constantinian settlement, evangelization continued to be important; it is a misleading stereotype of Christendom to think that it ushered in the cessation of outgoing mission or an era of 'automatic' Christians. In North Africa, for instance, where Augustine was based, the task of evangelization continued to be much larger than it was in Rome.[27] In Britain, though the gospel came quite early on with the Roman conquerors, the task had to be carried out all over again after they had left, as the work of both Celtic missionaries like Aidan, Cuthbert and Patrick, and the Roman emissaries from Gregory, attest.[28] Again, the fact that the task was often incomplete, and sometimes employed dubious methods, does not invalidate all the vital public sharing of the gospel that went on – regularly in the open air, in places where people gathered. The monastic communities often formed a base for the activities of outreach, a model that some are finding attractive again today.[29]

A similar pattern is seen in later periods too. The friars took the gospel to the people where they were, on the streets and lanes, at a time when a divorce had opened up between the few educated, powerful clergy and the majority of the population, who were dependent on their ministrations but largely untaught. This became a popular, indeed entertaining form of preaching. The missionary activities of the post-reformation Roman Catholic orders took the gospel into the open in various parts of the world.[30] In the eighteenth century, when the spiritual life of the established church was at a low ebb, John Wesley took to his horse and drew vast crowds to his open-air preaching. In the nineteenth century Charles Haddon Spurgeon would also preach to great crowds in out-of-church venues. In an offshoot of the Wesleyan tradition, William Booth and his 'Salvation Army' took the good news on to the streets of the great industrial cities and gathered the poor

27 Edwards, *History*, p. 139.
28 Edwards, *History*, p. 143.
29 See Duncan Maclaren, 2004, *Mission Implausible: Restoring Credibility to the Church*, Carlisle: Paternoster, pp. 187–200.
30 Edwards, *History*, p. 332.

and damaged into the fold through a ministry that combined (as it still does) proclamation and care in a powerful way. The 'seeker service' movement pioneered by Willow Creek Church in the late twentieth century deliberately set up meetings that were shaped upon the expectations and comfort-zones of those *outside* the church.

Nor is this model confined to those identified as 'evangelicals'. Hyde Park in London provided the platform for the great Methodist preacher Donald Soper, while the streets of industrial Glasgow offered a pulpit to George MacLeod, founder of the Iona Community.[31] And today, preachers of various backgrounds are exploring again the potential for an out-of-church proclamation that attracts by its holy folly.[32]

A trend from the early nineteenth century onwards particularly exemplifies this model of taking the 'word beyond the walls'. It has been dubbed 'frontier religion', and dates back to the time when the colonizers of America and their descendants were spreading west into new territory.[33] When there were few church buildings, Christians saw the potential for camps and outdoor gatherings where the gospel could be proclaimed. There was an advantage in the lack of traditional 'baggage' a church building represents, and preachers such as Charles Grandison Finney and later Dwight Moody would make full use of it, proclaiming the gospel in an earnest, often emotional manner that addressed the heart and won many adherents. This movement came also to encompass gatherings for the encouragement of the already converted (such as the Keswick Convention in Britain), and could espouse at various times a range of spiritualities and doctrinal positions (as the history of Keswick again shows). It influenced many evangelistic groupings, such as the Children's Special Service Mission (later Scripture Union), Pathfinders, Crusaders, Youth for Christ, and most prominently in the twentieth century, Billy Graham and his evangelistic association.

It is natural that such movements should arise when the 'mainstream' churches of Christendom either do not exist or are on the wane. A gospel for the world demands to be taken 'beyond the walls', and it will go out perhaps especially when those within the walls are less than hospitable to it. But it is interesting that in all these instances, the

---

31 On MacLeod's open-air preaching see Stuart Blythe, 2009, 'Open-Air Preaching as Radical Street Performance', unpublished PhD thesis, University of Edinburgh, ch. 5.

32 See Stanley P. Saunders and Charles L. Campbell, 2000, *The Word on the Street: Performing the Scriptures in an Urban Context*, Grand Rapids: Eerdmans; Blythe, 'Open-Air Preaching'.

33 See also Geoffrey Stevenson and Stephen Wright, 2008, *Preaching with Humanity: A Practical Guide for Today's Church*, London: Church House Publishing, pp. 22–4.

preacher appears not simply as a lone pioneer, but as one who remains dependent on a community of faith, indeed often bringing that community and even its worship into the arena with him or her. The friars were rooted in a community of their order. The Methodists had their connexion and their classes which both supported and were increased through their travelling preaching ministry. 'Frontier religion' regularly comprises not just preaching but worship, as any who have attended a Billy Graham crusade will know. It seems to be a pattern that though preaching from time to time needs to take place 'outside the walls', it is unnatural for it to be a solitary exercise. It is always bound up, in some way, with a worshipping community.

Questions for the local church

- What streams of tradition have influenced the preaching in your church?
- Which of the three settings for preaching outlined in this chapter corresponds most closely to the preaching in your church?
- How does your church's understanding of its role in society affect its preaching?

Areas for research

The influence of various preaching movements on others across history would provide a fascinating area of study. So would a comparison between two or more such movements, even if no actual influence was being investigated or assumed. The way in which the social setting and self-understanding of a church affect its preaching would be an important topic for some careful empirical study.

Further reading

O. C. Edwards Jr, 2004, *A History of Preaching*, Grand Rapids: Eerdmans.
Hughes Oliphant Old, 1998–2007, *The Reading and Preaching of Scripture in the Worship of the Christian Church*, 6 vols, Grand Rapids: Eerdmans.
Paul Scott Wilson, 1992, *A Concise History of Preaching*, Nashville: Abingdon.

2

Contemporary Functions of Preaching

Having briefly surveyed the historical phenomenon of preaching in Chapter 1, in this chapter we will outline four contemporary contexts which condition the event of preaching and within which it fulfils a distinct function today.

First, we will consider *shared worship*, which has been the dominant context for preaching over two millennia. Next we turn to *contemporary culture*. The Church is placed in the world as a missionary body,[1] and that means that preaching, while inevitably influenced by intellectual and social currents, can also exercise influence on the cultures in which it is set, and the individuals and groupings which inhabit them. The third context is that of *theology*. Preaching has sometimes been the spearhead of the Church's continuing theological conversations and debates about the meaning of God's revelation in Christ for our lives and the world. Although the study of theology now extends more widely than the Church and is carried forward in a variety of arenas of discourse, it undoubtedly remains true that for many Christians, the theology they have learned has come mainly or solely through preaching. There is an obvious link here to the fourth context, that of *pastoral care*. The Church and its pastors exercise such care for a wide range of people who may or may not be identified as Christian. An aspect of this care is the Christian education involved in both evangelism and Christian nurture: education understood in the fullest sense as not just an intellectual process but a transformational one, enabling people to be renewed not only in their thinking but in their living, according to Christ's pattern (cf. Rom. 12.1–2). And in this process preaching continues to play a pivotal, yet again contested, role.

---

1 We will consider this further in Chapter 9.

Shared worship

The context of worship exercises a considerable influence upon the preaching that takes place within it, and preaching, conversely, fulfils a distinct function when it is part of a service of worship. We will discuss this mutual influence first in general terms, and then with reference to the diversity of kinds of worship practised in today's Church.[2]

The effect of worship on preaching is profound, though often unnoticed. The worshipping context reminds speaker and hearers that preaching is meant to glorify God before it is meant to edify people – and that its purpose is certainly not to boost the ego of the preacher. Prayer, song, Bible reading, sacrament and silence all have a part to play in the Godward focus of the gathering, and together contribute to an atmosphere which becomes 'second nature' to the regular worshipper, including the preacher. Thus all are reminded that the sermon, like the rest of the service, is not a time for mere information, entertainment or displays of skill, but for drawing near to God.

Conversely, preaching can effectively function as an enabler of worship. This is because it can bring the recollection of God's past revelation in the biblical story together with the reality of the present, in which God is still to be discerned. It can do so in a focused way which claims the attention of the minds, hearts and consciences of the worshippers. Putting it simply, it can take the praises that we have sung and the Scriptures we have heard, and connect them with the world for which we intercede and the longings we express in the silence. Praise of God and reading of Scripture, if left on their own, may risk leaving us in 'the language of Zion', the great formulations of theology and the story of the past. Intercession for the world and silence before God bring us very much into the present, yet if left on their own may cut us loose from the depth of our tradition and the anchor of God's own promises. Preaching negotiates a way between past and present, between the sure foundation of Christ and the uncertain waters of the

---

2 For an attempt at a representative survey, with examples, of what preaching looks and sounds like in the range of worship settings in Britain today, see Geoffrey Stevenson and Stephen Wright, 2008, *Preaching with Humanity: A Practical Guide for Today's Church*, London: Church House Publishing, pp. 12–28. Seminal influences on my thinking on this subject have been Neville Clark, 1991, *Preaching in Context: Word, Worship and the People of God*, Bury St Edmunds: Kevin Mayhew; Ian Paton, 2004, 'Preaching in Worship', in Geoffrey Hunter, Gethin Thomas and Stephen Wright (eds), *A Preacher's Companion: Essays from the College of Preachers*, Oxford: Bible Reading Fellowship, pp. 114–17, and the longer lecture on which it was based. See also Carol M. Norén, 'The Word of God in Worship: Preaching in Relationship to Liturgy', in Cheslyn Jones et al. (eds), 1992, *The Study of Liturgy*, rev. edn, London: SPCK, pp. 31–49.

contemporary world, between the safety of an eternal, faithful God and the disturbing dynamism of a living, speaking God.

It does this by announcing a gospel that concerns both past and future, and interprets the present as a time of grace in the midst of judgement.[3] It may thus fundamentally shape the consciousness of the worshipper, who needs constant reminders of the 'grace in which we stand' (Rom. 5.2),[4] and for whom that grace is the only basis for self-offering to God (Rom. 12.1–2). Many churches believe that it does this in a creative partnership with the sacrament of Holy Communion. The word of grace, spoken and heard in the sermon, is enacted and received at the Lord's Table.

These mutual connections between preaching and worship are made in a multitude of ways, of which those gathered – both preacher and congregation – probably remain largely unconscious most of the time. A service is a network of signs which interact with each other and with the participants in dynamic complexity. Words of songs may echo, or sometimes question, words of sermons. Bible readings stand alongside sermons not simply as their jumping-off point, but as the sounding-board against which the preacher's words vibrate. Preaching may shed new light on the meaning of the sacraments and enable worshippers to participate at greater depth. The compassion evoked by a preacher may find expression in the outpouring of prayer led by an intercessor. Thus we might continue.

The existence of different traditions of worship lends yet more complexity to the picture, for sermon will relate to service differently depending on whether one is in a Methodist, Catholic, Pentecostal church or any other. The sacramental ethos of churches in the Catholic tradition yields a different atmosphere for preaching from the strongly word-centred approach of traditional Protestantism and the strongly experience-centred approach of the Pentecostal and charismatic branches of the family.

---

3 See Dietrich Bonhoeffer, 'The Proclaimed Word', in Richard Lischer (ed.), 2002, *The Company of Preachers: Wisdom on Preaching from Augustine to the Present*, Grand Rapids: Eerdmans, pp. 31–7, here p. 37. On the combination of grace and judgement in preaching see Paul Scott Wilson, 2004, *Preaching and Homiletical Theory*, St Louis: Chalice Press, pp. 73–115; 1999, *The Four Pages of the Sermon: A Guide to Biblical Preaching*, Nashville: Abingdon. Wilson here develops an approach to preaching based on the recognition of 'trouble' in the world and the text, and the announcement of 'grace' in the world and the text.

4 For a penetrating account of how important it is that worship and preaching should usher worshippers into the sphere of the kingdom, in which God's grace is found, see Clark, *Preaching*, pp. 35–8.

To give one example: where, in the service, does the sermon come? Its location says much about the implied meaning of the whole gathering, and therefore of the preaching within it. In Protestantism it is regularly at the climax of the service, occupying the longest single section. In Pentecostal and charismatic churches the situation is often similar to this, with the important difference that the sermon is followed by a time where response of one kind or another is specifically encouraged. In sacramental traditions the sermon is usually at the centre of the Eucharist, while the actual climax of the service is the distribution of bread and wine towards the end. Many local variations and permutations complicate the picture. We cannot ignore the existence of such variables in seeking guidance about if, what and how to preach, because the way a sermon is conceived, spoken and heard is inextricably entangled with them.

Contemporary culture

'Culture' is the network of customs, practices, preferences, beliefs and languages which makes up the fabric of our daily life. Just as worship and preaching influence each other in many subtle ways of which we are often unconscious, so it is with culture and preaching. Before we make any conscious decisions about *whether* or *what* or *how* to preach, we are affected by culture; and so, before they begin listening to any sermon, are our hearers. But preaching in turn can function as an influence within and upon the cultures around it.

This reality is made more complex by the fact that most Western societies today are 'multicultural'. Whatever the majority of people think about this, or how it should be handled, a great variety of *different* cultures jostle alongside each other. Moreover, as immigrants become naturalized, cultures start to blend in confusing but enriching ways. Shared Christian faith adds a dimension to this picture but it does not contradict it. All of us have received faith embedded in cultural clothing (translations of the Bible, church customs, habits seen as 'normative', whether weekly Communion or daily 'quiet time' and so on). As human beings, we have no other means of receiving it, or of passing it on. Churches themselves become 'subcultures', or groups of subcultures, and it is helpful to raise to consciousness those practices, forms of speech, rituals and so on which identify them as such. This is not for the purpose of trying to escape from being a subculture, which is impossible. It is simply so that we can take stock of how we behave, as the basis for bringing our common life under the light of God's direction.

An important mediator of that direction can be preaching. Through preaching, the gospel can influence culture, if the subcultures of particular churches themselves remain open to the gospel. The preacher himself or herself is in an interesting position, in that he or she may be immersed in the church's subculture, or may be (or may be perceived as) at least partly an 'outsider' to it. Over time, he or she may shift along this spectrum, one way or the other. Awareness of one's cultural location as a preacher enables sensitivity to the ways in which one's own embodiment of the gospel may be peculiar to a particular culture and the ways in which it transcends such particularity.

As we saw in Chapter 1, the transformation of culture has been seen as one of the classic aims of Christian mission.[5] Preaching's role in such transformation is well-documented, although as preaching is a fallible cultural act itself, it has produced not only positive transformation but less benign effects as well.[6] Moreover, we should not think of such transformation of cultures as something set apart from the transformation of individuals within them. As individuals are persuaded, whether through preaching or any other means, of the transforming truth and power of the gospel, they will start to exercise a transforming influence on the culture(s) in which they are embedded. Conversely, cultures influenced by the gospel may be hospitable settings for its transforming influence on individuals.[7] I am therefore treating preaching's function in transforming culture as its 'evangelistic' function in the widest sense.

It is important to distinguish two levels at which this function is fulfilled. First, it is fulfilled by means of the preacher's theological appropriation of God's revelation in order to interpret the present and mediate

---

5 See H. Richard Niebuhr, 1951, *Christ and Culture*, New York: Harper & Row, pp. 190–229.

6 For examples of the positive effect of preaching in transforming cultures we might look to the effect of Augustine's preaching in the fourth and fifth centuries on a decaying imperial culture, the social effects of Wesleyan preaching in the eighteenth, or those of Spurgeon or the Salvation Army in the nineteenth. On Augustine see the important work by Ronald Boyd-Macmillan, 2009, 'The Transforming Sermon: A study of the preaching of St. Augustine, with special reference to the *Sermones ad populum*, and the transformation theory of James Loder', unpublished PhD thesis, University of Aberdeen. Preaching, of course, was not the sole vehicle of such transformations, nor were they, naturally, complete and without negative aspects. The negative influence of preaching is seen in its use in warmongering, as in the Crusades.

7 This is, I am aware, a complex and contested matter. See Duncan Maclaren, 2004, *Mission Implausible: Restoring Credibility to the Church*, Carlisle: Paternoster, pp. 57–93, for a fascinating discussion of the persistence of religion in what is often called a 'secularized' society, and the openings this offers for a gospel that will transform individuals.

God's wisdom for life within it. That is, the *content* of preaching can be transformative of people's thought-world and therefore their lives. Insofar as the preacher's theology reflects contemporary fashions more than the historic revelation, this transformation will be lessened or eliminated. I consider this theological function of preaching in the next section.

Second, preaching can fulfil a transformative function with respect to culture by means of its *form*. This too can have a surprising effect. But here, too, if preaching imitates too closely *either* the communication style of a previous generation *or* that of today, its transformative potential will be reduced. The question is not whether our preaching 'looks' or 'sounds' strange in a culture accustomed to many other media, but whether that strangeness is a vehicle of transformation or a mere eccentric relic.

Roger Standing has given an excellent concise and up-to-date overview of cultural characteristics of contemporary British society, together with reflections on how these characteristics are inspiring preaching to adapt.[8] He cites eight: entertainment, narrative, consumerism, an ethos of suspicion in public life and reluctance to commit oneself deeply, 'virtual' relationships, celebrity, 'liquid modernity' and a 'post-Christendom' era in which there remain remarkable signs of Christian life and influence. He proceeds to give an incisive account of the potential of this atmosphere for Christian communication of the gospel, as well as the paradoxes entailed in becoming so immersed in it that the influence is predominantly one-way, from culture to preaching.

Here I want to take Standing's argument a little further and summarize some ways in which preaching with its own 'strangeness' might already be positively influencing this strange contemporary British cultural pot-pourri, and could influence it further.

First, preaching may be a voice of reconciliation within the mistrustful and often polarized arena of public discourse. Deborah Tannen writes about the 'argument culture' which shapes so much of this discourse, especially in the media and politics.[9] Tannen is not at all opposed to argument per se, but rather to '*ritualized* opposition, in contrast to the

---

8 Roger Standing, 2010, 'Mediated Preaching: Homiletics in Contemporary British Culture', in Geoffrey Stevenson (ed.), 2010, *The Future of Preaching*, London: SCM, pp. 9–26.

9 She comments that this culture owes much not only to the Western philosophical emphasis on disputation and formal logic, but also to the militaristic language and ethos of the Christendom atmosphere of the universities, in which modern science came to birth: Deborah Tannen, 1998, *The Argument Culture: Changing the Way we Argue and Debate*, London: Virago, pp. 264–6, drawing on David Noble, 1992, *A World without Women: The Christian Clerical Culture of Western Science*, New York and Oxford: Oxford University Press.

literal opposition of genuine disagreement'.[10] Prime Minister's Questions and tabloid journalism are examples which immediately spring to mind. One hopes that the echoes of a past in which the pulpit itself was a place for ritualized denunciation of 'the world', or other Christian traditions, are getting fainter now – though the memory of more adversarial times may linger, not least because 'preaching' has become associated with repeated scares about the 'extremism' of a minority of Muslims. But if preaching is allowed to be truly a vehicle for God's own act of reconciliation (2 Cor. 5.18–19), its positive influence could be incalculable. The fact that many congregations are multicultural now places particular demands on the preacher, but also offers a glorious opportunity for the reconciling nature of this ministry to be manifested.

Second, preaching may come as a moment of refreshing and personal simplicity after the frenetic virtual world of internet exchange in which 'friends' may be 'online', yet are not 'there'. This might particularly be true when preaching directly, interactively and without notes.[11] Preaching might call people out of over-immersion in the virtual and the impersonal. Tannen points out how one-way communication, such as the blanket email from boss to workers, or a message on an answerphone, can express aggression and therefore feed defensiveness in a way which does not happen in face-to-face communication.[12] Preaching may be largely one-way at the time, but at least the preacher is standing before the hearers, able to gauge their responses, and receive them orally afterwards. It may offer a salutary reminder to our culture of the vulnerability at the heart of personal relationships, expressed most clearly when we are physically present to each other.

Third, preaching can also function as a necessary and reassuring voice of *wisdom* in an ether awash with 'knowledge' which few know how to judge. Maybe the very difficulty and strangeness of preaching – sometimes – is a vital pointer beyond the immediately exciting, ever-changing yet ephemeral world of the small screen.

Fourth, preachers can use a language which deliberately eschews some of the debased forms of speech in circulation today. For example, the ideology of consumerism spreads in a sinister way from the economic to the linguistic sphere, and language shapes perceptions in all sorts of subtle ways (one hears, for instance, about the way people 'consume

---

10 Tannen, *Argument Culture*, p. 4 (my italics).

11 See Joseph M. Webb, 2001, *Preaching without Notes*, Nashville: Abingdon; also his 'Without Notes', in Paul Scott Wilson (ed.), 2008, *The New Interpreter's Handbook of Preaching*, Nashville: Abingdon, pp. 429–31.

12 Tannen, *Argument Culture*, pp. 247–9.

new media'). This is a sign of the central place the desires of the self, and the desire for things *now*, have in the psyche of today's society. All too easily, Christians may play along with this in the way that a variety of forms of church life and practice are 'marketed'. Indeed, some forms of preaching can be in reality an exercise in self-marketing or church-marketing, whereas a conscious resistance to using such language can help preaching to be a truly transformative event. Our words can evoke another world, a sphere of free giving, a sphere in which others are as important as ourselves, a sphere in which patience is possible because the future is *known* to be far more glorious than the present, a sphere in which the human-driven 'success' of the Church counts for nothing in comparison with the God-empowered growth of his kingdom.

It is important to think particularly about the way in which the influence of preaching on culture (and vice versa) may change if it happens in the open air rather than within the safe walls of the church.[13] We will return to this topic in Chapter 8 when we consider patterns and practices of preaching. In the open, the preacher is much more obviously a competitor. There is no hiding-place. He or she may choose to imitate some of the tactics of other 'open-air performers' such as street actors, or to offer a 'performance' in stark contrast to theirs. Neither option should be prejudged as the more potentially transformative. The judgement and response of the public, if any, will be thoroughly conditioned by their expectations and preferences concerning what may happen in such 'public space'. In church, the preacher is in an important sense on his or her own turf, in a position of control, and members of the general 'public' who enter will probably be aware on some level that they are moving into a different cultural arena. This may make them somewhat disorientated and vulnerable. Church buildings, therefore, certainly act to some extent as cultural 'screens' which may shield Christians from contemporary culture as well as shielding contemporary culture from Christian witness. Yet those individuals and groups who have the courage to take the gospel to the 'streets' may find that it yet has more influence there than many of us have dared to hope.

Theology

Christian theology is the Church's continued reflection on the meaning of God's revelation and its implications for our lives. It never stands

---

13 On this topic I am indebted especially to Stuart Blythe, 2009, 'Open-Air Preaching as Radical Street Performance' unpublished PhD thesis, University of Edinburgh.

still, for as the world changes, so our interaction with God's unique self-disclosure, in Israel and above all in Christ, must change too.[14] For a simple example, we might take our response to the phenomenon of consumerism, just mentioned. The Bible and Christian doctrine give us much practical and challenging guidance about attitudes to money and possessions, and a vision of that which is of true worth. But consumerism as we know it is a new phenomenon, which requires new thinking about how we relate this teaching to our own culture. The depth, or shallowness, of our thought about what it means to be a Christian in a 'consumer society' will be evident to others. To what extent is it hypocritical to enjoy its benefits (which are real) while decrying its practices? Simplistic challenges to 'give' when most people are in debt will be heard for what they are. Is it possible to 'give' when, in truth, you don't actually 'have'? In wealthier churches (which includes churches composed of people who can just afford high mortgages), how can preachers and congregations remember the poor, who are precisely those most taunted and excluded by consumerism? Such questions require careful and creative theological thought, not simplistic answers.[15]

Preaching and theology (as we might say) 'go back a long way' together. In the early centuries of Christianity, before the Bible and other literature were widely accessible to the general public, and long before Christian theology broke from being an area of study confined to Church circles, preaching was the main means of both doing creative theology and voicing the theological thinking that had been shaping the Church. Indeed, some of those known as the greatest theological thinkers of the early Church are also those known as some of the greatest preachers, and **vice versa**: Origen, Gregory Nazianzen, Augustine.

If preaching is not such a 'spearhead' for theology today, this is not necessarily because either discipline has either declined or is discredited (though some say that both these things are true, of either or both discipline). It may be precisely because those early preacher-theologians did their job so well. For their preaching, and especially the Scriptural interpretation it contained, have survived to a remarkable degree in written form; nor did they see any divide between the oral and written aspects

---

14 See Dave Tomlinson, 2008, *Re-enchanting Christianity: Faith in an Emerging Culture*, Norwich: Canterbury Press, pp. 15–33; Maggi Dawn, 1997, 'You Have to Change to Stay the Same', in Graham Cray et al., *The Post-evangelical Debate*, London: SPCK, pp. 35–56.

15 For theological reflection on this subject see, for example, Peter Selby, 2009, *Grace and Mortgage: The Language of Grace and the Debt of the World*, 2nd edn, London: Darton, Longman & Todd.

of their activity. Both were subsumed under what Michael Pasquarello (following old terminology) calls 'sacred rhetoric',[16] the entire enterprise of forming Christian minds and lives through the Church's ministry of proclaiming and teaching the gospel. In the sixteenth-century attempts to reform the Church, the Fathers' preaching and teaching was a vital guide.[17] And as, in the same period, both the Bible and other theological writings became available to vastly more people through the invention of printing and the growth in literacy, preaching no longer needed to be the gateway to theology that once it had been.

So it was that increasingly people did not need to listen to sermons to engage with what the theological thinkers were saying, nor did theological thought necessarily reflect the sorts of things that were being preached. A more radical step, however, came with the post-Enlightenment attempt to treat theology as a discipline that could, in principle, be subjected to the same standards of 'objective' rationality as any other, and thus be equally accessible to those beyond the Church as those within it. High academic standards had been nobly blended with theology in the mediaeval schools and above all in the faith-and-reason synthesis of Thomas Aquinas. But the overall framework remained an ecclesiastical one. The founding of the modern 'secular' university by Wilhelm von Humboldt in Berlin in 1810 signalled a fundamental questioning of why the study of theology should be confined to the one social grouping which had a deeply vested interest in it (even though that grouping, since the Reformation, had been internally divided).[18] This flew in the face of the Enlightenment ideals of detached reflection and the possibility, in principle, of any human being attaining growth in knowledge through the universal reason possessed by all. At the same time, there was a seminal attempt to divide up theology so that the descriptive, academic task of identifying 'biblical theology' was separated from the normative, constructive task of developing 'dogmatic theology'.[19] The fact that a place was allowed for the constructive task shows that preaching, and other forms of Church-based

---

16 Michael Pasquarello III, 2005, *Sacred Rhetoric: Preaching as a Theological and Pastoral Practice of the Church*, Grand Rapids: Eerdmans.

17 See for instance the quantity of references to them in Calvin's *Institutes of the Christian Religion*.

18 On this event see Timothy Clark, 1999, 'Literature and the Crisis in the Concept of the University', in David Fuller and Patricia Waugh (eds), *The Arts and Sciences of Criticism*, Oxford: Oxford University Press, pp. 217–37, here pp. 222–5.

19 This division is especially associated with the name of J. P. Gabler. See Craig G. Bartholomew, 2005, 'Biblical Theology', in Kevin J. Vanhoozer (ed.), *Dictionary for Theological Interpretation of the Bible*, Grand Rapids/London: Baker/SPCK, pp. 84–90, here pp. 85–6.

theologizing, still had their place; but to carry credibility they had to be based on the biblical theology done in the academy.

One might argue that preachers have been on the back foot ever since. Distinguished theologian-preachers such as Schleiermacher and Barth (in very different ways) sought to reassert the *Church's* authority in preaching: Schleiermacher by emphasizing the hearers' actual experience, and the evocation of their innate sense of transcendence in preaching; Barth by emphasizing the power of God's word to break into human experience in unpredictable and world-challenging ways. But they themselves produced works of academic theology which, arguably, have proved much more influential than their actual preaching. Can (and should) the preaching of the Church once again *be an influence* on the highest and most rigorous realms of study and exploration? If not – if the influence must inevitably be the other way round – does that mean that the Church is doomed to remain in the inappropriate-sounding role of handmaid of academic theology, even though such theology is not necessarily carried out within a Christian ethos? Given our contemporary awareness that the Enlightenment goal of 'neutrality' is a chimera, this must surely mean that the Church must open itself to being enslaved to presuppositions and modes of thought which, at least sometimes, fly in the face of 'the mind of Christ'.[20]

Large philosophical questions are raised here, but our concern is to pursue the implications for preaching. Two very practical matters can be identified: the way in which a preacher's own theological thinking is formed, and the operative frameworks or 'ordinary hermeneutics' by which a congregation's theological mind is shaped.

The hope of ministerial training institutions is to enable those called to ministry to articulate the Christian gospel in a way that is faithful to orthodox Christian tradition, and both comprehensible and applicable to their contemporaries. This is a matter not only of imparting knowledge but also of inducting students into ways of thinking and practices of ongoing theological reflection which stimulate lifelong growth as preachers, as well as in all other dimensions of ministry.

Reality, of course, is messy, and the processes of learning and development are as unpredictable and non-linear for ministers as they are for anyone else. It is appropriate, though, for any preacher reviewing their ministry at any stage to ask what theological sources and modes of thought are most influencing their preaching ministry. The question is bound to reveal the haphazard nature of the influences upon us.

---

20 See Bartholomew, 'Biblical Theology'.

We will all (probably!) have read the Bible. But we are all children of particular traditions; even those who come later into church life find themselves caught up in one tradition or another (or indeed choose one for themselves). We will have been directed to particular books and authors; we have heard particular teachers and preachers. Other writings or speakers we have come across quite by accident. Any or all of these we may have warmed to, reacted against or remained fairly neutral towards. Moreover, we are formed deeply by our theological friendships. The fact that a particular person is (or is not) sympathetic to a particular view may have great influence on the extent of our own sympathy to it.

Given the history of the academic 'takeover' of theology which I have outlined, preachers are bound to be influenced by such studies in many ways. Even if a preacher's reading is restricted (say) to popular devotional Bible commentaries, only those from the narrowest 'stables' will have been uninfluenced by academic biblical study and theology – to the extent, very likely, of remaining unhelpfully naïve. Any more 'mainstream' commentary, or theological work, will have been written in dialogue with a range of others, including, normally, at least some – often many – holding different views and perspectives from those of the writer himself or herself. If God's truth may potentially be found anywhere, it is not a matter of 'popular Christian' theology being 'right' and 'academic theology' being (at the very least) 'dangerous'. It is rather that the simple awareness – at least in outline – of the ways in which our theological minds are being shaped is the crucial first step to learning, appropriate critique of ourselves and our 'sources' and more sensitive mediation of the gospel for congregations.

In this light, the old jibe that you can tell when preachers have stopped thinking by the latest date of the books on their shelves needs revising – and not just because, these days, they probably haven't been able to afford to buy many new ones! It is not the date of the books alone, but their provenance which is significant. Although many publishers now offer a wide theological spectrum, some are still known for the particular perspective they take. A preaching diet that is dependent on the preacher's reading from the output of just one or two publishers (worse still, one or two authors) will be thin, narrow and very unlikely to contain the full sustenance of the gospel. 'Old' can be wonderfully refreshing – as those now rediscovering the riches of the Patristic tradition are learning. The question is whether our reading is enlarging our horizons in helpful ways, and whether we are learning to apply our critical faculties to everything, including that which we find most congenial.

Reflecting on the theological influences upon us should disabuse us of any notion that we might ever aspire to being pure channels for pure doctrine. Our theological outlook is mediated through many streams, and we have had our own, mysterious ways of absorbing those into our system and rejecting elements that do not seem to us to fit. The fact that we have had some sort of systematic training should be an advantage to us, but it does not make us the 'expert' who 'knows it all' in comparison with hearers who are (in this way of thinking) empty vessels waiting for our 'knowledge' to be offloaded. We 'know' genuinely, yet we 'know' in part (1 Cor. 13.12), like everyone else.

Our other concern here is the way in which the *congregation's* theological mind is shaped. Preachers need to reckon with the fact that preaching is only one element (maybe quite a small one) in this process. The fascinating study of 'ordinary hermeneutics' is starting to open up something of the picture for us.[21] Not only have people (sometimes) been influenced by a variety of preachers before the one they are listening to now. They may also (quite often) have read at least something of the Bible, maybe with accompanying notes. They may have dipped into theological reading, of the lighter or heavier variety. A preacher is profoundly mistaken and arrogant to assume general ignorance on the part of hearers. Many of them, while not being theologically trained, will be immersed in areas of life and learning – often practical, but sometimes academic too – of which the preacher is all but totally ignorant himself or herself. These areas may have considerable bearing on the theological thinking of those concerned even if they do not articulate it. Moreover, they must surely have a vital contribution – if somehow it can be tapped – to the developing theological reflection of the congregation in question, as they continue to wrestle with the application of the gospel to life.

Preachers and congregations should also take account of the more subtle ways in which shared theological attitudes and views are being shaped. The structures, symbols and words of worship are very influential on the reception of the sermon, as we noted above. However, they are also extremely influential on the entire theological mindset of the congregation. What a congregation *does* in worship week by week, and perhaps especially what it *sings*, forms its thinking about

21 See Andrew Rogers, 2007, 'Reading Scripture in Congregations: Towards an Ordinary Hermeneutics', in Andrew Walker and Luke Bretherton (eds), 2007, *Remembering our Future: Explorations in Deep Church*, Milton Keynes: Paternoster, pp. 81–107; Andrew Village, 2007, *The Bible and Lay People: An Empirical Approach to Ordinary Hermeneutics*, Aldershot: Ashgate.

God and his relationship with his world in almost frighteningly powerful ways. In addition, churches today are no longer so purely 'local'.
Many Christians are regular attenders at conferences and festivals,
regular readers of online Christian material or printed notes, regular
receivers of Christian magazines, regular listeners to Christian radio
stations, and so on. What is said and done in these various forums
may be far more penetrating of people's perspectives than the preacher's words. It may hold far greater sway over how, in practice, congregations interpret the Bible and construct a theology that appears to
be both faithful and applicable.

The need for an awareness of such influences on congregational
thinking is brought into sharp relief when it is realized that sometimes
the messages given by the preacher are in *conflict*, maybe unwittingly
so, with the messages being received openly or subliminally from elsewhere. For example, a preacher may want to draw people's attention
to Paul's theology of power through weakness, yet the songs the congregation most loves to sing may all emphasize the power rather than
the weakness. A preacher may want to give the congregation permission to lament as the Psalmist did, but some in the congregation may
have been schooled (in deeper than conscious ways) in the idea that
encounter with God must be celebratory and joyful or else it is not
genuine. A preacher may have been influenced (say) by reformed theology or catholic spirituality, whereas the congregation might be (say)
more 'liberal' or more 'charismatic' – something which can come out in
tensions between the discussions in home groups and what is preached
on Sundays.[22]

Unless we reckon as honestly as we can with this diversity and complexity of influences, we will not be in a position to discuss the important normative and practical questions of 'whether', 'why', and 'how'
which we shall approach in Parts 3 and 4 of the book – whether we are
thinking of preaching in general, or the preaching ministry of a church
in general or particular sermons. Yet even to attempt an examination
of such influences runs the risk of falling into two traps. On the one
side, the preacher may regard such an exercise as an attempt to expose
the 'inadequate' theologies the congregation is imbibing from various
quarters, as a prelude to being able to 'correct' them with more insight.
This would be foolish, given – as we have seen – that the preacher's
store of 'truth' is, in its way, as partial and haphazardly garnered as
anyone else's. On the other side, the preacher may be in danger of

---

22 Cf. Rogers, 'Reading Scripture in Congregations'.

losing confidence altogether in the calling and formation they have received. To say that the congregation is a mediator of truth as well as the preacher does not mean that the preacher has nothing distinctive and vital to contribute.[23]

Pastoral care

The final arena within which preaching has an important function is that of pastoral care.[24] Most preachers are also pastors of those to whom they preach, whether as a sole minister or as part of a team; whether 'full-time' or 'part-time'.

Whether or not the preacher has an official pastoral role among a specific congregation, the presence or absence of pastoral concern in preaching, and consistency or otherwise between pastoral care and what is preached and how it is preached, will make themselves felt. Beyond anything to do with sermon content or method, hearers can sense whether the preacher cares. They feel instinctively (if not always articulately) whether what is being offered them is nourishing and nurturing (even if they cannot take the full meal on that occasion), or whether it is vacuous, tasteless or downright poisonous. And whatever the preacher's role – regular pastor, 'lay preacher', visitor – their attitude to their hearers will show.

To identify the preaching encounter as a 'pastoral' one does not imply anything about the hearers with respect to their prior commitment, allegiance or church membership; it encompasses 'evangelistic' preaching as much as 'teaching'. Whatever kind of spiritual life our hearers have or do not have, we are their pastors inasmuch as we co-operate, or not, with the desire of Father, Son and Spirit to bring fullness of life to all.

The pastor who preaches to his or her congregation most weeks in the year is not just engaged in the delivery of necessary information to an anonymous group (like the radio or TV news presenter), nor the regular performance of scripts to equally anonymous groups (like an actor). He or she is in a peculiar and privileged relationship to these people, and preaching is neither an interruption to this relationship nor the main driver of it. It is an integral part of it.

---

23 On the theological function of preaching see also Trevor Pitt, 2010, 'The Conversation of Preaching and Theology', in Stevenson, *Future of Preaching*, pp. 65–83.

24 On the connection between preaching and pastoral care see Michael J. Quicke, 2005, 'The Scriptures in Preaching', in Paul Ballard and Stephen R. Holmes (eds), *The Bible in Pastoral Practice*, London: Darton, Longman & Todd, pp. 241–57.

Again, we must recognize this as a fact before we begin to talk about 'what' and 'how' we preach. Whatever we as preachers may think we are doing – if, for instance, we imagine that we can get away with a distinctly non-pastoral tirade on Sunday morning and resume normal church meetings on Monday evening or pastoral visits on Tuesday afternoon – we will soon find out that the congregation thinks differently. *There is a relationship there*, and preaching holds out the possibilities of either deepening it or damaging it.

Yet the relationship is not an ordinary one, but is inevitably bound up with the preacher's role. Across the spectrum of theologies of ministry, there is common ground in the recognition that where there are ministers, they are set apart by the Church under, it believes, the guidance and inspiration of God, for guiding his flock. Not only the preacher's compassion and motivation, therefore, are at stake, and his or her sensitivity to the fact of pastoral relationship, but the fittingness of the way in which he or she exercises the entire pastoral role. Thus a preacher may avoid the danger mentioned above of real damage to the relationship, yet still court weakening the preaching event if it is not seen in a healthy balance with other elements of the ministerial calling. Others apart from the preacher will, one hopes, share in the pastoral care of a congregation; but a preacher who preaches about care yet appears to give little time to caring, or to leave it all to others, risks damaging the pastoral relationship in perhaps a less immediate, but more long-term way than the one who offloads grudges or hostility in a single sermon. The same is equally true, conversely, of those who spend large amounts of time on personal pastoral caring but insufficient time reflecting how most helpfully to advance the pastoral cause in preaching. No minister should be thought of – or think of themselves – as omnicompetent, but there are central ministerial tasks which rightly require to be held in proper balance.

An aspect of exercising a pastoral function through preaching is leadership. The relationship between preaching and leadership is a delicate one.[25] The tasks of preacher, pastor and leader come together in the calling to build Christian community based on the word of God.[26] On the one hand, a pastor who preaches is **de facto** exercising leadership.

25 See Michael J. Quicke, 2006, *360-degree Leadership: Preaching to Transform Congregations*, Grand Rapids: Baker.

26 'Because the word conveys the new humanity, by its very nature it is always directed towards the congregation. It seeks community, it needs community, because it is already laden with humanity', Bonhoeffer, 'The Proclaimed Word', p. 35.

He or she is acting at the very least as a guide to those hearing. And the preacher who is sensitive both to the revelation of God and to the needs of the people will rightly seek a sense of how God may be wanting to lead the people on in their specific circumstances and their Christian community life. On the other hand, when preaching is understood purely as a function of leadership, the Godward dimension is easily lost (even if God-language is used). Preaching as an event which serves to enable worship, transform cultures and shape theology cannot at the same time be preaching that is equivalent to motivational management.

The relationship of preaching to pastoral care is intimately linked to its relationship to theology. It is the pastoring impulse which motivates and directs the preacher to articulate not necessarily what the congregation *wants* to hear, but what it is *able* to hear of the gospel vision the preacher has received. It is this same impulse which drives the preacher to utter not just a resumé of their own beliefs, but whatever from Scripture and Christian tradition will most helpfully enlarge, redirect and engage with the various beliefs and perspectives already held by the congregation. The reality is that people will be adjusting those beliefs and perspectives all the time – notwithstanding the periods of resistance to change which we all live through. The pastoral preacher fulfils an important function contributing to that process.

Questions for the local church

- In what ways is the preaching you experience, whether as preacher or hearer, fulfilling or seeking to fulfil these functions?
- Does it fulfil one or more of them better than others, and if so, why?
- Are there other functions which preaching is fulfilling, or could or should fulfil?

Areas for research

The way in which preaching *in fact* fulfils any of the four functions identified in this chapter is an important topic for empirical research. For example, one could build on the foundations being laid in the study of 'ordinary hermeneutics' to study the way in which preaching in fact contributes to the worshipping life and theological development of a congregation.

Further reading

Martyn D. Atkins, 2001, *Preaching in a Cultural Context*, Peterborough: Foundery Press.

Neville Clark, 1991, *Preaching in Context: Word, Worship and the People of God*, Bury St Edmunds: Kevin Mayhew.

G. Lee Ramsey Jr, 2000, *Care-full Preaching: From Sermon to Caring Community*, St Louis: Chalice Press.

William H. Willimon, 2005, *Proclamation and Theology*, Nashville: Abingdon.

PART 2

Introduction

The second stage of practical theology is called by Osmer 'The Interpretive Task: Sagely Wisdom'.[1] This is the stage at which we bring various theories from the sciences or humanities to bear upon the phenomenon on we which we are reflecting, in order to be able to understand better from a human perspective what is going on. Thus in Chapters 3 and 4 I seek to interpret preaching with the aid of several theories related to human communication. We will consider aspects of language, media, rhetoric, sociology and psychology. If as theologians we are tempted to doubt the necessity or worth of this stage – preferring to move straight on to the next stage, in order to develop a theological perspective – the wisdom tradition of Scripture should be sufficient to convince us otherwise. Osmer gives an excellent account of the pertinence of the wisdom tradition to the practical theological task.[2]

Some might still feel, however, that preaching is such an irreducibly theological event that to postpone a properly theological consideration of it till Part 3 is to give in to reductionism. Are we not allowing our basic understanding to be dictated by 'secular' categories? I offer three responses to such a fear.

First, the phenomena of preaching which I seek to analyse here are, to my mind, thoroughly conditioned by God himself. In no sense do I regard preaching as merely a 'secular' occurrence. There is no wish to claim that the various 'human' categories applied to the study can fully encompass or explain the divine realities inherent in the event. In Osmer's helpful analogy, human theories provide a map of the territory that may be found more or less suitable for the expedition, but they are not the territory itself, and of necessity leave much out.[3] This is true even when the 'territory' is purely mundane. Yet such theories and

---

1 Richard R. Osmer, 2008, *Practical Theology: An Introduction*, Grand Rapids: Eerdmans, pp. 79–128.

2 Osmer, *Practical Theology*, pp. 81–100.

3 Osmer, *Practical Theology*, p. 80.

categories, with all their limitations, stem from the creativity implanted in us by God himself. They are not 'secular' at all. They mediate his creative wisdom to us and are meant to be used, alongside what we call the 'special' revelation he has given in Christ and through Scripture.

Second, I make no claim that these categories from the human sciences, or my application of them, offers us a 'neutral' analysis. There can be no such thing. Therefore, although I do not make theology an explicit part of the framework in this part, I am very happy to acknowledge that a theological perspective undergirds the way I seek to understand everything – preaching included. In practice that means I have chosen frameworks of analysis that seem to me to accord with such a theological perspective and usefully fill it out. Most importantly, I adopt a fundamentally positive view of the potential of human communication, grounded in the belief in a God who communes with his children and enables their mutual communion to be real and not sham.

Third, the truth of God's incarnation in Christ suggests that to ignore the human dimensions of our knowledge, our practices and our discipleship would be profoundly un-theological. If, as we continue to claim, God still speaks, somehow, through human beings, our aim should be to seek to understand with all our (God-given!) human powers what that claim entails and what are its practical consequences for us. History is littered with the wreckage caused by those who have been so confident in the possession of divine inspiration that they have (unwittingly) wrought abuse of some kind on their many hearers. Such speakers (if Christian) have often, I suspect, not grasped this implication of the incarnation: that far from neglecting the human, we are called to embrace it and enable it to be God-filled. For preaching, this means that it would be sub-Christian to neglect the human capacities, conditioning and categories of thought which enable us to make the most of who we are and what we might be. When all that has been attended to, the question of whom, how, when and where he will inspire is for God's free choice alone. The danger for us is precisely that we will be so sure of God's inspiration that we seek to act as God instead of being ourselves. This, to me, is amply sufficient to justify bringing all the relevant tools of human knowledge, skill, creativity and hard work to the task of preaching itself, and of understanding what it is we are about.

Central to reflection on the nature of preaching must be an awareness of the dynamics of human communication, and the various theories considered in Chapters 3 and 4 all bear in some way upon this phenomenon. Preaching's place in Christian tradition and contemporary Church life gives it a unique character among communicative events –

a uniqueness greatly enhanced by the divine dimensions claimed for it in Christian theology. But to overlook what it shares in common with other acts of communication would be a grave mistake.

The simple model of communication in which a 'sender' (usually a speaker or writer) encodes a 'message' (usually in words) and delivers it to a 'receiver' (usually a hearer or reader) is now widely and rightly regarded as inadequate. Even if we expand the model to allow for a possible act or acts of translation somewhere along the way (in other words, bringing a third person into the frame as an interpreter, or envisaging the necessity of a specific process of decoding by the receiver), it should be clear that an event of communication is more complex than the simple 'delivery' of a message.[4] Such a model implies, essentially, a mind-to-mind procedure that excludes the subtle but highly important elements of personal interchange that take place within and beneath the outward signs of words (or other signals).

Thus we are wrong if we imagine that preaching is simply a matter of words. In a helpful application of contemporary communication theory to preaching, Achim Härtner and Holger Eschmann explore the model of the 'message square' offered by the Hamburg psychologist Friedemann Schulz von Thun.[5] The 'message square' recognizes that the 'message' is not simply a one-dimensional piece of encoded 'content'. Rather, this 'content' is but one aspect of the message, one side of the square. Along with it go three other sides: disclosure of self (the sender is saying something, at least implicitly, about themselves), relationship (the sender is saying something, at least implicitly, about his or her relationship to the receiver(s)), and appeal (the sender is saying something, at least implicitly, about how he or she desires the receiver(s) to respond).

Thus in a sermon and in any particular section of it, the preacher is not only 'delivering content' (even if they *think* that is all they are doing). They are also disclosing something about themselves, something about their relationship to the hearers, and something about how they wish the hearers to respond.

The unity and force of the act of communication will depend considerably on the consistency between these elements. For instance, let us suppose the preacher is explaining 1 John 4.7: 'Beloved, let us love one

---

4 For an explanation, expansion and critique of this basic 'cybernetic' model see Achim Härtner and Holger Eschmann, 2004, *Learning to Preach Today: A Guide for Communicators and Listeners*, Sheffield: Cliff College, pp. 167–71.

5 Discussed in Härtner and Eschmann, *Learning to Preach*, pp. 171–98.

another; for love is of God, and the one who loves is born of God and knows God.' The 'content' of the explanation may be well encoded, in a language that the hearers will easily understand. But the hearers will also be 'hearing' what the preacher's manner and the wider context of their words is disclosing about him or her. Is this preacher a loving person? If so, the content of the explanation will be reinforced; if not, the communicative event will seem flawed – love is being spoken about, but not demonstrated. Further, they will also be 'hearing' something about the preacher's relationship *to them*: does this preacher *love us*? If he or she loves others but not the hearers themselves, the content of the message will not be much supported. Finally, they will also be 'hearing' an implied appeal. The preacher may simply be explaining the text, but the hearers will surely detect whether or not the preacher really means them to take the text's injunction as applying to them. The preacher may or may not go on to make that application explicit, but the hearers will know whether they are to take this text and its explanation seriously. Preaching, like all other communicative events, is a relational activity, involving not only the mind but also the emotions, the will, and the richness of person-to-person contact. Sometimes those who, for whatever reason, seek to suppress or deny this reality only succeed in making it more obvious.

The presence of this 'square' of factors puts certain obligations on both sender and receiver. When communication is working well, these obligations tend to be fulfilled quite automatically. It is the first stage of reflective practice to raise such unconscious or automatic levels of behaviour to consciousness. It is often a breakdown in behaviour or relationship – in this case, that of communication – which makes us conscious of these levels; one of the great hopes of the reflective practitioner, in whatever sphere, is to achieve prevention of such breakdown rather than to be always trying to pick up the pieces.

Thus whether they think about it long and hard or not, anyone who wants to communicate with another or others as a 'sender' will be putting a part of themselves into the words; will see the event as a relational one; and will reckon with the fact that their words will carry an appeal of some kind. Equally, anyone who wants to be involved in communication as a 'receiver' will be alert not only to the message contents, but also to the personal, relational and appeal aspects of the sender's message: they will be 'four-eared receivers', attuned to all four sides of the 'message square'.[6] Moreover, in any continuous piece of communication there is

---

6 Härtner and Eschmann, *Learning to Preach*, pp. 175–6.

constant interplay between sender and receiver, such that the sender is always responding to signals picked up from the receiver (seeking to discern whether the message is getting through, and on what levels), even as the receiver is always responding to signals picked up from the sender (seeking to detect the various aspects of the four-sided message, and how one should react to them).[7]

Although this interchange is most obvious in conversation or dialogue, in which the roles of sender and receiver are constantly being swapped, it is a mistake to think it is not also happening in a largely monological address. The receivers' signals may be silent ones, but they are there to be discerned nonetheless. And the *public* nature of preaching, as an event with multiple hearers, makes this process especially complex.

All this constitutes the most basic reason why preaching must be considered as a corporate, not an individualistic event. The previous chapters have already given strong backing to such a notion, as preaching has been located within the tradition and practices of the Church. But it is as a communicative event that it displays this corporate character most obviously.

In this part we will unpack the implications of the 'message square' for preaching. In Chapter 3 we will consider the mystery of language, the words (or images) which are the basic tools of communication, and the relationship of medium and message. This will lead to examining preaching as rhetorical journey, an event in time, with constant interplay between 'sender' and 'receiver'. In Chapter 4 we will explore preaching as a sociological event in which the identity of a congregation is shaped, as well as some of the psychological dynamics which feed into the preacher's self-disclosure and appeal, the relationship between preacher and hearers, and the hearers' response to the message.

Finally we will raise the question of preaching as an event of *spiritual* encounter. How are claims that preaching is a locus for meeting with God to be assessed? This will form an appropriate transition point to Part 3, in which we will turn to our theological appraisal of preaching events.

---

7 Härtner and Eschmann, *Learning to Preach*, pp. 176–7.

3

Language, Medium and Rhetoric

The mystery of language

Words are a preacher's stock-in-trade. As we have seen, live communication is a relational event, which invests words with tone and value which go far beyond anything that could conceivably be captured in a dictionary. Nonetheless, words themselves and the language-systems of which they are a part have a mysterious character and force which must be reckoned with.

A successful act of communication requires the adoption not just of a language but a particular 'register' of language appropriate to both speaker and hearers. For instance, a preacher who uses the language of a theological lecture will not communicate effectively with most congregations. There are, however, deeper questions to consider here, arising from the modern philosophy of language. Without getting mired in abstruse philosophical debates, we will seek to tread a path between extreme positions in order to identify some key facts.

First, it is now generally recognized that we are all *embedded* in language, yet have power to shape it. Language shapes our thinking and living in profound ways from the earliest stage of life. This recognition has come in response to the over-confident view of the Enlightenment that as humans we could be masters of language, deploying it at will for our purposes, and able to decode the language of others with the aid of authoritative guides such as dictionaries. Some have gone so far the other way as to say there can be no thinking without language. Without adjudicating on that point, we are wise to recognize that no speaker can simply select and control what they say at will. But this does not mean we are helpless tools of an impersonal system. Words can still work *for us* in creative ways. But they do this not so much as tools to be selected objectively from a toolbox, but rather as an internal lump of clay which invites being shaped into particular forms.

Perceiving this should save us from two unfortunate errors. On the one hand, it is futile to seek to escape from the ordinary language that has formed us – whether the common language of our upbringing or the specific 'Christian' cultural language that forms our heritage of faith. Both are a part of the 'givenness' of what we have to work with, and any attempt to leave behind either (in the interests, perhaps, of being more 'accessible' to our hearers) is doomed to failure. On the other hand, we should not imagine we are *imprisoned* by these inherited languages. We are free agents who can mould the clay in ways that are both authentic to us and available to our hearers to receive. Otherwise we are doomed to mere repetition. Unfortunately, some preaching seems to court this error. Cliché may be religious-sounding, and accord well with orthodox doctrine, but that does not stop it being cliché.[1]

Moreover, there is a creative element to being a receiver as well as to being a sender. Not only is it *possible* to invest creatively in the words we hear, bringing our own associations to what, to the speaker, might seem a perfectly ordinary sentence; we are actually doing it, consciously or unconsciously, all the time. We are interpreting beings, as linguistic philosophy since Martin Heidegger has recognized.[2] A single word – 'waves', 'rose', 'hospital', almost anything – may draw to the surface of a hearer's mind specific memories or expectations, as well as vague hopes, delights and fears. That sensation then shapes and colours not only the meaning the hearer receives from the word, but their reception of all the communication that is to come.

Without frank recognition of this combination of the given and the creative in our use of language, discussion of the subject of preaching and, indeed, of specific sermons will be fraught with pitfalls. As R. E. C. Browne put it, the sermon is to be located neither in the mind or script of the preacher, nor in the ears of the hearer, but in that uncertain yet fertile space between them, as the gift of language is moulded, almost simultaneously, by each.[3]

The second modern insight into language relevant to us here is that words do have meaningful reference beyond themselves to a 'real'

1 For incisive criticism of jargon and clichés in preaching, see Charles Smyth, 1940, *The Art of Preaching: Preaching in the Church of England 747–1939*, London: SPCK, pp. 141–3; on the importance of originality of language in preaching, see R. E. C. Browne, 1976, *The Ministry of the Word*, 2nd edn, London: SCM, pp. 91–100.

2 On the importance of Heidegger and his pupil Hans-Georg Gadamer for thinking about preaching, see John W. Wright, 2007, *Telling God's Story: Narrative Preaching for Christian Formation*, Downers Grove, IL: InterVarsity Press Academic, pp. 21–32.

3 See Browne, *Ministry of the Word*, pp. 28–31.

world, but also shape our perception of it. Although words are part of language-systems in which their relationship to each other is crucial[4] – thus, for instance, we cannot understand 'red' without reference to 'black', 'yellow', 'green' and so on – the label 'red' really can be applied to certain objects. The notion that there is no reality – or at least no accessible reality – outside language probably lies behind some of the nagging scepticism about words and their effectiveness which undermines preaching as well as other communicative events. Is E. M. Forster's jibe about 'poor little talkative Christianity'[5] the more stinging because words, in the end, refer only to other words?

Common sense as well as a Christian understanding of the creation, however, suggests that there is more to reality than language alone. Words evoke pictures, places, memories, ideas. At the simplest level, when we follow a sign saying 'exit' and then find our way out of the building, we have experienced the fact that there are words, and there is reality, and the two are not the same. This is one of the important senses in which words can be said to *work* (we will come to another shortly). They fulfil their function of pointing, not just to other words in the 'system' of language, but to reality beyond the system.[6] Whether they 'work' effectively on any particular occasion, of course, is another matter (someone might have mischievously turned the 'exit' sign to point in the wrong direction). But the preacher has no need to be hampered by the vague doubt that seeps into the atmosphere of the age about the power of words to do their 'pointing' job. Look around, and listen: they are doing it all the time.

The relationship between words and the world also, however, works the other way round. It is widely accepted that even though there is much more to reality than language, language certainly shapes our perception and experience of reality in penetrating ways. It does not simply point away from itself to 'things'; to a significant extent it controls how we will encounter those 'things'. This is true even for the 'exit' sign: it turns what might otherwise be a random opening in the side of a building into a passage from one space to another, a passage which may turn out to be fraught with significance.

It is true on a deeper level for the lazy jargon which now forms so much of our public discourse. For example, when the education or

---

4 As highlighted by Ferdinand de Saussure, 1977, *Course in General Linguistics*, trans. Wade Baskin, Glasgow: Fontana (originally lectures given in Geneva 1907–11).

5 E. M. Forster, 1961, *A Passage to India*, Harmondsworth: Penguin, p. 148.

6 Philosophers of language call this language's 'referential' function.

health services talk about 'delivering' patient care or teaching, it surely not only reinforces but helps to perpetuate (and create in the young) a sense that these things can be done in much the same impersonal way as a postman pushing a letter through the door.[7] When teachers or nurses are simply 'human resources', links in the chain of 'delivering targets', it is little wonder they are sometimes demotivated, lacking the inspiration to throw heart and soul into the task. When railway passengers turn into 'customers', it establishes the common perception that money is the only language that really talks: we can take our 'custom' elsewhere if we're not satisfied (which is largely an illusion, as it happens, with the British railway system). It tends to erase from the public mind the very idea that if people were motivated by noble ideals of service, a business *might* run as a monopoly in a way that was *both* financially successful *and* of outstanding service to its 'customers'.

The power of language to shape our view of reality and thus, in a sense, our 'world' is eloquently applied to preaching by Walter Brueggemann, who identifies the preacher's task as being to enable people to *imagine* the world differently, according to the way of God's kingdom. He emphasizes the vital force of language – above all poetic, imagistic language – to achieve this end.[8]

My third conviction about language that is pertinent to preaching is that *meaning is never final*, yet *words nonetheless have effects*. Here I seek to hold in balance (or tension) two positions sometimes seen as sharply opposite. On the one hand is that of Jacques Derrida, famous for his assertion that meaning is endlessly 'deferred' because the sign-system within which we operate is infinite. On the other is the speech–act theory developed especially by J. L. Austin and John R. Searle, which identifies the way in which words do have effects in society: a famous person names a ship and it is named; I call your name and you turn round; she promises to love me for ever and I her, and our relationship is fundamentally different thereafter.[9]

It seems to me that, paradoxical as it may sound, there is plentiful evidence that both these positions are correct. In support of Derrida, we

---

7 For an excellent critique of the 'delivery' metaphor as applied to preaching, proposing 'performance' as a much better one, see Jana Childers, 2008, 'Recovering Performance', in Paul Scott Wilson (ed.), 2008, *The New Interpreter's Handbook of Preaching*, Nashville: Abingdon, pp. 213–15.

8 For example Walter Brueggemann, 1989, *Finally Comes the Poet*, Minneapolis: Fortress.

9 On the debate between Derrida and Searle, see Kevin J. Vanhoozer, 1998, *Is there a Meaning in this Text?: The Bible, the Reader and the Morality of Literary Knowledge*, Leicester: Apollos, pp. 211–14.

have only to think of the multiplicity of associations evoked in 'receivers' by the 'senders' of particular messages, already highlighted above. In addition, we may say that the 'meaning' of a sermon, as of any other speech, is indeed 'endlessly deferred'. Its hearers, and indeed its speaker, both while it is remembered, and beyond the point of conscious memory, will in countless small ways adjust their sense of its meaning in response to the infinite number of 'signs' of which we are daily aware: words heard, sights seen, people encountered, interpretations offered. Any attempt to argue for an 'authority' of the preacher must take account of the essentially unstable nature of language exposed by Derrida, open as it is to ever-renewable meanings for its users.

This is most manifest in a preacher's use of figurative language – simile, metaphor and imagery of all kinds. By its nature, such language breaks the conventions, and strives to yield new insight. For example, the phenomenon of doubt is not actually visible, but a preacher might describe doubt as a 'dark cloud looming overhead'. Nor is a personal difficulty like unemployment, but a preacher might call it a 'seemingly insurmountable peak'. These (not particularly imaginative) examples show how easily metaphorical language may yield new meanings, not by any means confined to what the speaker had in mind, and thus effect a shift in the whole language-system within which the hearer makes sense not only of the sermon but of the world. Either metaphor may succeed in capturing the preacher's sense of sympathy with the problems mentioned and thus enhance the communicative bond between preacher and hearer. They may in addition form a helpful part of the mental furniture of the person suffering from them, a prelude to discovering a solution (aren't clouds eventually dispersed by the sun? are any peaks really insurmountable?) Thus they may positively shift the language-system within which the hearer operates.

It is equally possible, however, that the hearer will react adversely to such a metaphor. Perhaps 'dark cloud looming overhead' makes the doubt seem worse than it is; and because the image sounds exaggerated, it strikes the hearer as a sweeping comparison rather than a useful diagnosis. Or perhaps the unemployed person is a mountaineer, and 'seemingly insurmountable peak' makes his condition sound much more exciting than it really is.

Metaphorical language thus holds the potential both for enlarging perceptions and a sense of meaning, and also for allowing considerable 'slippage' between the ideal intentions of the speaker and the actual responses of the hearers. Moreover, the responses of the same hearer to the same utterance may change over time. All this demonstrates

Derrida's point that closure of 'meaning' is unattainable. We can go on finding 'meaning' in a sermon (or any other set of words), but there will never come a point when we can say 'that's it' – even as individuals, let alone as groups of hearers.

Yet in support of Austin and Searle, we can surely say that despite Derrida's point, language actually serves us remarkably well in achieving certain ends. We manage most of our daily transactions in family, social and working lives with fair success. Words convey what we want them to convey: the time of a meeting, the expression of a wish, the sealing of a deal, the desire to have a question answered. The failures in communication are the exceptions which heighten the fact that success is the rule. The key point is that we do not usually spend time dwelling on the possible range of *meanings* of words that we hear or speak. This is because our concern is with what the words will *do*, and we have a well-justified expectation, on the basis of past experience and established social patterns, that certain words in certain combinations will have a fairly predictable effect. This is the main interest of speech–act theory: what words actually *do*.

So what might a sermon *do*? It might issue promises, encouragements, warnings. It might pose questions and give information. It might affirm hearers in a belief that Christianity is dull, or that the preacher is eccentric, or that the gospel is true. The way it *does* these things is not necessarily related *explicitly* to its actual words. On a simple level, Thomas G. Long writes that the sermon's introduction should offer a 'promise' about what is to follow: in other words, it should have the effect of making the hearers feel that what is to come will be interesting and worth listening to.[10] But of course very few preachers will begin by telling their listeners 'What you are about to hear will be interesting and worth listening to'! The introduction achieves the effect of a promise by being, in itself, interesting and inviting – whatever it may actually be *saying*.

In a similar but more profound way, a sermon as a whole may achieve the effect of a promise, warning, encouragement or question without ever using words like 'promise', 'warning' and so on. The entire tone may do it. The whole matter and manner of a preacher's discourse may communicate the graciousness of God, such that the hearers sense that God has truly been making them a promise. Or the preacher might tell a provocative story without ever posing an explicit question to the

---

10 Thomas G. Long, 2005, *The Witness of Preaching*, 2nd edn, Louisville: Westminster John Knox, pp. 177–85.

hearers, yet achieve the effect of getting the hearers to face a clear question or questions that are crucially important. The presence of such effects is well attested.

So there are ways of using language which, notwithstanding the multiple associations and endless deferral of meaning highlighted by Derrida, do achieve important effects, in preaching as in any other form of discourse. However, a public speech such as a sermon poses more of a challenge than ordinary conversation when it comes to achieving desired and expected effects with words. This is partly because of its public nature, and the difficulty of saying something which will have a similar effect for all concerned (even more, of saying something which will have *different* effects appropriate to the different hearers!). Partly it is because a monologue, the normal sermon form, does not allow for interruptions to seek clarification, verbal responses and so on. The social setting of the sermon may therefore encourage more speculation on varieties of possible meaning than do everyday speech transactions. For example, a preacher's words of exhortation which he or she feels are 'just what they need' may, while achieving the desired effect in some, constitute a threat or an insult to others; instead of being encouraged, they may be affronted. The achievement of desirable and helpful effects by the preacher's speech–acts therefore calls for more careful attention to language and, especially, to the hearers than it does in daily conversation.

It seems healthy, therefore, neither to deny the multiple meanings that may emerge from a preacher's discourse, which certainly entail the possibility of misunderstanding, nor to deny the power of words to achieve certain effects which can be, at least to some extent, predicted. Language is both open to being ever shaped into new forms that may yield rich insight or trigger unhelpful associations, and yet stable enough to be used by us in bringing about a variety of goals in social interaction. Both realities are abundantly evident in preaching.

Medium and message

In the 1960s the communications theorist Marshall McCluhan made famous the slogan 'the medium is the message'. His point was that the content of a message and the form in which it is delivered cannot be neatly separated. It is simply wrong to imagine that a message can be detached from the form in which it is couched, or transposed into a different form without its actual content being adjusted in some way. The most basic example of this fact is translation. No text or even sentence can be translated from the form of one language into that of another without undergoing some shift, however subtle, in meaning or resonance. This is because forms of communication are not neutral shapes, empty receptacles for meaning. They carry their own baggage of associations which becomes bound up with the 'content' of the message they carry.

McCluhan's thesis is only one of the more well-known manifestations of the widespread conviction that stripping away 'rhetoric' from speech or writing in order to achieve a 'clean', objective presentation is impossible. There is no genuinely *communicative* language that is 'untainted' by the drive, in some way, to persuade, to evoke, to make a mark. And that drive is primarily expressed via the form in which the message is contained. That 'form' always consists of more than bare 'language' in the sense of words in combination. It comprises also the social vehicles for carrying that language – conversation, print, broadcasting, and so on. And often its 'language' will include elements other than words, especially pictures. Sometimes words will be eclipsed or excluded altogether.

McCluhan was writing at a time when the medium of television was on the rise. He provoked important questions about what that medium 'does' to the messages it conveys – and, more profoundly, about the message it conveys in itself. Those questions have only become more acute and interesting since the growth of other electronic media, particularly the internet. Let us take the example of a news report to illustrate his point.

Imagine a large meteorite has landed in a local park. Imagine too that reports on the event, the first ones each using similar words at their heart, are soon afterwards being relayed in a variety of different forms. Then consider the varied dynamics of the different reports:

1 A man who has been walking his dog in the park rushes home and recounts the event rather breathlessly to his wife.
2 A woman who has seen the meteorite landing from an upstairs flat types an entry on her blog, with a link to her Facebook page where she has uploaded some pictures she took with her digital camera.
3 National radio reports the event briefly, summarizing the eyewitnesses' words, on one of its late-afternoon two-minute news summaries.
4 The event is reported on the national TV news that evening, again largely in the words of the two eyewitnesses. It is accompanied by professional video footage of the scene. Immediately after the

news bulletin, by coincidence, there is a science-fiction film about UFOs.

5 The same report appears on the online news channel. It can be read as text, listened to or watched. In addition, users are invited to send in any of their comments or pictures. There is a link to a Science page where the nature and origin of meteorites are explained, with pictures, and there is a time chart listing previous meteorite landings.

6 In the morning, the breakfast-time radio and TV programmes repeat the report, interview one of the eyewitnesses live and get some expert comment from an astronomer.

7 The national newspapers include the report on an inside page, with pictures, where it jostles alongside stories about corrupt politicians, failed celebrities, drug-ridden sports and remarkably rescued animals.

8 The blogger gets some responses and a conversation opens up about the strange and unexpected.

9 Two days later the local newspaper prints a report largely consisting of the eyewitness accounts of the man and the woman, together with a picture and the banner headline 'The Aliens have Landed'.

10 A young girl writes about the event in her diary, which will be found by her own children after her death, seventy years later.

It is worth pausing over this scenario to spend some time imagining how, in each case, the medium is shaping the message. Several questions may be asked. In which medium is the message most trustworthy? How might we know? In which medium will it seem most trustworthy to its receivers? How do the various media make the message sound – serious, funny, entertaining, intriguing, fanciful?

Many points of significance could be drawn out here; let me just highlight two.

First, it should be clear that although the *words* of the report will not be exactly the same in the various different media or occasions, the varieties of 'message' caused by the differences of media are mainly conditioned by factors other than the words of the report themselves. They concern, especially, the way in which the words are conveyed (speech, writing, print, online, broadcast etc.); the way in which they are framed (headlines, discussions, background information, opportunity for 'receiver response/interaction'); the pictures with which they are or are not accompanied; and the other messages which are juxtaposed with them.

Second, the transition from report 3 to the subsequent reports high-lights a matter that has become even more pressing in social analy-sis since McCluhan. This is the question of whether 'information' has become so packaged as 'entertainment' that our basic conceptions of truth, goodness and beauty have undergone a perhaps dangerous shift. A brief radio report may still contain the authoritative echoes of the early days of the BBC. As soon as the report moves to television, the presence not only of pictures but of *seen* newsreaders and reporters who have clearly learned to make themselves presentable on screen subtly changes the whole communicative event. We are drawn into it much more immediately, but with the possibility that the visual dimen-sion so overwhelms our senses that our grasp of the details of the hap-pening is lessened.

This shift in dynamic is further pronounced when we get to the end of the news bulletin and start watching the sci-fi movie. The news has become, in retrospect, just another stage in the evening's entertainment. It may have been occasionally harrowing, but the excitement of the meteorite landing reminds us that life can be quite fun and safe really; so we sit back and enjoy the film. Of course, the film might get har-rowing too, but we know that it's not 'real'. And because most of what many people watch isn't 'real', why should we face up to the reality behind the news? Subsequent mutations of the report (5–8) partly help to balance this out, by including a greater element of serious reflection and background. But they also, arguably, start to blur the lines be-tween 'information' and 'entertainment' still further. At least, the bare 'information' of the early stages can get blurred or even forgotten as the story 'runs and runs', and is mediated now through online discus-sion. What had originally been a (nearly) spontaneous account of an event, inducing perhaps surprise and perplexity, has gradually become a 'story' with a life of its own which may be 'accessed' with a range of purposes (from scientific research through to online fantasizing) and effects (from the satisfaction of knowledge gained through to the titil-lation of our senses).

Neil Postman's 1987 book *Amusing Ourselves to Death* addressed this subject head-on, and it is interesting to note that the continuing debate warranted a new edition in 2006.[11] It seems that broadcast-ers, fully aware of what has happened here, have decided to embrace rather than resist it. Thus new genres have arisen such as 'faction' ('A

---

11 Neil Postman, 2006, *Amusing Ourselves to Death: Public Discourse in the Age of Showbusiness*, 2nd edn, London: Penguin.

literary genre in which fictional narrative is developed from a basis of real events or characters; documentary fiction; similarly, in film-making, etc.; an instance of this'),[12] the 'docu-drama' ('A dramatized film (usually for television) which is based on a semi-fictional interpretation of real events; a documentary drama'),[13] and 'infotainment' ('Broadcast material which seeks to inform and entertain simultaneously; information presented in an entertaining way').[14] A current affairs programme such as *Broadcasting House* (Sunday mornings on Radio 4) can combine a deliberately light and ironic element with serious journalism.[15]

The relevance of all this for an analysis of preaching is far-reaching. Preaching is not only an event of person-to-person communication, drawing on the rich resources of language. It has its own 'medium', or rather media. Clearly, one medium is most familiar from its long use: the speech of an individual, maybe clerically or otherwise formally dressed, frequently from a pulpit or lectern, normally within a church building, without immediate opportunity for interaction. Increasingly, newer media are making their appearance as vehicles for preaching, as the resources of film and data projection are brought to bear. 'Hearers' may now also be 'viewers', whether what they are viewing is pictures or words or both. In some contexts, the hearers' silence is broken as the preacher seeks some form of interactivity and explicit response. In others, the 'hearers' or 'viewers' are not limited to those physically gathered with the preacher, but include those to whom the event is broadcast on radio, television or the internet, and/or those who engage with the sermon later via a recording or transcript.

The vital question which thus arises, and which can only be answered with difficulty, over time, entailing careful empirical observation as well as a theoretical grasp of communication dynamics, is how the different media in which preaching may come affect the message. A book which helpfully opens up this question in relation to worship as a

12 *OED*: http://dictionary.oed.com/cgi/entry/50081508?query_type=word&queryword=Faction&first=1&max_to_show=10&sort_type=alpha&result_place=3&search_id=NOLO-ruVWzC-1009&hilite=50081508, accessed 09.10.2009. The first citation of the word is from 1967.

13 *OED*: http://dictionary.oed.com/cgi/entry/50068082?single=1&query_type=word&queryword=Docudrama&first=1&max_to_show=10, accessed 09.10.2009. The first citation is from 1961, though it is not cited in a British context till 1981.

14 *OED*: http://dictionary.oed.com/cgi/entry/00293375?single=1&query_type=word&queryword=infotainment&first=1&max_to_show=10, accessed 09.10.2009. The first citation is from 1980.

15 http://www.bbc.co.uk/programmes/b006qnj3, accessed 09.10.2009.

whole is Shane Hipps, 2005, *The Hidden Power of Electronic Culture: How Media Shapes Faith, the Gospel and Church*.[16] Drawing on McCluhan's work, Hipps issues a salutary warning that whatever we do with electronic culture, we should not imagine that it is neutral, or plays no part in shaping what is done and said in our worship. Naturally, the point must be applied equally to the traditional medium of the sermon. The question is what any particular medium is doing to the message in a given context. Let us explore this in relation to both 'traditional' and more 'contemporary' media, focusing on the aspects of the *familiarity* and the *associations* of particular media.

The *familiarity* of a medium can be both a strength and a weakness. A familiar medium may allow a message to be received with less 'interference' than an unfamiliar one, for it is largely the message, not the medium, on which one is concentrating. Thus a regular congregation used to traditional preaching may hear the message more fully when they are allowed to concentrate on it, without the (potential) distraction of, for example, a more informal, interactive or visual medium. But equally, it is possible that the content of the message may be *dulled* precisely because of the familiarity of the medium. The preacher may be speaking of Jesus and his informal, storytelling, interactive approach to instructing his disciples and the crowds. Yet if the preacher is safe in his pulpit and his robes, giving a formal monological discourse with no opportunity for response, will not the medium be *working against* the message and thus blunting its impact?

We must also ask 'familiar to whom?' The conventional form of preaching may often possess the *advantage* of familiarity for those who regularly attend church. For occasional visitors, however, the ten- or twenty-minute live formal monologue may well be a very strange genre. Its use may accentuate the cultural barrier between 'insider' and 'outsider', and the stranger may find themselves somewhat embarrassed to be in this position of listener, such that the message itself is not clearly received. For such people, a multi-media presentation might feel both safer and more familiar, and thus provide a more propitious emotional space for the message itself to be heard.

Yet generalization is dangerous. An 'old-fashioned sermon' might be a deeply refreshing experience for a visitor – whether because it awakens positive memories from long ago, or is such a change from the banalities of

---

16 El Cajon, CA: Youth Specialities. Some of the material in this book is reproduced in Shane Hipps, 2009, *Flickering Pixels: How Technology Shapes Your Faith*, Grand Rapids: Zondervan.

television, or some other reason. The very same sermon might be a deeply soporific experience for a 'regular' who, perhaps, has heard similar things said by this same preacher in similar ways many times before, and longs for a fresh approach.

The *associations* of a medium are powerful. Think again of the reports of the meteorite landing. The wife who hears her husband's first-hand account will immediately be struck by the fact that *something out-of-the-ordinary has happened.* Her prior knowledge of her husband and her observations of his manner will probably give her a fair idea of whether his words constitute an accurate report or result from an unfortunate accident to his brain (perhaps he bumped into a lamppost, rather than saw a meteorite?). There is an immediacy in the report, a preparedness to be awakened out of the ordinary everyday routines, resulting from her relationship to her husband, the medium of conversation and the purported recentness of the event. However, for a young man unknown to the witnesses, relaxing after work the following evening by browsing the internet or curling up on the sofa with his paper, the event is experienced differently. Almost certainly he doesn't feel that it requires any action or reaction on his part. He may be interested or not depending on his personality. He might be tickled by the way the report is written or intrigued by the picture. But all the *associations* of a conversation with an eye-witness to whom one is close are different from the *associations* of reading a paper or surfing the web (which are, of course, also different from each other).

So what associations does preaching, in its various media, carry? Let us start with the example of open-air preaching in an obviously 'public' space, for here perhaps the question is raised most acutely. On the one hand, the kind of open-air preaching that sounds like a rant, that seems to have little concern for its listeners (or whether indeed there *are* any listeners), that appears to be an attempt to impose a view on an unwilling public, may be precisely what has given 'preaching' a bad name in some contemporary quarters, and which instils in Christians, never mind others, an unusually strong urge to pass by on the other side.[17] On the other hand, the open-air spaces of towns and cities are home to all kinds of pressure-groups seeking to gain attention by one means or another, handing out leaflets, getting people to give their bank details to charities, selling things second-hand, and – most significantly – giving

---

17 See Geoffrey Stevenson and Stephen Wright, 2008, *Preaching with Humanity: A Practical Guide for Today's Church*, London: Church House Publishing, pp. 1–11, especially p. 1.

dramatic or musical performances. Is it not perfectly possible – in theory – that the preacher can take her place in this veritable market-place of ideas, like Paul in Athens, and gain a respectful hearing through a reasonably traditional form of monological address? Even if she does not gain such a hearing, does such preaching not bear the honourable hallmark of being a 'fool for Christ'?[18]

My point here is that a key factor if these questions are to be answered is the *associations* the medium bears. The 'ranting' street-preacher may be associated with all sorts of negative images of high-pressure, manipulative communication against which most people strongly react. (The preacher themself may well not be conscious of communicating in this way; even if they are, they may think they have theological justification for it; and their lack of hearers may be taken as a sign that they are faithfully suffering in the cause of Christ. I think there are dangerous misconceptions in such thinking, but my point here is not to discuss these, but rather simply to observe the importance of associations in responding to a medium of communication.) On the other hand, in a society where increasing numbers of diverse views, special interests and philosophies claim our interest, sometimes quite stridently, the response to the medium of street-preaching in itself may be neutral or even positive, if (say) it is associated in people's minds with an engaging piece of drama or a public salesman or advocate who manages to be attractive as well as assertive. (Reverting to our discussion of 'familiarity', it may also have novelty value.)

Here the example of the meteorite reports is suggestive, for 'communicating good news' is one of the most basic frameworks for thinking about the task of preaching. What kind of 'news' will preaching most be associated with? One might argue that the immediacy of the open-air announcement, the direct, pressing and surprising claim on people's attention, bears more resemblance to the immediacy and sense of importance attendant on the first eye-witness reports about Jesus than does the more reflective and (often) predictable event in church. The latter may sometimes seem more similar to an article in a newspaper, appearing as it does as part of an expected communicative format, able to be chewed over in comfort, whether that of the 'safe' church service/sitting room or, increasingly, via an electronic medium at another time.

---

18 See Stuart Blythe, 2009, 'Open-Air Preaching as Radical Street Performance', unpublished PhD thesis, University of Edinburgh; Stanley P. Saunders and Charles L. Campbell, 2000, *The Word on the Street: Performing the Scriptures in an Urban Context*, Grand Rapids: Eerdmans.

The question of the associations of a medium also needs careful scrutiny in thinking about the nature, validity and different forms of preaching *inside* church buildings. One cannot easily predict what such associations will be. Traditional forms of preaching will have nourishing, wholesome associations for some, domineering, disillusioning associations for others. Similarly, the use of contemporary media in church will, for some receivers, have many positive associations, whether of pleasure in the stimulation of the senses or of excited learning. But for others it may seem like yet another business presentation, an amateur version of what the TV producers do much better, or a painful reminder, through strong visual content, of an experience they would rather forget.

The big question implied by the studies of McCluhan, Postman, Hipps and others is whether the use of contemporary technology and visual media undermines a sense of immediacy and seriousness in the event of preaching. If our message is 'good news' of unique importance, do we not need to retain something of the raw eye-witness feel of the husband reporting on the event to his wife, or at least the crisp summary of the radio news? The genuine fear is that the further we move from simple, oral, person-to-person reportage, the more the basic story will get blurred, the less its impact will be felt, and the further it will be unconsciously co-opted into a culture where the default mode of public communication is entertainment rather than information or, still less, spiritual formation. We may rightly have rejected the idea that preaching is mere 'information', but what if sometimes it is in danger of becoming 'infotainment'?

Again, generalized answers are impossible here, and important distinctions need to be drawn. The words we are using and the concepts behind them need to be clarified. It is a fallacy, for a start, to separate 'news' from 'pleasure'. Good news, if received as such, imparts pleasure. Its messenger informs, but also refreshes (as noted in Prov. 25.25). But 'pleasure' in the giving and/or receiving of a message is not the same as 'entertainment' in the sense of having pleasure as one's sole motivation, as giver or receiver. Nor should 'entertainment' in itself be seen as anything other than the good gift of a Creator God (like his other gifts, capable of being distorted or idolized). It is rather that the associations carried by any communicative medium will inevitably shape the message being conveyed. Christians thus have the task of finding a medium whose associations distort the message least and extend it best in directions that allow its authentic heart to be disclosed.

The unique nature of the good news preachers are called to convey surely implies that while the medium of preaching, as a human event, will naturally evoke a range of associations, it will not be simply aligned with any other event. It may, at various times, remind one of a political speech, a motivational talk, a news bulletin, a storytelling session or even a TV programme, but there will always be something in it which escapes easy categorization as one of these or anything else. It is hard to see how we can improve on Augustine in the early fifth century, who identified the basic rhetorical aims of preaching, in terms drawn from classical writers, as 'to teach, to delight and to move'.[19] If one or more of these elements is regularly lacking, there will be a danger that the associations of the sermon will become limited, such that it becomes an educational or an entertaining or a motivational event, or maybe a combination of two, but lacks the roundedness of including all three. Yet Augustine and the other Fathers recognized that this trio alone could not form a foundation for Christian rhetoric, since unlike classical oratory, Christian preaching was uniquely tied to a historical event (the coming of Christ), a person (Christ himself) and a book (the Scriptures which bore witness to him).[20] The sermon was thus to be centred on Christ and shaped around him. In practice, this meant a high value being placed upon Scripture, its forms and arguments, as over against the preacher's own rhetorical devices. Recent times have seen a revival of this basic Augustinian sense that Scripture itself should be allowed to constitute the central 'medium' of the sermon.[21]

This might be heard as a thinly veiled argument for the revival of a particular traditional form of 'expository preaching', but it is not. It is dangerous to assume that any particular form of preaching can carry the mantle of being the 'true' medium that alone can adequately bear the message. We should not be misled by the wide availability of the Bible in book form into thinking that the only 'biblical' medium for preaching is a book-based one. Contemporary visual media may turn out to be equally appropriate and effective vehicles in some circumstances for

---

19 Augustine, *De Doctrina Christiana* 4.12.27. For discussion of Augustine's approach, see André Resner Jr, 1999, *Preacher and Cross: Person and Message in Theology and Rhetoric*, Grand Rapids: Eerdmans, pp. 45–58.

20 See Ronald Boyd-Macmillan, 2009, 'The Transforming Sermon: A Study of the Preaching of St Augustine, with Special Reference to the *Sermones ad populum*, and the Transformation Theory of James Loder', unpublished PhD thesis, University of Aberdeen; Wright, *Telling God's Story*, pp. 159–63.

21 Fred B. Craddock, 2001, *As One without Authority*, 2nd edn, St Louis: Chalice Press, p. 45; Thomas G. Long, 1989, *Preaching and the Literary Forms of the Bible*, Philadelphia: Fortress; Mike Graves, 1997, *The Sermon as Symphony: Preaching the Literary Forms of the New Testament*, Valley Forge: Judson Press; John D. Woods, 2008, 'Bearing Witness: The Homiletic Theory and Practice of Thomas G. Long', unpublished DMin thesis, University of Wales, Lampeter.

'teaching, delighting and persuading' a congregation in Christ-centred biblical truth, or more so. The main question to ask about the medium in which preaching comes today, however, may be whether it appears, first, too like a dry lecture to delight or persuade; or second, too like contemporary entertainment to teach or persuade; or third, too like contemporary motivational management to teach or delight.

A journey in time

As an event of public communication, preaching is more than a moment of encounter. It is an event that unfolds over time. This fact is crucial to understanding its dynamics.

At root, this means that hearers are attending not only to what the preacher is saying at that moment, but are fitting that together with what he or she has just said, and anticipating what he or she is about to say. It is in that constant, instinctive process of fluctuating absorption and expectation that 'understanding' of the sermon takes place. And 'understanding', in the full sense in which I use it here, is more than an intellectual matter. It is a *relational* reality, entailing emotional and volitional response to a person.

It is easy to see how this works in preaching. A preacher's opening story, though perfectly 'understandable' on an intellectual level, may be tasteless or alienating to some hearers, such that they find it not only difficult subsequently to respond warmly to the preacher's message, but even to comprehend mentally all that he is saying. Another preacher may use powerful imagery for a while which provides insight and excitement for the hearers, but then descends into prosaic, predictable moralizing, which disappoints the hearers and leaves them wondering what the overall message really is – not only of this preacher, but perhaps also of the God in whose name she claims to speak. Yet another may announce at the outset a clear three-part structure for the sermon, and follow this through admirably, satisfying expectations, such that all the hearers can grasp, intellectually, what the message is; but the lack of any emotive content is perceived instinctively as a gap, and wills are not engaged as they might be. Some hearers will be perfectly satisfied with this, but others, sensing that this is an occasion when the deepest springs of human behaviour should rightly be stirred, even at the cost of some discomfort, will feel inadequately fed.

So the ideal, we might say, is an event in which the hearers, as they receive the speaker's communication in the present moment, reflecting on what has just been said and anticipating what is going to be said, are enabled to enter into the journey on which the speaker is taking them, not only following the thought but feeling positive about the journey itself – positive enough to embrace an element of discomfort from a genuine challenge along the way. We might compare this to following an obviously reliable guide on an exciting mountain hike in which we do not get hopelessly lost, but are nevertheless led through some tough terrain, which seems well worth the effort because of the stretching pleasures of the whole experience. We are learning much as we go along, if we keep our senses alert, about the countryside around us – and also, in a less obvious way, about our fellow travellers and ourselves. But there is much more to the journey than 'learning' in the sense of absorbing information.

There are, however, two important qualifications to this picture of an ideal 'speech'. First, the speaker cannot realistically expect every hearer to be 'with her' every step of the way. All hearers have the habit of wandering off the path now and again, and then rejoining the main group. Second, although the speaker aims to have the full party of hearers with her – and on good terms with her! – by the end of the journey, that does not imply that all the hearers will have received the same – mentally, emotionally or volitionally – from the sermon. They may all have been following the same guide down (mostly) the same track, but what they have made of the scenery around them, how they feel about the whole experience, how it has changed them, will be quite different. To recognize that this is the case with preaching is not imposing some ideology of individualism upon it (as if hearers each have 'rights' to make what they want of the sermon). It is simply realism; this is what happens, in preaching as in any other speech.

The question then is: what does it mean for the preacher to be a 'reliable guide' when our hearers will inevitably have a range of views about what makes a satisfying journey, and are bound to wander off from time to time anyway?

No choice of *method* on its own is going to be foolproof or without pitfalls. But the speaker must make basic moral choices concerning his relationship with the hearers: here are three of the most important.

First: is the speaker going to be honest? This does not mean 'baring all', any more than it does in our day-to-day conversations – indeed, the public speaker who wishes to have a good relationship with the hearers will be more restrained in self-revelation than when speaking to individuals. The respecting of our own and others' privacy – and therefore our freedom to choose our level of openness – is fundamental to genuine equality of relationship. There is no need for a preacher to inflict self-harm by making himself or herself over-vulnerable. And the larger the group of hearers, the more distant the speaker is bound to seem – at least to some. But this still allows for a transparency which enables communication to be personal rather than merely impersonal.

Second, is the speaker going to give himself or herself to the task? All communication entails giving and receiving. This may seem obvious, but what does 'giving' mean for the *public* speaker? One quality that it entails is *creativity*.

All preparation for public speech, including preaching, is a *creative* act. It involves an element of planning, thought and decision-making which makes it akin to a work of art. However, this is sometimes neglected – whether through sheer laziness, or a belief (unfortunately sometimes held by preachers) that we are supposed to be impersonal channels rather than creative agents. Consideration of how to plan a 'rhetorical journey' that will engage the hearers at an appropriate level, however, should make the need for creativity very obvious. It is possible to repeat a formula or summarize a text without much creativity. But if good rhetoric entails the attempt to engage responsibly and relationally with a group of hearers, that means thinking carefully about the journey on which one is planning to take them. That is inevitably a creative business.

Creativity often means hard work. A good rhetorical journey is not planned without a deep level of personal engagement in the task. The joy of it, however, is the permission to engage all one's faculties of mind, emotion, imagination and will in an act of self-giving, and the realization that the end result does not depend *merely* on hard work but on springs of inspiration. This is daunting in those times when the springs seem to run dry. But sources of replenishment are always available, and need to be constantly drawn upon by the speaker.[22]

What exactly is it that we seek to create in a sermon? We have spoken thus far of *rhetoric*, but we have also touched on the idea of preaching as a *work of art*. The distinction between rhetoric and poetics, between persuasion and the fashioning of objects of beauty, is notoriously difficult to draw, and there is certainly overlapping between different categories. However, any genuinely creative public speech is likely to have elements of both. It will seek to achieve certain attitudes of mind

---

22 A useful book on sources of refreshment for the preacher is Mike Graves, 2006, *The Fully Alive Preacher: Recovering from Homiletical Burnout*, Louisville: Westminster John Knox.

and responses of will in the hearers. But it will also create a work of art in which, as with a painting, a poem or a sonata, the creator's aims are more subtle and complex than rhetorical persuasion. Hearers will respond in different ways, but if they allow it, that response will come from a deeper place than it does when someone is simply trying to persuade them.

In recent times there have been welcome reminders and explorations of the essential 'poetic' dimension of preaching.[23] Yet the 'rhetorical' element continues also to be highlighted, rightly, in all the various discussions about how to engage hearers – not least through Thomas Long's carefully phrased encouragement to preachers to plan not only a 'focus' but a 'function' for a sermon.[24] Few would go as far as Browne's daring suggestion that it can be good for sermons to be downright *difficult* for the hearers, since that is the way that poetry often works its magic best![25] David Buttrick's phrase adopted by Eugene Lowry, 'dancing the edge of mystery', catches better the balance most seek to strike.[26]

It is important not to fall into false stereotypes here. In particular, we should not think of rhetoric and persuasion as being biased towards the intellect, and poetics and artistry as being biased towards the emotions. Indeed, recognizing the emotional element in rhetoric is vital to handling it honestly and well, while the best art certainly entails intellectual efforts by both creator and receivers. Intellect and emotion both contribute to the touching of volition. Perhaps the question is not so much whether we should focus on rhetoric or poetics in our thinking about taking listeners on a journey, but whether both the intellectual *and* emotional ways in which we seek to engage them genuinely touch them (so that they feel that the journey is worthwhile setting out on) and genuinely take them somewhere (so that they feel, at the end of the sermon, that they have actually been on a journey, not stood still).

The third moral question concerning the journey through time is this: Is the speaker going to respect the hearers and their freedom? Relational speech demands no less. The particular quality to highlight in this regard is *attention*.

---

23 See Browne, *Ministry of the Word*; Peter K. Stevenson, 2007, 'The Preacher as Poet', *Ministry Today* 41, pp. 29–38.

24 Long, *Witness of Preaching*, pp. 99–116.

25 *Ministry of the Word*, especially pp. 58–71 on 'the essential untidiness'.

26 Eugene L. Lowry, 1997, *The Sermon: Dancing the Edge of Mystery*, Nashville: Abingdon.

Attention emerges from the same wellspring as creativity: the desire to enter or maintain a relationship in which giving and receiving are both genuine. In delineating an ethical model for rhetoric generally, Wayne C. Booth advocates what he calls 'listening-rhetoric', seeking truth *beyond* different positions, in contradistinction to 'win-rhetoric', which is merely out to win the argument at all costs, and 'bargain-rhetoric', which merely seeks a truce *between* different positions.[27] In personal conversation, attention to the other is a sign of respect; of openness to receive, as well as the giving of time and the giving-up of one's own voice. Such attention enables one then to respond as and when appropriate on a genuine, personal and not merely stereotyped level. Similarly, if the public speaker wants genuinely to respect her hearers, she will need to attend to them and their likely backgrounds, situations and responses. Sometimes they will be (at least relatively) 'anonymous', but the speaker needs to recognize how much she does not know even about those she 'knows'.[28] A lot of guesswork is involved here (but so it is in all relationship, even on a one-to-one level). Yet the simple act of attention may make all the difference to the journey. Without, of course, ever being able to predict or plot how each one will experience the journey, the simple process of attending to the hearers, before the event, will enable some routes to be rejected and one, eventually, to be chosen.

'Attention' to the hearers is also crucial *during* the event. Not all speakers (or hearers) will feel that a highly vocal level of interaction is helpful or natural for them, but the speaker's attention to the whole atmosphere of the event, and the signals – usually non-verbal – that the hearers display during the speech, does at least three things. It allows for an element of genuine, spontaneous self-giving in response to the needs of the moment – departing from what has been prepared, omitting, embellishing and so on; it demonstrates respect for the hearers as they are rather than as we had imagined them or hoped them to be; and it thus secures *their* attention to the speaker.

The goal of such attention is that the hearers will be able to respond to the speech in real freedom, without any sense of being browbeaten

27 Wayne C. Booth, 2004, *The Rhetoric of Rhetoric: The Quest for Effective Communication*, Malden, MA and Oxford: Blackwell, pp. 43–50.

28 Compare Craddock's helpful comments on the need for preachers to treat their hearers as a (relatively unknown) 'audience' as well as a (relatively known) 'congregation': Fred B. Craddock, 1985, *Preaching*, Nashville: Abingdon, pp. 86–98.

or manipulated. There must be no embarrassment about giving them something to respond *to*. That is the speaker's gift. But nor must there be any coercion. The speaker must show himself or herself genuinely open to a free response.

These three moral attributes – honesty, self-giving leading to creativity, respect leading to attention – are called for in hearers as well as speaker if the journey is to be a productive one. Unless we are honest with ourselves, we will not be able to engage with what we are hearing on a deep level: a part of us will be shielded from what we might receive, and therefore prevent us from making an appropriate response. Without the self-giving of creativity, the process of working through the implications of what is said will be aborted. Without respect for the speaker, there will not be openness to receive a message.

The journey of a public speech, therefore, brings into play some basic phenomena of communication which those who preach and listen to preaching need to be aware of as much as anybody else. These are phenomena relating to the openness of speaker and hearers to one another and their readiness to invest in the event. Yet none of this can provide us with a model of structuring a sermon which will be 'right' for a range of hearers on any particular occasion. This is because rhetoric (and poetics too) are relational and ethical matters before they are technical matters. 'Effectiveness' in public speech – including, especially, preaching – is not a matter of giving people an 'experience' (whether comfortingly predictable, or excitingly new), nor of achieving immediate but perhaps superficial comprehension or response. It is to be defined in the much more subtle, but elusive terms of the way in which over a long period one human being exercises a wholesome influence upon others.

Questions for the local church

- Is the preacher using a language which not only connects with the hearers but also sparks their imaginations and communicates God's transforming grace?
- What media do people engage with most, in or out of church? In what ways might preaching helpfully be imitating other media and in what ways would it be better to be different from them?
- How varied are the 'rhetorical journeys' on which preachers take the congregation? What might be gained by introducing a greater variety?

Areas for research

The question of how the language of the preacher is understood (or misunderstood) by the hearers is certainly worthy of exploration. So is the way in which hearers respond to different media used in preaching, and the structure of preaching journey which they find most satisfying. All these could be the subject of carefully constructed empirical research projects.

Further reading

Wayne C. Booth, 2004, *The Rhetoric of Rhetoric: The Quest for Effective Communication*, Malden, MA and Oxford: Blackwell.

Rosalind Brown, 2009, *Can Words Express our Wonder? Preaching in the Church Today*, Norwich: Canterbury Press.

Jolyon P. Mitchell, 1999, *Visually Speaking: Radio and the Renaissance of Preaching*, Edinburgh: T & T Clark.

4

Insights from Sociology and Psychology

In this chapter we will outline aspects of what sociology and psychology may teach us about what is going on in preaching. Let us underline again that it would be reductive to claim that these disciplines, or any other, could *explain* what is going on. But equally, it would be remiss to ignore what light they may be able to shed on the human dimension of the event.

Sociology: the forming of identity

From a sociological point of view, preaching may be seen as an *identity-forming* event. It is a means by which a particular group of people has its sense of who it is continually reinforced. It regularly fulfils this role as part of the larger event of a service of worship. This sense of shared identity will influence the worldview and behaviour of those people, as a group and as individuals.

The way in which preaching may form the identity of a congregation may be illustrated by two contrasting models. In a 'church for the community' model the boundaries of church membership are often highly flexible, indeed invisible. Gathered in the congregation on any occasion may be a wide mixture of people whose Christian commitment ranges from deep to non-existent, but all held somehow within the embrace of a 'church' so deeply involved in its local community that it is often hard to tell the difference between 'church' and 'community'. In such a setting, the preaching is likely to speak very inclusively of the love of God for all people, the purposes of God for the whole world, and of those present as all 'on a level' in their acceptability to God and his church. In a 'gathered church' model, however, where the boundaries of church membership are more tightly drawn, there is likely to be a stronger core of committed Christians worshipping at one time. Others will be present, but the preaching is likely to seek both consciously and unconsciously to reinforce the sense that true believers in Jesus Christ are a 'special people' who should be grateful for their status and privileges, and whom others should aspire to join.

Of course there are few churches which fit such models so neatly. However, the illustration points to the fact that preaching is indeed a 'social act'.[1] It plays a part in shaping the identity of a group. Naturally, a preacher may not only *reinforce* an existing identity (for example, by frequently using the word 'family' to refer to a church, which already thinks of itself like that), but also seek to *adjust* the identity (perhaps deliberately shifting the emphasis from 'family' to 'pilgrim people').

Over time, the identity-forming role played by preaching may be highly significant, especially in churches with a strong emphasis on preaching. It may be one of the most powerful means of establishing and perpetuating a particular tradition of faith in that community. In due course it may happen that the deeper effects of the evolution of social groupings noted by the classic study of Berger and Luckmann show themselves.[2] The content of, and approach to, preaching may assist in the 'institutionalization' of a particular form of Christian community. The preaching may further serve a process of 'sedimentation' whereby the congregation gets 'stuck' in a particular rut, and the *living* character of tradition gets lost. The entire 'symbolic universe' of a congregation may be shaped by the preaching of a particular figure. They then 'internalize' the reality set forth by that preaching to the extent that their faith and outlook are entirely conditioned by it.

How one evaluates such a process will depend on a variety of factors. The solidifying of the identity of any group may be seen as a basically benign process insofar as it strengthens and nourishes the members and (at least) does no harm to others. However, most groups (at least when observed from outside) lose elements of life and health when reaching the 'sedimentation' stage, and the dangers of a group mentality so strong that its members deeply share the same 'symbolic universe', such that they find it difficult to perceive or acknowledge reality beyond the way it is defined by the group, are well known.

The key thing for Christians, and especially for preachers – occupying the influential position that they have – is to be aware that the Church is far from being immune to such processes. On the contrary,

---

1 See Arthur Van Seters (ed.), 1988, *Preaching as a Social Act: Theology and Practice*, Nashville: Abingdon.

2 Peter L. Berger and Thomas Luckmann, 1971, *The Social Construction of Reality*, Harmondsworth: Penguin.

there are dynamics at work in the 'society' of churches of which it is crucial to take account. The question of what kind of 'identity' it is healthy to develop and establish as a church is fundamental to debates within the New Testament and throughout Christian history. How, in practice, can one maintain a distinctive character without becoming exclusive, even superior? How can one maintain tradition in a healthy way, preserving the riches of the past, without the fossilization that goes along with refusal to respond to the circumstances of the present? How can one build up a sense of congregational fellowship and purpose without expecting that everyone will share the same points of view on everything? How can one exercise a wise and godly influence without seeking simply to shape hearers in one's own image? How might one, wittingly or unwittingly, severely disrupt the identity of the congregation, and in what circumstances, if any, might that be called for? In what ways might the development of a congregation's identity affect that of the wider community?[3]

These questions open up theological and practical matters which will be revisited in Parts 3 and 4. In the meantime, however, they lead to a consideration of the *psychological* factors affecting preaching.

Psychology: the interchange between persons

If preaching is a community event, it is also a personal one. The preacher and hearers are socially influenced, but they are also persons, all different, affected by a range of psychological factors which may be more or less obvious or obscure. Such factors may be revealed from time to time in specific words, but it is in the dynamics of non-verbal communication that they are at work most powerfully.

A contemporary secular handbook of communication identifies three areas of psychological theory which particularly underlie the study of human interaction and non-verbal communication.[4] The first is Neuro-Linguistic Programming (NLP).[5] NLP 'concentrates especially on face-to-face communication and provides techniques for building rapport by picking up on and *consciously* "mirroring" voice, speech

---

3 For a readable insight into some contemporary sociological dynamics of churches see Duncan Maclaren, 2004, *Mission Implausible: Restoring Credibility to the Church*, Carlisle: Paternoster.

4 Nicky Stanton, 2004, *Mastering Communication*, 4th edn, London: Palgrave Macmillan, pp. 45–7.

5 See http://www.anlp.org/

and body-language signals of others, and learning how others perceive the world so you can present ideas in ways they will accept'.[6] Another definition says:

> NLP is a collection of models, tools and techniques that enables its Practitioners to:
>
> - Communicate more effectively.
> - Achieve excellence in their chosen field.
> - Overcome performance-limiting behaviours.
> - Programme their unconscious mind.
> - Programme themselves to improve performance and results.[7]

These definitions have a strongly pragmatic feel, stressing the goal of NLP in making us better communicators. However, a third definition places the emphasis much more on NLP as a means to achieve health in one's own psychological responses:

> NLP is a therapeutic technique to detect and reprogramme unconscious patterns of thought and behaviour in order to alter psychological responses. The basic principle of NLP is that it is in an individual's power to change their own subconscious programming for the better.[8]

This highlights the fact that though NLP might be seen ultimately as a technique for 'improving' communication, it has a deeper purpose in the one who engages with it. It is a 'therapeutic' technique, enabling an individual to adjust their own responses in a positive direction. It thus has affinities with Cognitive Behavioural Therapy (CBT), which seeks to adjust attitudes and behaviour through the examination and challenging of a person's thoughts and their associated feelings.

Any means of discerning the roots of psychological disorder and empowering healthy human responses to situations and to other humans is surely to be taken seriously by those concerned with preaching. Individuals who are so well adjusted psychologically that they need *no* such therapeutic action (from whatever source) are surely rare indeed, and the effect of one damaged individual on others may be considerable – not least if that one regularly addresses a large

---

6 Stanton, *Mastering Communication*, p. 45.

7 http://www.anlp.org/index.asp?pageid=51

8 http://www.anlp.org/index.asp?pageid=51

group. Thus however the theory and techniques of NLP itself are assessed, the field of enquiry opens up the whole area of relating well to the world outside the self in a way which is vital to preaching.

It would be wholesome for a preacher to consider the range of psychological responses to the world and ask if there are unhelpful attitudes, maybe originating in the unconscious, which show themselves quite unbidden in preaching. It might, indeed, be their manifestation in preaching (and their obviousness to the congregation) that brings the preacher to a crisis point, leading to the search for healing. For example, a desire always to be in control may be revealed in preaching that is domineering. A fear of self-exposure and intimacy may lead to preaching that is stiff and distant. A deep unmet need for love may lead to preaching that focuses inappropriately on the preacher, appealing for the hearers' sympathy.

The second area of psychological theory underlying the study of non-verbal communication is Emotional Intelligence (EI). Overlapping in many ways with the concerns of NLP, EI is 'the capacity for recognizing our own feelings and those of others, for motivating ourselves and for managing emotions effectively in ourselves and in others . . . a learned capability that contributes to effective performance'.[9] The final phrase is suggestive: EI 'contributes to effective performance', yet there is more to it than simply a pragmatic goal. It is regarded as a sign of a healthy person. It entails self-control and empathy.

Again, we can easily see the relevance of such emotional competencies to preaching. Fully rounded human communication will embrace emotion, but in a controlled way. An analysis of preaching on the basis of the emotional intelligence of both preacher and hearer could lead to fascinating results, though it would be very difficult to conduct. It would give nuance to the blunt idea of 'effective communication'. A 'good' preaching event might be seen not as one in which the preacher simply informs, persuades or entertains the hearers, but one in which the preacher acts with a healthy degree of assertiveness, confident but not aggressive, while the congregation's own right to assert themselves is respected. They feel able to disagree or see things from a different perspective – and to voice this at a suitable moment, if they wish, to the preacher, without him or her feeling there is something wrong with such difference, and without *fearing* that this will be the response. All are comfortable and relate well in an environment within which all are not expected to agree.

The final area of psychological theory underlying contemporary understanding of non-verbal communication is Transactional Analysis

---

9 Stanton, *Mastering Communication*, p. 45.

(TA). Eric Berne's identification of the three 'ego states' out of which we act – parent, child and adult – has extensive implications for public communication, not least for preaching. Our 'parent' is 'our ingrained voice of authority', our 'child' is 'our internal reaction and feelings to external events', and our 'adult' is 'our ability to think and determine action for ourselves, based on received data'.[10] Successful 'transactions', or communication, according to Berne, depend on the stimulus receiving the appropriate response: the 'cry' of a child needs the authoritative calming of a parent; the warning of a 'parent' needs the heeding of the 'child'; the 'adult' seeks 'adult' conversation and engagement in response. Inappropriate responses spell a breakdown in communication – whether it is meeting a 'child's' cry with adult conversation, or meeting a 'parent's' instructions with the competing instructions of another 'parent', or responding to an 'adult' initiative with either a 'childish', passive response or a 'parental', authoritarian one.

It might be that Transactional Analysis would go a long way towards explaining some of the unfortunate miscommunication which can take place in preaching, as well as the 'successful' communication. When Christians are provoked into declaring that 'preaching has had its day', it may be that what many are reacting to is a kind of preaching in which preacher and hearers collude in the preacher playing the 'parent' role and the hearers the 'child', when it would be more appropriate for the relationship to be 'adult' to 'adult'. It is all too possible that such collusion helps to keep the hearers in a state of immaturity. If worship is seen in some sense as the occasion when we can come to 'know ourselves' most deeply as children of God, this awareness may be threatened by an overpowering sense (probably not articulated as such) that we are children of the preacher. More common, perhaps, now, rather than collusion, is a mismatch between the ego-states of preacher and hearers. The preacher may continue in the content, manner and structure of their speaking to adopt a 'parent' posture, while many in the congregation understandably feel that as they relate 'adult' to 'adult' in most other spheres of life, there is no reason why they should not also do so in church. Alternatively the preacher may strive to communicate as 'adult', but some in the congregation prefer the safe dependency of being 'child'. Either scenario is a recipe for failure in communication; but if the failure is analysed in terms of TA, there is the prospect of understanding and growth.

---

10 http://www.businessballs.com/transact.htm

Eric Berne is also famous for his analysis of the 'games people play'.[11] It would be very illuminating to analyse preaching, sometimes, in terms of the 'game' being played. Is the preacher seeking to gain control of the congregation by 'stroking' their egos, flattering them? Or conversely, is he/she using the platform of preaching to assert personal authority, to lend weight to an opinion which found little favour in discussion at the church council, but can perhaps carry the day with the implicit spiritual wind of a sacred occasion in its sails? There are no doubt many other possible lines of enquiry like this.

The realms opened up by NLP, EI and TA are all effective, in various ways, at exposing flaws in the communication process. But the psychological theory which has been developed most in relation to preaching is that relating to personality preference, and this is especially helpful in developing communication in positive ways, rather than just countering the negative. We will now devote a section to it.

In discussing the 'message square' in the introduction to Part 2, we noted that communication always entails an element of self-disclosure by the communicator, that it always implies a message about the relationship between communicator and receiver, and that it always contains an appeal, however tacit. We have already touched on some of the basic implications of these elements. Here we will consider especially the influence of personal differences on the *appeal* which a message carries.

Bound up in the processes of communication along with language and the broader media in which a message is couched is the variety in human personality and preference among communicators and receivers of communication. It is this variety which often gives communication its excitement and unpredictability, but also allows it to elude precise analysis. So our aim here is not to try to map, in a pseudo-scientific way, the different ways in which personality may have an impact on communication, but to present the basic presence of that influence so that we may at least take proper account of it. I use the term 'personalities and preferences' here as a shorthand for the full range of 'human' dimensions which affect communication, including not only the individual's inherited psychological makeup, but also gender and cultural influences – all of which are closely intertwined. Many other variables could also be brought into the picture, such as age, family background, stage of faith (or unfaith), spirituality, life experiences and so on, of

---

11 Eric Berne, 1964, *Games People Play: The Psychology of Human Relationships*, Harmondsworth: Penguin.

which space forbids exploration. I focus here on the central factors of personality, gender and cultural influences by way of illustrating the rich complexity of the process.

Psychologists have developed ways in which to chart the range of human personalities, not so that people can 'pigeon-hole' themselves or others, but so that through understanding our differences we may be able to have more confidence in who we are, more understanding of others, and more skill in working together positively. One of the most well-used tools, based on Jungian psychology, is the Myers-Briggs Type Indicator (MBTI®). The implications of this for understanding and developing preaching have been explored in various places.[12] The examples I give here are just a tiny snapshot of the many insights which may emerge when we face up to the variety of human personality in an analysis of preaching.

First we must stress that *difference* does not, in itself, mean *difficulty* in communication. The appeal of a speaker may be precisely in his or her difference from the hearer, just as in our social interactions, opposites may attract. None of us wants other people to be just the same as us! So, for instance, an introvert may enjoy listening to an extravert and vice versa; the appeal of one to another may be highly effective. This is all a part of the mystery and wonder of diversity within the human family.

Yet effective communication does entail the establishing of a bond between speaker and hearer, that sense that concerns are shared, perspectives are understood, and the communicator's appeal, whether open or tacit, is something to which the receiver can respond positively. Thus in our everyday relationships with one another we instinctively reach out beyond our own *preferences* as individuals in order to establish these bonds. If and when this becomes difficult for any reason, relationships either do not begin, or having begun, are weakened or in extreme cases destroyed.

---

12 See especially Leslie J. Francis and Andrew Village, 2008, *Preaching with all our Souls: A Study in Hermeneutics and Psychological Type*, London: Continuum; Angela Butler, 1999, *Personality and Communicating the Gospel*, Cambridge: Grove. For wider studies relating the MBTI® to Christian life and ministry, not specifically focused on preaching but highly relevant to it, see Leslie J. Francis, 2005, *Faith and Psychology: Personality, Religion and the Individual*, London: Darton, Longman & Todd; Malcolm Goldsmith and Martin Wharton, 1993, *Knowing Me, Knowing You: Exploring Personality Type and Temperament*, London: SPCK; Julia McGuinness, 2009, *Growing Spiritually with the Myers-Briggs Model*, London: SPCK. Another valuable and ancient tool for understanding personality difference is the Enneagram. I am not aware of any substantial published work specifically relating this to preaching.

The permutations of personality preference identified by the MBTI®
are therefore extremely useful in analysing the communication process,
in two ways. First, they teach us as both communicators and receivers to have confidence in who we are, in our instinctive preferences;
to realize that our personality is a gift that we have received and can
give to others. If we seem to have more difficulty in either communicating to, or receiving communication from, certain people, remembering
the reality and richness of difference will enable us to see this not as
a problem to depress us but as part of the human adventure. Second,
understanding the range of personality preferences gives us clear leads
as to how, as communicators, we can reach out beyond our own preferences to create a bond with as wide a range of others as possible; and as
to how listeners can also reach out beyond *their* preferences to receive
communication productively from a speaker who may be very different
from them. Here are some examples, related to the four pairs of the
Myers-Briggs model, of how this may work in practice for preaching.

The extravert preacher (E) may struggle with devoting time to solitary sermon preparation, but is likely to form an excellent bond with
hearers, for the act of public communication is just the setting where
she feels at home. Maybe she would benefit from more shared preparation in which ideas can be bounced around a small group. Maybe too
some introverted hearers will find her enthusiasm a bit breathless and
overwhelming. But her extraversion is only a *preference*; without ceasing to 'be herself', she can include quieter, more reflective stages in the
sermon.

The introverted preacher (I) just loves his time in the study. In fact,
he would often be quite happy to stay there. As a human being, he also
longs to communicate with others, but is likely to find the public setting
of preaching strange, if not intimidating at first. The very act of communication will therefore be more of an effort. Hearers, too, may find
it more of an effort to receive his message than that of his extraverted
sister. The effort may well be rewarded because of the care that has
gone into preparation. But the introversion of this preacher, like the extraversion of the other, is only a *preference*. He too, without ceasing to
'be himself', can learn to reach out with those moments of 'extraverted'
self-disclosure through which a bond with hearers is made.

The sensing preacher (S) is a keen observer of details – in the Bible
and the world. She may be skilled at presenting those details in an
ordered and vivid way, often painting pictures or even evoking smell,
taste or touch with words. Her preaching will naturally appeal to those
of a similar preference. Yet she may forget the overarching, visionary

element, the 'big picture' which is so important to the listener with an iNtuitive preference (N), and thus needs to work at a presentation which keeps the 'wood' in view and not just the 'trees'. Conversely, the intuitive preacher may be inspiring and profound, yet lack the earthing in specifics which the sensing listener craves. So he needs to work at bringing his big visions down to earth. Here we may also give an example of how closely the different preferences depend on each other. If the sermon is to contain *imaginary* pictures, stories or details that will appeal to 'sensers', the 'intuitives' with their creative urge may in fact be *better* at providing these than sensers themselves, who instinctively stick to observable realities!

Similarly, the preacher who prefers 'feeling' as the key to decision-making (F) will effortlessly communicate a sense of sympathy with her hearers and with situations referred to in the sermon, while the one who prefers 'thinking' (T) will instinctively want to give himself and his hearers an intellectual challenge. 'Feeling' listeners will be disappointed by a preaching ministry that sounds to them mostly 'head' not 'heart', while 'thinkers' will be frustrated by what they may perceive as warm words without anything really to get their teeth into.

The final polarity is between 'judging' (J) and 'perceiving' (P). Those with a 'judging' preference like to make decisions and get things sorted. Preachers like this will be inclined to decisiveness both in their preparation (wanting to finish the process in good time, with a clear sense of what they are going to say) and in their message (setting out truths in such a way as to make the need for decision about them plain). It may all come over as too tied-down for the 'perceiving' listener, who likes the open-endedness of 'going with the flow'. On the other hand, preachers with a 'perceiving' preference will tend to remain more open to fresh ideas right up to – and even during! – the sermon. This may communicate a genuinely living message, but be a little unsatisfying for the 'judging' listener who is looking for clarity of direction.

Gender provides a further matrix within which some of the contours of human communication may be traced. It interacts with personality in complex ways. While it is unquestionable that both males and females may have any permutation of preferences within the Myers-Briggs model, it is also true that there are often *perceptions* that certain preferences predominate in one gender rather than the other. In particular, women may often be *expected* to be those who decide on a 'feeling' basis, while men may be expected to decide on a 'thinking' basis, even if empirical observation does not necessarily bear this out. Such perceptions may subtly control expectations by preachers of how those of different genders will hear them, as well as expectations by listeners of how those of different genders will preach. This may require an effort of adjustment to overcome unwarranted stereotypes. Why should a preacher with a largely female congregation be always appealing to the 'feeling' preference, denying the hearers the mental stimulation of a more 'thinking' sermon – or vice versa? Listeners, too, need to be prepared for their expectations to be overturned, in order to receive what a preacher may give. Positive reactions to the person of the preacher, even if they have to be learned over time, will enable more benefit to be derived from their message. 'Isn't it good that he allows us to see a more feminine side' is a much more healthy response than 'I just can't get used to a woman being so assertive'.

The widely accepted reality is that our sense of gender is controlled by both biology and culture. The male–female dichotomy is a useful working classification, but neither cultural convention nor even biological sex allows hard and fast distinction. This means that gender stereotyping is always unhelpful. Yet valuable studies have been done on gender tendencies in communication. Tannen, for example, puts it like this:

Are men more likely to engage in ritual opposition, nonliteral attack? Are they more likely to take an oppositional stance toward other people and the world? Are they more likely to find opposition entertaining – to enjoy watching a good fight, or having one?
The short answer is, Yes.
The long question is, Why?[13]

Beverly Zink-Sawyer has noted the way in which women preachers have been naturally drawn to narrative preaching.[14] An analysis of gender and preaching might usefully start from observations such as this, but would need to be open to the possibility that generalizations might need considerable revision in the light of the data.

Undoubtedly an inherited cultural bias against women having prominent public positions, not least preaching, continues to form the background for preaching in many settings today. Such a bias is one which both women and men, both preachers and listeners, need to work at

---

13 Deborah Tannen, 1998, *The Argument Culture: Changing the Way we Argue and Debate*, London: Virago, p. 173.
14 Beverly Zink-Sawyer, 2008, 'A Match Made in Heaven: The Intersection of Gender and Narrative Preaching', in Mike Graves and David J. Schlafer (eds), *What's the Shape of Narrative Preaching?*, St Louis: Chalice Press, pp. 41–53.

countering if communication by women is to be received as effectively as that of men. Such work is simple to describe but more difficult to achieve. It will surely entail having the confidence to be ourselves and giving others the permission and the confidence to be themselves. This will involve especially men in adjusting inherited perspectives and prejudices which may show themselves in careless assumptions or language. It may involve a change of attitudes by denominational or congregational bodies. It may also involve a readiness to adjust the medium and structure of preaching where appropriate so that it is more hospitable to what a woman has to give. Again, we should beware of stereotypes: women preachers will not *necessarily* be more inclined to empathy, interactivity or storytelling, for instance, though these may indeed be neglected emphases which they bring to the preaching 'table'.[15] But if a woman *does* have a quiet voice and *is* uncomfortable proclaiming a message from a high pulpit in a large church, yet has a clear call from God to share his word, would it not be better for both preacher and listeners to create spaces within the life of that church where she could feel at home in sharing the word, rather than squeezing her ministry into an alien shape?

Similar considerations arise, *mutatis mutandis*, from variety in cultural background and influences among preachers and hearers. We must stress again that difference in itself is not to be bemoaned as a 'problem' but celebrated as a gift. An African preacher may be hugely refreshing to a group of European hearers, and vice versa. Yet there are also challenges involved in maximizing the appeal of a message when, as we saw in Chapter 2, the congregation may contain people from a wide range of backgrounds, most of which may be quite different from the preacher's own.

One of the most obvious ways in which culture affects preaching is through language. We have all learned our native language more or less unconsciously, and we continue to adapt our speech and writing as language evolves – again, largely unconsciously. Even where preacher and hearers share a common language, there are different registers and styles of speech which roughly correspond to different subcultures or cultural preferences. Words, phrases, figures of speech and so on can be identical in the various branches of English, yet mean very different things depending on whether the speaker is British, American, Indian, Australian or from somewhere else. The consequences for the unwary can be amusing, offensive or both! The effort to 'extend oneself' in

---

15 See Heather Walton and Susan Durber (eds), 1994, *Silence in Heaven: A Book of Women's Preaching*, London: SCM.

understanding the other – whether that be the listeners or the preacher – will be well repaid here, as much as with the variety of personalities and with different genders.

Differences of linguistic nuance, however, are less difficult to pinpoint than some deeper but also more nebulous differences in cultural preference. We might think here of the different radio stations people listen to, the different newspapers they read, the different kinds of work environment they inhabit. What happens when a 'Radio 4' preacher addresses a group of people who mainly listen to Radio 1 or Radio 2? Can a *Guardian* preacher get through to hearers who mainly read the *Sun* or the *Mail*? Or what about a preacher with a background in management – how will her speaking be heard by those who spend their working lives on a shop floor?

Experience suggests that in such situations there will be little problem with basic comprehension. By and large, preachers and hearers will share a common level of education and a common immersion in at least some aspects of culture, and these will ensure that the message will be more or less understood, provided the preacher steers clear of abstruse unexplained jargon. The problem is more likely to arise on the subliminal level. If a preacher, over time, consistently *sounds* 'different' from the hearers, they may sense a distance which, however sympathetic they are, prevents a full 'owning' of the preacher's message. Conversely, of course, the hearers may begin to 'talk like the preacher', which may not be a healthy thing.

This problem of cultural distance should not be exaggerated. Particularly in a multicultural setting, we are all adjusting our 'ears' and our speech to some extent much of the time, to enable communication. But our concern in this part of the book is to underline the dynamics of what happens, rather than propose normative ways of dealing with it. And language is just the tip of the iceberg of culture. All the time, mostly unintentionally, we are yielding cultural information about ourselves, and others are responding (openly or not) in a way which indicates their own cultural makeup. Our everyday dealings with each other say something about the cultural values which shape us, and it is no different with preaching.

The way a preacher 'applies' the message will therefore be influenced by cultural assumptions. Our modelling of the habits of Christian life will inevitably be coloured by the way we have learned, and seek, to 'inhabit' that life culturally. This does not mean it is impossible for us to imagine others doing so differently, but that it may be difficult for us to do so. For example, if it has been ingrained in us that a 'right' application of Paul's injunction to 'Pray constantly' (1 Thess. 5.17) is to have daily set times of prayer, it might be difficult for us to see that for others, a habit of spontaneous prayer at different times might be equally 'right' for them, shaped as they are by different cultural expectations.

In all these ways, and countless others, personal differences play an enormous part in the nature and effectiveness of communication, including preaching. In concluding this section it is worth noting that the extent to which preacher and hearers interact *outside* the sermon time plays a big part in the way in which preaching is received. No obstacle of communication is too great once people build up trusting relationships. Where there is perceived difficulty, on one side or another, in the preaching ministry, open discussion in a friendly atmosphere may resolve it, and the relationship between preacher and hearers may deepen as a consequence. Positively, a relationship between preacher and hearers in which the character of the preacher becomes known, open to view, not as a perfect example but as one in the process of being shaped and formed by Christ, surely does far more for the effectiveness of preaching than any academic brilliance or rhetorical skill.[16]

A meeting with God?

There is one final element of the communicative encounter of preaching which must now be mentioned. I have tried scrupulously to avoid discussing it so far, in order to highlight just how much preaching shares with any other public speech. But the phenomenon which must now come to the fore is the claim that somehow, in the preaching event, people meet with God.

I do not leave this point to the next part, in which we will specifically try to understand the event of preaching through a theological lens, because that might imply that preaching can only be a meeting with God *if and when we interpret it that way*. The Church's historic claim which I wish to echo, however, is that such a meeting is a reality, not just a perception. It is right, therefore, to include it at the climax of our interpretation of what is going on when preaching happens.

Such a meeting is, of course, mysterious, just as God is mysterious. It is not amenable even to the kind of analysis to which we have subjected human communication – and that, as we have seen, is mysterious enough. It is not a meeting which can be attributed directly or solely

---

16 On the importance of the *ēthos* or character of the speaker in ancient rhetoric, and of the preacher, see André Resner Jr, 1999, *Preacher and Cross: Person and Message in Theology and Rhetoric*, Ground Rapids: Eerdmans.

to preacher or hearers or Scripture or the gathering as a whole. It cannot be engineered (if it is to be a meeting in which God gives himself freely), nor timed (as if we could pin God's presence down to particular moments). But an analysis of preaching is not only incomplete without it; it is impossible without it. Without such a meeting, I believe, preaching loses its entire *raison d'être*.

All we need to say at this point is that this claim about preaching makes it *sui generis*, not ultimately subject to the dynamics of language and rhetoric, society and psyche. And yet preaching remains a human reality, which can to a considerable extent – as we have tried to show in this part – be subjected to human canons of scrutiny. For the moment, let this remain a caution to all who would analyse and discuss preaching. It is a divine *and* human event, and should not be reduced to either one or the other.

Questions for the local church

- In what ways does preaching help to form the identity of your congregation? Are these ways healthy?
- Does there seem to be a healthy relationship between preachers and hearers? Can anything be done to make it healthier?
- How do you see the human and divine aspects of preaching coming together in practice? In what ways does God speak to people through, and apart from, the preacher's gifts, character and relationship with the congregation?

Areas for research

It could be valuable to do a historical study of a period in a church's ministry, seeking to identify through interviews or other means how people perceive the church's identity to have been shaped by the preaching ministry. To explore the preaching of a church in terms of the emotional intelligence of preachers or hearers, or to analyse it in terms of Transactional Analysis, would be a demanding and sensitive, yet potentially highly revealing study. A number of studies of personality and communication, and gender and communication, are available, but there is much more to do in discovering how these factors affect the preaching and hearing of sermons. There is also much work to do in exploring how preaching in a multicultural congregation can effectively connect with a range of hearers.

Further reading

Susan Durber, 2007, *Preaching Like a Woman*, London: SPCK.

Paul G. Hiebert, 2008, *Transforming Worldviews: An Anthropological Understanding of How People Change*, Grand Rapids: Baker Academic.

Joseph R. Jeter Jr and Ronald J. Allen, 2002, *One Gospel, Many Ears: Preaching for Different Listeners in the Congregation*, St Louis: Chalice Press.

Arthur Van Seters (ed.), 1988, *Preaching as a Social Act: Theology and Practice*, Nashville: Abingdon.

PART 3

Introduction

We now move to the third stage of practical theological reflection, described by Osmer as 'The Normative Task: Prophetic Discernment'.[1] Here we examine the practice of preaching from a theological perspective. This is not just one more theory to add to those we considered in Part 2, but, for Christians, the *normative* framework of understanding, which embraces the other frameworks without erasing or superseding them. Given all the human history, contexts and dynamics of this practice of the Church, preaching, what are we to say about its place and significance in the purposes of God?

Osmer helpfully breaks down this stage of the process into three elements, which will form the structure of Chapters 5 to 8. He outlines them as follows:

> First, [the normative task] involves a style of theological reflection in which theological concepts are used to interpret particular episodes, situations and contexts. In light of what we know of God, how might God be acting? What are the fitting patterns of human response? Second, it involves the task of finding ethical principles, guidelines and rules that are relevant to the situation and can guide strategies of action. Third, it involves exploring past and present practices of the Christian tradition that provide normative guidance in shaping the patterns of the Christian life.[2]

Thus in Chapters 5 and 6 we will seek to interpret the event of preaching in the light of the biblical narrative and Christian theology. Chapter 5 will recount key elements of that narrative and Chapter 6 will draw their threads together with some central theological claims about the divine and human elements in preaching. In Chapter 7 we move from

---

1 Richard R. Osmer, 2008, *Practical Theology: An Introduction*, Grand Rapids: Eerdmans, pp. 129–73.
2 Osmer, *Practical Theology*, p. 8.

this basis to ethical principles that may guide our practice of preaching. In Chapter 8 we consider some of the central kinds of preaching practice, with the purpose of assessing how adequately they express the theological realities and ethical requirements just outlined.

This part of our investigation cannot stand alone, but is intimately linked to Parts 1 and 2. Thus Chapter 5 is not an attempt to deduce timeless truths from Scripture, but to take the *story* of preaching outlined in Chapter 1 back a stage further into the 'normative' period of revelation, so as to conceive what an authentic continuity of preaching in the present would look like. Chapters 6 and 7 do not attempt to devise a list of 'pure' theological bases and ethical norms for preaching, but to set the various functions of preaching discussed in Chapter 2 and the human dynamics of preaching discussed in Chapters 3 and 4 within the open-ended narrative outlined in Chapter 5. Chapter 8 seeks to crystallize how some important varieties of preaching practice do, or do not, express this integration of human realities within a theological framework.

So it is in this part of the book that one of the essential characteristics of practical theology, its interdisciplinary nature, comes to the fore. As Osmer points out, there is a necessary cross-disciplinary task entailed in all four stages of the practical theological process – the 'descriptive', 'interpretive', 'normative' and 'pragmatic' tasks.[3] But it is here at the 'normative' stage that it is most crucial to make this explicit. *If, with the tradition of the Church, we are to continue to see preaching as a 'divine' event, we must give a robust account of how its theological character embraces and does not erase the human dimensions which we have studied.*

Osmer describes various models of 'cross-disciplinary dialogue'.[4] It is not necessary here to outline or discuss these, but only to say that the 'revised correlational model' associated with the names of David Tracy and Don Browning is the one which approximates most closely to my purpose in developing this practical theology of preaching.[5] This model allows theology and other disciplines to pose questions to each other. I believe that theology need not be threatened by this process, for its inherent cogency and truth will both be hospitable to questions and show its worthiness to be the dominant, inclusive framework for understanding. There will also be elements of the 'revised praxis method of correlation' associated with the names of Matthew Lamb and Rebecca

---

3 Osmer, *Practical Theology*, pp. 161–3.
4 Osmer, *Practical Theology*, pp. 160–73.
5 Osmer, *Practical Theology*, p. 166.

Chopp.[6] In this model, the conversation is not just a matter of rational exchange, but also one of dialogue between different forms of *praxis* aimed at human liberation. I believe that the praxis of preaching can emerge from this dialogue (in contrast to what some have claimed) as a genuinely liberating activity.

---

6 Osmer, *Practical Theology*, p. 167.

5

The Biblical Grounding of Preaching

We begin our theological appraisal of preaching with attention to the Scriptures. The Scriptures possess 'normative' status for most Christians. However, this status may be understood in a wide variety of ways, and the theological appraisal of current practices in the light of the Bible is far from being a straightforward process. We need to pay rigorous attention to how we use Scripture in such an appraisal, if it is to carry weight.[1] Before I outline my preferred method, I will mention three others which often appear in arguments about the Scriptural grounding for preaching and say why I think they are inadequate.

The first is to do a word-study of biblical words related to preaching, especially in the New Testament. This can be fruitful, not least in showing the range of words used, and the rich variety of practice they suggest. However, there are two main pitfalls with it. The first is the fallacy of linking words to concepts – long recognized as such in linguistics, and identified devastatingly by James Barr in much of the biblical theology of the mid twentieth-century.[2] It is simply not the case (for instance) that we can tie a Greek word for 'preach' or 'teach' to a single, timeless concept. Nor can we precisely demarcate the semantic ranges of different, but similar words, even in the same language.[3] To draw precise equivalences or boundaries between words in *different*

---

1 In an article based on research among theological students, Roger Walton identified seven potential strategies, ranging in sophistication from casual 'links and associations' through crude proof-texting to careful mutual critique between Scripture and the present: Roger Walton, 2003, 'Using the Bible and Christian Tradition in Theological Reflection', *British Journal of Theological Education*, 13.2, pp. 133–51.

2 James Barr, 1961, *The Semantics of Biblical Language*, London: SCM, *passim* but see for example pp. 38–40, 242–3.

3 This is a danger of a simplistic adoption of the distinction drawn by C. H. Dodd between the notions of *kerygma* (proclamation), *didachē* (teaching) and *paraklēsis* (exhortation or encouragement) in the New Testament. See C. H. Dodd, 1936, *The Apostolic Preaching and its Developments*, London: Hodder & Stoughton, pp. 7–8. For a discussion of the relationship between preaching and teaching see Arthur Rowe, 1999, 'Preaching and Teaching', *Evangel* 17.2, pp. 48–50.

languages (such as English, Greek and Hebrew) is still more perilous. This fact, together with the span of time over which the Scriptures were written, means that great caution must be exercised in any attempt to establish a 'theology' of some subject such as preaching even partly on the basis of individual Scriptural words. It is the *immediate* context of a word in a text or an activity (like preaching) in life which is the decisive determinant of its meaning and character – and even then the precise range of 'meaning' or 'character' will differ for different speakers and hearers, writers and readers.

This leads to the other pitfall of word-studies, which is to abstract words from the larger units of text where they are found, and especially from a *narrative*. To suppose that the authority of Scripture for today is mediated to us through the occurrence and meaning of particular iso-lated *words* is to truncate and skew that authority, which must surely come through the narrative as a whole. A better pattern is that found in Peter Adam's *Speaking God's Words*, in which he takes from the New Testament not only words and images, but also model sermons, the epistles as models, Paul as a model preacher and Paul's teaching on the ministry of the Word as all contributing to a full-orbed 'biblical' view of preaching.[4] I will seek to offer a fuller and deeper account below, in-corporating the Old Testament, but Adam's approach certainly points in the right direction.

The second inadequate method of basing a theology of preaching on Scripture is to see the sermons in the book of Acts (or indeed the 'ser-mons' of Jesus) as direct models for contemporary preaching. As we saw above, Adam draws on these as a part of his delineation of the NT basis for preaching, but complements them with other elements. There are at least three dangers of treating such biblical 'sermons' as models. First, we may make the unwarranted assumption that the texts record the actual words of a sermon, rather than a summary of the salient points by the book's author. This is certainly how the sermons in Acts are best regarded. In the case of Jesus, the differing accounts of Jesus' Sermon on the Mount (Matt. 5–7) or Sermon on the Plain (Luke 6.20–49) seem to indicate clearly that the Gospels are arranging remembered sayings of Jesus in a particular way for their own purposes; undoubtedly there was at least one such large gathering as Matthew 5 and Luke 6 record, but this does not mean that we have, in either account, the very words of a sermon of Jesus. Second, we may overlook the inherent uncertainty

---

4 Peter Adam, 1996, *Speaking God's Words: A Practical Theology of Preaching*, Leices-ter: InterVarsity Press, pp. 75–84.

about whether, either in human intention or divine providence, these accounts of 'sermons' are to be taken as models for future generations of preachers. Clearly many Scriptural narratives record events which are not to be imitated, and it remains an open question which occurrences recorded by Scripture are to be regarded as in any sense 'normative'. Many parts of Scripture simply testify to past events, without implying that those events should be taken as examples for future generations. Third, it is naïve to ignore the huge historical and circumstantial gap between first-century 'sermons' and those of today. No one, even those who take these sermons as normative in some way, is going to preach today a sermon which resembles The Sermon on the Mount or Peter's sermon in Solomon's portico (Acts 3.12–26) or Paul's sermon in Athens (Acts 17.22–31) in the form in which they are recorded for us. There are important patterns to discern in such texts, and of course the content of what was said remains highly significant for us. But it is idealistic and simplistic to treat such records of preaching as 'models'.

A third inadequate method is to seek throughout Scripture occurrences of 'word ministry' which is then taken as being a kind of prototype for, and in effect a justification of, a particular contemporary practice of preaching. This is a danger of the approach of Hughes Oliphant Old, who in the first of a multi-volume series covers the biblical and early Christian periods of preaching.[5] Thomas Long commented that Old tends to see in the biblical (and later) history 'a parade of precocious Presbyterians'.[6] There are rich insights to be gleaned from Old's work, but the tendency is to a static view of Scripture as a source-book of precursors for present practice.

My fourth, preferred pattern is more dynamic. It sees Scripture as an unfolding narrative in distinct stages, during which the character and purposes of God attain fuller clarity and his revelation extends from individuals and a small nation to the ends of the earth. We today are still a part of this narrative, and can understand our Christian identity as belonging to the final stage of the story which the New Testament outlines for us.[7] We look back to Scripture as our 'founding narrative'

---

5 Hughes Oliphant Old, 1998, *The Reading and Preaching of the Scriptures in the Worship of the Christian Church*, vol. 1: *The biblical period*, Grand Rapids: Eerdmans.

6 Review in *Christian Century*, December 2 1998, p. 1154, cited in O. C. Edwards Jr, 2004, *A History of Preaching*, vol. 1, Grand Rapids, Eerdmans, p. xxiii.

7 Cf. for such an understanding N. T. Wright, 1991, 'How Can the Bible be Authoritative', http://www.ntwrightpage.com/Wright_Bible_Authoritative.htm, originally published in *Vox Evangelica* 21, pp. 7–32; Craig Bartholomew and Michael Goheen, 2006, *The Drama of Scripture: Finding our Place in the Biblical Story*, London: SPCK.

and seek to discern within it patterns which enable us to make some sense (though not yet ultimate sense) of our current world and our current Church practices. We will see that an authentic 'performance' of Scripture does not require the imitation of all apparent 'prototypes', but may, if we take the progression of the narrative seriously, require us to leave aspects of some behind.[8] This is at the other extreme from a 'proof-texting' approach which takes individual texts out of context as direct promises, commands, prohibitions or models to be transferred in an uncomplicated way to the present. I would argue that a framework of thought which places us in a chain of life continuous with the biblical narrative, seeking to advance its logic and goals in authentic ways, respects the authority of Scripture far more deeply than one which extracts words or even stories in an essentially arbitrary manner as normative or exemplary.[9] It allows us, in fact, to go on *listening* to Scripture, rather than trying to bring our own premature closure to its interpretation.[10]

It should be clear that this is no easy route to a set of templates for contemporary preaching. The possible Scriptural patterns for preaching differ; they are all at a considerable remove from our own setting, and 'application' of them must therefore be thoughtful and creative rather than mechanical and slavish. Indeed, even patterns or models of this kind are identified and chosen *by us* (in this case, me!) rather than imposing themselves *upon us* in an uncontested and obvious fashion. It will be safest if rather than speaking of 'models', we call them 'moments' in the chronological unfolding of God's purposes.

---

8 See Keith Ward, 2004, *What the Bible Really Teaches: A Challenge to Fundamentalists*, London: SPCK. Ward's fourth principle of biblical interpretation is that of 'sublation', which he defines as follows: 'To 'sublate' means to negate and yet to fulfil at the same time ... Many biblical passages are sublated by later teachings, so that they no longer apply literally, but can be seen to point towards a deeper spiritual meaning' (p. 23). On the idea of the interpretation of Scripture as 'performance' see Frances Young, 1990, *The Art of Performance: Towards a Theology of Holy Scripture*, London: Darton, Longman & Todd.

9 Among various works which approach contemporary theology and ethics in a 'narrative' and/or 'performative' manner such as this see John E. Colwell, 2001, *Living the Christian Story: The Distinctiveness of Christian Ethics*, Edinburgh and New York: T & T Clark; Samuel Wells, 2004, *Improvisation: The Drama of Christian Ethics*, London: SPCK.

10 For a succinct account of the kind of theology of preaching to which the Bible seems to lead see Gail R. O'Day, 1993, 'Toward a Biblical Theology of Preaching', in Gail R. O'Day and Thomas G. Long (eds), *Listening to the Word: Studies in Honour of Fred B. Craddock*, Nashville: Abingdon, pp. 17–32. O'Day draws the threads together under these headings: 'The Language of the Gospel', 'A Word of Hope Spoken in the Face of Fear', 'Preaching God's Promises in Exile', 'The "Fear Not" News of the Church', and 'Preaching as Salvation Oracle'.

The first two moments are taken from the life of Israel as reflected in the Old Testament. The way in which God's *Torah* (teaching) and Wisdom were passed on regularly to his people through intermediaries of one kind or another is an obvious place to start. The prophets, those who forcefully called Israel back to obedience to that teaching, provide an equally obvious next step.

We then move to the New Testament, and to Jesus himself. We recognize in him the decisive new beginning in God's purposes: he proclaims, enacts and incarnates good news from God. Surely we can use him as (in a sense) a model, and yet, as we shall see further below, his uniqueness as well as his historical location forbid us from doing so in any simplistic way. The ministry of apostleship, prophecy and teaching in the New Testament churches, our next 'moment', also offers in one way a paradigm, in another an unrepeatable example.

First, though, let us find an appropriate starting-place for the story.

Teaching from God

If we were to trace the pedigree of Christian preaching back all the way through the many turns of its history, we would finally reach a point beyond which it is both impossible and pointless to try to go. That point is the ancient Israelite practice in which particular, recognized individuals spoke to their people, often in cultic settings, words which were held to come with authority from the God they believed had bound himself to them in covenant: Yahweh, whom they came to acknowledge as the Creator of the whole world.

In the nature of the case, precise details of the historical circumstances in which this practice arose are lost to us. But the Hebrew Scriptures, though not history-writing in the modern sense, give us stories from which we may not only reconstruct a plausible, if tentative and fragmented, outline of development, but also, more importantly, understand the importance and meaning of this practice in the life of the nation within which the Christian movement had its birth.

Central among those stories is that of a single great figure, Moses, through whom Yahweh had spoken in a uniquely authoritative manner, and who was to become the reference-point for Jewish understanding of what God had called them to be and to do, down to the present day. The teaching that Moses delivered from Yahweh became known as *Torah*, normally and inadequately translated as 'law', better rendered simply as 'teaching'. Although its central precepts were committed to writing, *Torah* was never confined to a written text or collection of texts. *Torah*, or pieces of *Torah*, was what the priests delivered orally on a regular basis in the temple, rulings or advice on particular matters that needed attention. In a wider sense, it was also the 'wisdom' or *Hokmah* that was handed on in other settings, especially in the home from parent to child: the kind of teaching preserved for us in the book of Proverbs. *Hokmah* and *Torah* alike had one great centring foundation: love for Yahweh himself (Deut. 6.5) also expressed as 'fear', deep reverence (Deut. 10.20; Prov. 1.7). Three points about this ancient Israelite practice of teaching or *Torah* are crucial for our reflection on how it might, or might not, point forward to the role of preaching today.[11]

First, the immediate purpose of the words of *Torah* given through Moses, the priests and others was to shape and order the life of the community of Israel, to preserve its distinct identity. This was a holistic purpose. Though in modern times it has been customary to divide the definitive instructions of *Torah* in the books Exodus to Deuteronomy into 'moral', 'civic' and 'cultic' laws, this is an anachronistic and often misleading distinction, and does not reflect the way in which the 'laws' or elements of teaching are actually arranged in these books (in which these three elements are notoriously difficult to disentangle).[12] The evidence suggests rather that, in common with other ancient societies, no distinction was perceived in Israel between what we call 'personal morality', 'law' ('civil' and 'criminal'), and 'religion'. All were bound together. *Torah* was thus not merely a set of rules for the individual's behaviour, nor just a set of laws to regulate a society, nor only a handbook for 'religious observance' (along the lines of a set of denominational principles, liturgical standards or 'canon law', perhaps, today). The individual behaviour, corporate practice and faith-expression of Israel were inseparably tied to each other.

This has great implications. God's teaching was identity-forming in a total sense. It was not simply a matter of 'what you should/shouldn't do' in various settings – as an initial, superficial reading of much of Exodus to Deuteronomy might suggest. Rather, it was a matter of *'this is who I Am: this is what and who you are: therefore this is how you*

---

11 See Philip Stern, 1993, 'Torah', in Bruce M. Metzger and Michael D. Coogan (eds), *The Oxford Companion to the Bible*, Oxford: Oxford University Press, pp. 747–8. Stern notes that kings, too, could promulgate *Torah*, as well as being expected (like everyone else) to obey it.

12 See for example Leviticus 19, where precepts from all three categories are bound together within the overarching instruction to be holy as Yahweh is holy (v. 2). On the function of *Torah* see Hetty Lalleman, 2004, *Celebrating the Law?: Rethinking Old Testament Ethics*, Carlisle: Paternoster.

should be'. Most memorably, this is expressed in the command 'You shall be holy; for I the LORD your God am holy' (Lev. 19.2). God's 'teaching' consists as much of reminding the people of his mighty acts as their father and protector, and their belonging in his family, as it does of specific commandments. It is *because* they are a particular kind of community belonging to *this* God that they are to live *this* way. Deuteronomy, especially, is full of this logic. And it is this identity-forming purpose of *Torah* that binds what we call the 'cultic', 'civic' and 'moral' elements together. The purpose of the sacrificial system outlined in such detail in the first part of Leviticus is not mere arcane religious ritual, but is to reinforce the nature of the God whom Israel serves, to whom they are bound as a covenant family. When this 'cultic' *Torah* is observed aright, it will inevitably shape the 'civil' life of the community and the 'moral' life of its members – and also the reverse, for as the prophets were to point out, one could not hang on to one or two of these elements without the other(s) and escape the displeasure of Yahweh (for example Isa. 1.10–17). Further, the identity-forming purpose of *Torah* is seen in that the books which became recognized as *Torah* in its definitive sense – what we call the Pentateuch, Genesis to Deuteronomy – contain long stretches of *narrative*, notably the entire fifty chapters of Genesis. Such narrative is best seen as one long summons to Israel to remember and ponder who they are, as a result of God's gracious acts.

Second, the central place for the transmission of *Torah* was the community's worship, and the normative channels for it were the priests and Levites. Those who administered the cultic rituals were also those who communicated the teaching of Yahweh, for whose sake and in obedience to whom those rituals were enacted.[13] These moments – whether focused on tabernacle or Temple – were the opportunity to draw near to God in a holistic way that was both a *sign* of the presence and power of God which was promised for *all* the hours and days of the community's life, and a *motor* to enable his people to remember and experience that. The speaking and hearing of words from God was not an isolated event, but one bound up at the very centre of Israel's life with the shared drama of its worship and remembrance of Yahweh who had bound them to himself in covenant.[14]

This did not mean, however, that *Torah* could *only* come in worship, through the mouths of the priests and Levites. As we have seen, the concept of 'wisdom', *Hokmah*, is closely associated with *Torah*. In the

---

13 See Old, *Reading and Preaching*, vol. 1, pp. 30–1.
14 Cf. Old, *Reading and Preaching*, vol. 1, pp. 25–6.

book of Proverbs the two seem to be more or less interchangeable; see the many references to *Torah*, 'teaching', in the book (for example 1.8; 3.1; 4.2; 6.20, 23; 7.2; 13.14; 28.4, 7, 9, 18; 31.26). It is clear that one of the main arenas where *Hokmah* was passed on was not in the temple or even (later) the synagogue, but the home. It was the wisdom of a father and mother that children were to heed (Prov. 1.8 etc.). The influence of *Torah* away from the cultic setting is important. But it is clearly the public delivery of *Torah* in the cultic setting that provides the most immediate analogy here for our reflection on contemporary preaching.

The third point about *Torah* worth pausing over here is the fact that when the priests and Levites taught, they were (at least ideally!) both rooted in the definitive teaching of Yahweh given in the past through Moses, and communicating a fresh word for particular situations. When (at a time in Israel's history difficult to pinpoint with precision) *Torah* became the label attached more specifically to the teaching of Moses, and then to the five 'books of Moses', the task still remained of interpreting, applying and obeying the teaching in each new generation. The book of Deuteronomy is the earliest written encapsulation of such an act of interpretation. In Judaism in later times, the sacredness of this ongoing task became expressed in the belief in an 'oral' *Torah* that had been passed on through the generations of elders and teachers.[15] This could lead to an over-valuing and fossilizing of the oral teaching, as seems to have happened in the Pharisaism criticized by Jesus. But it can also be understood as a vital metaphor for the creative tension inevitably involved in communicating the teaching of a God who was both faithful and living, a tension that involved being true to the past as well as alive to the present and future.

Our first scene for reflection, then, is the gathered community of Israel, worshipping Yahweh their covenant God, seeking to hear his teaching through the mouth of his authorized spokesmen: teaching which would foster their shared identity as his people, shape their common life, preserve the definitive revelation of his character and will, and be used to apply it freshly to new circumstances.

Voicing prophecy

Our second 'moment' is that of the classical period of Old Testament prophecy, from the eighth century BC onwards. The prophets essentially were doing nothing more or less than continuing to pass on

---

15 Stern, 'Torah', p. 748.

God's *Torah* to his people. Like the priestly teachers, they aimed to form and re-form God's people according to their true identity as his covenant family. In several striking ways, however, they constitute a new twist to the tale, a fresh pattern worthy of reflection in its own right as a dialogue partner for understanding our preaching ministry. The prophets come from a period when Israel's obedience to God's *Torah* had grown stale, routine or altogether dead. This makes their fresh characteristics readily comprehensible.

First, they often seem to have operated outside the setting of cultic worship, and where they still seem close to it, they sometimes critique it fiercely (see Jeremiah's tirade against the temple in Jeremiah 7, delivered in its very gateway). They thus act as a reminder to Israel – quite apart from the actual content of their message – that it is important to listen out for *Torah* in unaccustomed settings, and not to assume that what goes on, or what is heard, in the regular rituals will necessarily be above criticism.

Second, they were not authorized as prophets by anyone but Yahweh, even though some, such as Jeremiah and Ezekiel, were priests from the line of Aaron (Jer. 1.1; Ezek. 1.3). Amos, the earliest prophet whose words are collected in a book, is the archetypal case. Perceived as a threat to the established order of monarchy and cult, he famously responded to the bullying of Amaziah the priest:

> I am no prophet, nor a prophet's son; but I am a herdsman, and a dresser of sycamore trees, and the LORD took me from following the flock, and the LORD said to me, 'Go, prophesy to my people Israel.'
>
> (Amos 7.14, 15)

The force of this is to emphasize Amos's total lack of dependence on any authorization through birth or official appointment; at his time there must have been 'prophets' who were, as we would say, socialized into Israel's 'establishment', earning their living as 'prophets' (7.12) and thus in a weak position to be able to challenge the nation with the word of a God who refused to be tamed by custom.[16] Amos is an ordinary farmer gripped by conviction that Yahweh was speaking through *him* to his people. In due course, his people came to recognize that it was indeed so; hence the presence of his book in their Scriptures. He

---

16 On the significance of Amos's financial independence see Hans Walter Wolff, 1977, *Joel and Amos*, Hermeneia – A Critical and Historical Commentary on the Bible, Philadelphia: Fortress, pp. 313–14.

epitomizes the fact that Yahweh's teaching, though having its 'official' channels, can never be limited to them.

The third point is closely connected to this. From the eighth century, the prophets' intended audience was much wider than that of the priests and Levites who regularly taught in the temple. Nor was it only directed to the leaders – kings, priests and (phoney) 'prophets' – but also towards the nation as a whole.[17] This is appropriate to the fact that a prophet could spring up anywhere, whether it was Amos out 'in the sticks' at Tekoa, or Isaiah at the king's court. This is not to drive a false wedge between prophecy and the regular priestly teaching. The latter surely did not consist merely of individualistic advice; we have seen how *Torah* encompassed 'national' and 'cultic' as well as 'personal' morality. It is rather that – just like today – regular bread-and-butter teaching and preaching, whether good or bad, went unreported. Maybe we still have the prophets' words precisely *because* they were issuing outspoken rallying-cries to the nation and its leaders, rather than simply reminding the people of the basis of their faith and how it should apply. And maybe such a message could often be heard better when it came from outside the hallowed temple courts. (It is sobering, though, to realize that, as far as we can tell, the prophets saw little fruit from their labours.)

A fourth point must be made. The prophets' vocation took them beyond the borders of the covenant community, sometimes geographically, but more often in vision. This also follows from what we have said about them thus far. The shattering experience of exile was to make Israel herself a radical 'outsider', fundamentally questioning Yahweh and his covenant purpose. We find prophets totally identifying with them in this state, and continuing to be mouthpieces for Yahweh far beyond Israel's traditional borders: Jeremiah, dragged off to Egypt (Jer. 43.6, 7); Ezekiel by the river Chebar in Babylon (Ezek. 1.1); 'Isaiah of the Exile' (the hypothetical author of Isa. 40–66) assuring his compatriots that Yahweh was with them. No temple was needed as the setting for these sermons; they did not even need to be in the 'holy land'.

Further, some prophets had a *message* for the nations too. Sometimes a message of judgement *concerning* the nations seems to be mainly for 'home consumption', such as Jeremiah 46 to 51, or the prophecies of Obadiah and Nahum: Israel needs to be assured that her God is in charge of events beyond her borders. Sometimes the vision is wider, more positive, but still essentially directed to Israel, as

---

17 R. N. Whybray, 1993, 'Prophets – Ancient Israel', in Metzger and Coogan (eds), *Oxford Companion to the Bible*, pp. 620–2.

when she is told by 'Isaiah of the Exile' that as God's servant, she is to be a 'light to the nations' (Isa. 42, 49). And we have one memorable story of Yahweh's message actually being proclaimed in another nation (Jonah), though Yahweh has to take extreme, even comical action to reverse the prophet's reluctance to carry out the commission.

The prophets therefore represent a widening of the channel of proclamation at the far end of which, after much further journeying, we stand today. In them we see God's word coming in often unexpected places, through often unexpected people, to challenge and later encourage the nation and its leaders, declare the whole world to be God's business, and even begin, with extreme hesitation, to take his word right to the power-centres of that world.

The voice of prophecy was widely regarded as falling largely silent for four hundred years. The final representative of the era of 'the law and the prophets', according to the New Testament, was John the Baptizer (Luke 16.16). All the classic features of the prophet's ministry are seen in him. He operated away from the centre of cultic power. Though from a priestly family (Luke 1.5), he 'appeared' in the wilderness, in rough garb like that of Elijah: unauthorized, simply a 'voice' preparing the way for Yahweh to visit his people (Mark 1.1–8). His message was for all and sundry, and all and sundry came to hear it. Agents of the Roman regime (soldiers and tax-collectors) were left in no doubt that there was a word for them (Luke 3.12–14); nor was King Herod himself (Luke 3.19). And though John, like most of his predecessors, was sharply focused on calling Yahweh's own covenant people back to him, his warning to them contains both a threat and an implied promise: 'Do not begin to say to yourselves, "We have Abraham as our ancestor"; for I tell you, God is able from these stones to raise up children to Abraham' (Luke 3.8). The characteristic note of Isaiah of the Exile and others is heard again: the special covenant relationship with Israel is not to be taken presumptuously, nor thought to exclude Yahweh's power over and care for the world as a whole.

Jesus of Nazareth

In close succession to John, yet sharply distinguished from him, was Jesus himself. Known as a prophet (for example Luke 7.16),[18] his followers came to recognize that he was much more than that.

---

18 For discussion of the characteristics of a 'prophet' in the time of Jesus see N. T. Wright, 1996, *Jesus and the Victory of God*, London: SPCK, pp. 147–74.

John and Jesus were united in their emphasis on Yahweh's coming to fulfil his purposes, and the consequent need for his people to repent. It is not accurate to say that John preached judgement while Jesus preached mercy; for though he spoke of coming judgement (Luke 3.9), John's baptism was with a view to the forgiveness of sins (Luke 1.77; 3.3), and though Jesus announced the year of Yahweh's favour (Luke 4.19), he did not shirk giving warning of judgement (for example Luke 12.16–21; 21.6). The difference, rather, is seen in their symbolic representation of two eras. John's austere lifestyle bespoke the age of preparation and longing, while Jesus' habits of celebration signalled that the longed-for reign of God had finally dawned (Luke 7.18–35). But both John and Jesus were Wisdom's children, in their different manners 'vindicating' Wisdom's way (Luke 7.35).

How then might we sketch the contours of Jesus' ministry, so that its significance for contemporary preaching may be assessed? It may be helpful to think of the four characteristics of the prophets' ministry noted above, and consider how Jesus both continued and transcended them.

First, Jesus, like the prophets and John, proclaimed his message outside the religious fulcrum of the nation. The Synoptic Gospels agree in depicting the original arena for Jesus' ministry as being in Galilee;[19] though John places the focus on Jerusalem, the overall effect is similar, because there Jesus finds himself in intense conflict with the Jewish dignitaries. It was precisely his implied claim to be speaking and acting for God *outside* the normal cultic channels which aroused ire in the establishment early on (Mark 2.6, 7). The main distinction from the prophets in this respect is that accompanying Jesus' words were mighty works which, though not totally unprecedented, took place on a scale and with an immediacy which set apart his ministry as mediating the real presence and power of God. The prophets had often criticized a temple cult that had become ineffectual through compromise and injustice; Jesus actually provides an alternative to that cult.[20]

Yet we must not exaggerate the picture of Jesus as an 'outsider'. It is clear that, like some of the prophets, he had strong links to the 'system'. Luke's portrayal of his upbringing in a faithful Jewish household is particularly telling. As a boy, Jesus was at home with the teachers in the

---

19 On the significance of Galilee as the geographical location for Jesus' early ministry see R. T. France, 2007, *The Gospel of Matthew*, The New International Commentary on the New Testament, Grand Rapids: Eerdmans, pp. 5–7.

20 See Mark 1.40–5; Luke 17.11–19. The cleansed leprosy sufferers are sent to the temple, but only as a demonstration of healing that has taken place elsewhere. On the significance of the 'miracles' of Jesus, see Wright, *Jesus*, pp. 191–7.

Temple (Luke 2.41–52). In his later fierce denunciations of the Temple, his motivation was love for the one who had chosen it as a house of prayer for all nations (Luke 19.46), and the context was his weeping over the holy city (Luke 19.41). Whether or not he had had any rabbinic training,[21] he was clearly an acceptable and attractive speaker in the synagogues, at least at the outset of his ministry (Luke 4.15). He discussed and disputed with Pharisees and scribes, as well as Sadducees and others, right up to a few days before his death.

All this suggests a person who was not so marginal as to be irrelevant. He had the ear of many, including some who were his enemies. Indeed, as compared with John, he may be seen as moving into the mainstream. His ministry took place not in the wilderness, but in synagogues, homes, market squares, hillsides, lakeshores, roads and the Temple itself. Moreover he deliberately and conspicuously took part in celebratory feasting, often raising eyebrows about the company he kept. He took part in the regular round of Jewish festivals (John 5 — 10).

Second, like the prophets, Jesus had no 'official' authorization for what he was saying and doing. Especially in the early stages of his public ministry, he took the initiative to call people to be disciples (Mark 1.16–20), a contrast to standard rabbinic practice in which the student would choose the teacher. His ministry marked a new stage in the coming of God's word, for he was bringing it back into the heart of the nation's life. Though judgement still hung over the heads of all who practised injustice, Jesus demonstrated that the feast of God's kingdom had begun among the people at large, including many who could make no particular claim to piety but were simply struggling on seeking to be faithful to Yahweh in the midst of economic exigency and political oppression.

Third, like the prophets, Jesus had a message for his people, for the nation as a whole. He directly challenged its religious authorities and ultimately would stand before Herod the 'king' of Galilee and Pilate the Roman governor (Luke 23.1–25). Yet, again, he seems to bring the prophetic message down to earth, in his ministry to the crowds and small groups who gathered around him. Of course we have very little in the way of narrative concerning the lives of the Old Testament prophets. We know that Isaiah, at least, had disciples (Isa. 8.16), and no doubt he and others addressed themselves from time to time to the everyday concerns of the people as well as to the direction of the nation.

---

21 France comments that 'Rabbi' as applied to Jesus 'was apparently an honorary title, based on his reputation rather than his official status': *Matthew*, p. 862.

Indeed, Walter Brueggemann has pointed out that the stories of some of the earlier prophets, Elijah and Elisha, seem to represent a 'counter-tradition' to royal ideology and historiography, in their emphasis on these men's ministry among the poor and, indeed, non-Israelites.[22] But with Jesus this is a defining feature of his work. Much of his teaching was given to a small band of disciples. And in his encounter with wider groups, he was concerned to give hope, warning and practical wisdom for people to grasp in their daily lives. In this sense, he represents a coming together of the priestly and prophetic traditions: the regular giving of *Torah*, applying the Mosaic word to everyday life, alongside the summons to the nation as a whole.

Fourth, what of his concern for those beyond Israel? At first glance, it might seem as if Jesus here takes a step back from Isaiah of the Exile: according to Matthew, he said 'I was sent only to the lost sheep of the house of Israel' (Matt. 15.24). Yet all the Gospel writers see the decisive significance of Jesus' ministry in the history of God's dealings with the world as a whole. Jesus was rooted in his own people, loved them, and longed for them to become what God intended them to be. But in his words and actions, he emitted clear signs that their destiny was not to be an exclusive or domineering one. He aroused anger by implicitly associating himself in Nazareth with the ministry of Elijah and Elisha beyond the borders of Israel (Luke 4.24–28). He healed a Samaritan (Luke 17.11–19), a Canaanite (Matt. 15.21–28) and a Roman (Matt. 8.5–13). In fact he both proclaimed and enacted the fulfilment of the calling of Yahweh's servant to be a light to the nations (Isa. 42, 49; cf. Matt. 12.15–21).[23] Reading from that same section in Isaiah, 'The spirit of the Lord GOD is upon me, because the LORD has anointed me . . .' (Isa. 61.1), he declared: 'Today this Scripture has been fulfilled in your hearing' (Luke 4.17–21).

The link which both Jesus himself and the Evangelists perceived between him and the prophets is summed up in Jesus' explanation of his parabolic teaching (Mark 4.10–12). Just as Isaiah had been warned of resistance to his message (Isa. 6.9–10), so Jesus discerned that his words were bringing near a time of judgement. The somewhat veiled and indirect form of teaching so characteristic of Jesus was to be a means whereby Israel's true desires, for obedience to God or otherwise,

---

22 Walter Brueggemann, 2003, *An Introduction to the Old Testament: The Canon and Christian Imagination*, Louisville: Westminster John Knox, pp. 152–4.

23 On the importance of Isa. 40–55 for Jesus' self-understanding and kingdom proclamation see Wright, *Jesus*, pp. 601–4.

would be made manifest. In Jesus, however, the secret revealed to those who are open to receive it is nothing less than the secret of the kingdom of God (Mark 4.11). There is a uniqueness to Jesus' parabolic teaching. It is set apart from both the earlier ministry of the prophets, and the later ministry of the apostles and the Church. Judgement and grace are continued effects of God's revelation in all periods, but it was in the ministry of Jesus that the crisis of God's kingdom came to a head.

Apostolic announcements

The New Testament is largely a reflection – mostly at some remove, to be sure – of the proclamation of the apostles about Jesus. No less than the teachers of *Torah*, Israel's prophets or Jesus, the apostles and their associates understood themselves to be preaching the word of Yahweh himself. For example, in what is probably the earliest NT document, Paul tells the Thessalonian Christians he thanks God 'that when you received the word of God that you heard from us [Paul, Silvanus and Timothy], you accepted it not as a human word but as what it really is, God's word, which is also at work in you believers' (1 Thess. 2.13). Moreover, 'the word of the Lord has sounded forth' from the Thessalonians far and wide (1 Thess. 1.8). No defining social limits are set upon the channels through whom God's word may spread. One did not have to be known as 'priest', 'prophet' or 'apostle'; one *could not*, of course, be Jesus! Luke sees this symbolized in the events of Pentecost, when the proclamation of the gospel in many languages by a group of ordinary Galileans fulfils Joel's prophecy:

> In the last days it will be, God declares, that I will pour out my Spirit upon all flesh, and your sons and your daughters shall prophesy, and your young men shall see visions, and your old men shall dream dreams. Even upon my slaves, both men and women, in those days I will pour out my Spirit; and they shall prophesy.
>
> (Acts 2.17, 18; cf. Joel 2.28, 29)

In keeping, then, with the way that Jesus brought the word of God right back to the centre of Israel's life, the apostolic age opens with a vivid display of the breaking down of all social and cultic divisions in the perception of where and how that word might come. Yet it is the *public* proclamation of the word in this period in which our particular interest here lies: and understandably, it is those most prominently charged with this – the apostles and their immediate colleagues and successors – to whose preaching we mainly have access, although even that is only indirect. What characterized the social settings and dynamics of their preaching?

Like Jesus, the apostles preached outside the official channels. They were not authorized by the Jerusalem authorities, but spoke in the 'name' and authority of Jesus alone (for example Acts 3.16; 4.10). Like him, they could point to transformed lives as evidence that it was through *this* channel that the power of God was now directed. Yet also like him, they did not reject the Temple in itself. They attended its worship, at least in the early days, and taught there (for example Acts 5.21). Paul's first preaching after his conversion was in the synagogues (Acts 9.20). When Paul and his colleagues started taking the gospel further afield into the Gentile world, their first port of call in any place was the synagogue (Acts 13.5 etc.). When they 'preached' among Gentiles, Acts suggests that they did so in the place and manner appropriate to that setting: in Athens, Paul debated in the marketplace and on the Areopagus (Acts 17.17–34). In other words, whether among Jews or Gentiles, the apostles were not marginal figures. They were in the thick of it, wherever they could get a hearing – whether they got a positive response or not.

We have seen that the priests applied *Torah* to ordinary people's daily lives; the prophets called the nation and its leaders back to fundamental obedience; Jesus did both. To whom was the apostles' message directed? A striking shift is noticeable here, as the message goes out beyond the borders of Israel.

According to Luke, the death and resurrection of Jesus was a fateful moment for Israel, when her leaders had rejected her Messiah. This certainly did not mean that there was no good news for Jews, or that God had abandoned them. At the end of Acts Paul is still trying to persuade Jewish people to believe in Jesus (28.17–31). Some show the signs of hard-heartedness noted long before by Isaiah, but others are convinced (vv. 24–28). But Acts leaves us with the picture of Paul under house arrest welcoming *all* who come to him (v. 30) – presumably both Jew and Gentile – 'proclaiming the kingdom of God and teaching about the Lord Jesus Christ with all boldness and without hindrance' (v. 31). The message being proclaimed is now quite openly *for all*. There is an order of priority in Paul's mission, as seen in Acts and in his summary statement in Romans (1.16: '. . . to the Jew first and also to the Greek'). But there is no order of priority in the kingdom whose arrival the apostles proclaim. The prophetic vision of God's servant being a 'light to the nations' (Isa. 42.6) is now explicitly enacted as the apostles bring the good news of Israel's Messiah not only to Israel, but also to the Gentiles.

This widening of focus beyond national Israel does not mean that the apostles' message was directed to people as a more or less random assortment of individuals. It continued to have highly political ramifications, now not merely for Israelites but for the Roman empire itself. To say that Jesus was Lord could not but be subversive in a political climate where Caesar alone was supposed to be Lord. It is highly significant that Luke should leave us with that picture of Paul 'proclaiming the kingdom of God and teaching about the Lord Jesus Christ' (Acts 28.31). It is often noted that 'the kingdom of God' is the main theme of Jesus' teaching in the synoptic Gospels, but rare in Paul's letters. Granted that Luke may have wished to show the continuity between Jesus and the early Church by explicitly using 'kingdom' language in Acts, it is nonetheless important to note that he can summarize the early Church's message as 'the kingdom of God', that divine new order which calls all human authorities to account. It is the world itself that God is going to judge by the standard of Jesus (Acts 17.31).

We have seen that Jesus, like the early teachers of Israel, not only proclaimed a message of hope and warning to the nation, but also taught the disciples and the crowds, the general populace who sorely needed encouragement and wisdom from God. What about the apostles? Did they have a similar 'popular' touch, or did they just operate on the grand scale? The glimpses of their ministry which we gain from Acts and the epistles are instructive. While the actual 'sermons' recorded in Acts appear to be simple summaries of their core message, the descriptions of Paul's ministry in places such as Corinth and Ephesus suggest personal, daily, down-to-earth, warm human contact as he shared the gospel and encouraged believers (Acts 18.1–18; 19.10–12; 20.18–21, 31–35). Within this daily ministry we have little clue as to what the more public elements of teaching or preaching might have looked like. But from Paul's letters we can gain an excellent idea of the kind of subjects which concerned him in his dealings with local churches. We see him applying the gospel to the specific and pressing pastoral and ethical challenges these churches faced. Though these words of advice have come down to us in the form of letters rather than transcripts of 'sermons', it is not fanciful to see here a real continuity with the regular teaching of Israelites by priests and Levites.

The one small peep we get into what actually went on in these early Christian gatherings (1 Cor. 11–14) shows us that neither the Church nor Paul believed that 'the word of God' was confined to the OT Scriptures. It was a living reality, mediated in 'prophecy' through any member of the congregation. Paul's concern here is not to squash such utterances – far from it. He simply wants to maximize their benefit by getting the Corinthians to be more disciplined, so that they listen to each other instead of all trying to get in at once, and so that they value the comprehensible words more highly than the incomprehensible ones. For Paul, hearing the word of God is too important a matter for the spirituality of a Christian community to be merely equated with spontaneity. Without the consideration of love, it will descend into ungodly chaos. All this underlines the fact that the word of God which burst out in a fresh way at Pentecost was alive and active in the local congregations, directing them in his way.

Paul's letters too can be seen as vehicles of the word of God. J. Louis Martyn has argued that a letter such as Galatians would have been read out in a context of worship, with the faith and hope that by the power of the Spirit it would have been heard not just as an argument, but as a 're-proclamation' of God's good news.[24] The public reading of a letter from Paul would have been a sacred moment – as well, no doubt, as a rather uncomfortable one at times! The writing of a pastoral letter became a medium for the speaking of a pastoral, applied word. (And it is hard to believe that this was not followed at some point by lively discussion.)

It is important to see the extent to which the apostolic proclamation and teaching concerned not only Jesus himself, but also the way in which Jesus had fulfilled the promises contained in the Jewish Scriptures. Clearly, Jesus *could* be proclaimed without direct reference to the Scriptures, as in Athens, the centre of Greek culture (Acts 17.22–31). But the other sermons in Acts place heavy emphasis on Jesus as the climax of Israel's narrative, and Paul's most mature writing – Romans – shows that he is still wrestling with just how this can be, and that he feels it necessary to do so for a mixed congregation of Jewish and Gentile believers. The Gospels too reveal a pervasive concern, worked out in different ways, to present Jesus as the true fulfilment of Israel's history and hopes. Two other NT voices, those of Hebrews and Revelation, equally express this concern, in their diverse ways.

What of the role of specific Christian leaders *other* than the apostles in the transmission of this gospel word? Acts records that Paul and Barnabas appointed elders in every gathering of believers that was formed through their missionary endeavours (13.23). The impression given by the

---

24 J. Louis Martyn, 1997, *Galatians*, Anchor Bible 33A, New York: Doubleday, p. 21.

NT, with its various designations for such people – not just 'elders', but 'overseers' and 'deacons' (Phil. 1.1) – is of a still-fluid, rather than settled Church order. However, prominent among the gifts mentioned by Paul in the various lists that have come down to us are the 'word' ministries of prophecy, teaching and evangelism (Rom. 12.6; 1 Cor. 12.28; Eph. 4.11). Those who demonstrably had such gifts were to be encouraged to exercise them, whether or not they were official leaders, but one can imagine that the discernment of such gifts in a person would soon become an obvious criterion for appointment as an elder.

It has been common to emphasize the immediacy of the inspiration of the NT 'prophets' by the Spirit. No doubt there was an evident element of liveliness and inspiration in the ministry of the word in NT times. But as Richard Bauckham has convincingly pointed out, there was also a strong emphasis on faithfulness to eyewitness testimony about Jesus.[25] This is seen in Paul's writing, in which he stresses how he not only received a personal revelation of Christ, but also the testimony of those who had witnessed his life, death and resurrection appearances (1 Cor. 15.1–11; Gal. 1.18—2.10). But it is also seen in the Gospels. Luke underlines how he has received his information from those who were 'eyewitnesses and servants of the word' (Luke 1.2), and Bauckham carefully traces the signs of debt to eyewitnesses owed by the four Evangelists.[26] Ancient historians placed a high value on eyewitness testimony, and it must have been eyewitnesses, and those who had known them, as well as those with evident gifts of the Spirit, who were entrusted with the task of being 'servants of the word' in the early Church.

To summarize: the apostles and their contemporaries exhibit a lively picture of God's word coming through any and all upon whom his Spirit had fallen. In the name of Jesus, a word was to be spoken which called not only Israel, but all the nations, to repentance in the light of God's kingdom, whose arrival had been confirmed through Jesus' resurrection from the dead. Any could speak this word; but via the leaders of the Church, the representative figures who became known as apostles, together with other eyewitnesses to Jesus and gifted and/or appointed people in the churches, we can trace a pattern which may be particularly fruitful for our thinking about preaching today. This was a pattern in which preaching in the established centres, Jewish and Gentile, was combined with preaching anywhere and everywhere; in which

---

25 Richard Bauckham, 2006, *Jesus and the Eyewitnesses: The Gospels as Eyewitness Testimony*, Grand Rapids: Eerdmans.
26 *Jesus*, especially pp. 116–24, 155–239, 358–471.

prophecy to the nations was combined with care and teaching for communities and individuals; in which the immediacy of a living word was grounded in faithful tradition based on eyewitness testimony. The word was making its way into the world in both its centres and its margins.

Gathering the testimony together

A survey of the Scriptural narrative with a view to how it grounds our preaching ministry today would be seriously incomplete without highlighting the way in which that narrative makes God's self-communication not only a striking element of the history it recounts, but also a foundational motif in the way that God has both created and redeemed the world.

The Old Testament, as we have seen, recounts the giving of *Torah* to Moses and to his successors as teachers and priests. It also recounts the sayings of the wise, rooted in the fear of Yahweh, and the words of prophets who have stood in Yahweh's council. But it goes further than this, for it proclaims that it was by the word of Yahweh that the heavens and the earth were made (Ps. 33.6–9; Gen. 1.1–31). The picture of divine Wisdom being present with Yahweh at creation, and actively assisting in it (Prov. 8.22–31), is but a slightly different image for the same reality;[27] as is the later Jewish belief that it was through *Torah* itself that the world was made.[28] All these are ways of claiming that the revelation of God which Israel had received through Moses, priests, sages and prophets was indeed the revelation of the *true* God through whom all things had been created. The corollary of this was that for those whose eyes were opened by God's teaching, however it came, the witness of the creation to his truth was entirely consistent with the witness of the specific words that he spoke. Psalm 19 illustrates the point beautifully. Verses 1–6 speak of the wordless, soundless declaration of God's glory by the heavens; verses 7–11 speak of the specific function and power of the words of *Torah*. *Torah* can *do* things which God's revelation on its own in creation cannot (revive the soul, make wise the simple, rejoice the heart, enlighten the eyes), but there is no discrepancy between what each displays about God. The Psalm clearly celebrates both.

---

27 On the nature of God's Wisdom and its relationship to Christ, see Peter K. Stevenson and Stephen I. Wright, 2010, *Preaching the Incarnation*, Louisville: Westminster John Knox, ch. 2.

28 Stern, 'Torah', p. 748.

Closely related to this testimony to the seamless nature of God's revelation in his creation and in his specific words to Israel is the sense that 'words' may be visible as well as audible. Genesis 1, for example, represents God 'speaking' in an audible fashion so that the universe comes into being. But once the universe is there, it continues to 'speak', displaying God's glory, in a noiseless but highly visible way (Ps. 19.1–6). And God's specific revelation in *Torah*, wisdom and prophecy throughout Israel's history comes not only in words, but also in multi-sensory form. Quintessentially this was so at the revelatory high-point of Sinai, where thunders, lightnings, a thick cloud, a trumpet blast and an earthquake preceded and attended the actual reception of God's *words* (Ex. 19.16–19). The prophetic books often include claims that the prophet has *seen* Yawheh's 'word' before it is actually put into 'words' (for example Isa. 1.1; Ezek. 1.1; Ob. 1; Mic. 1.1; Nah. 1.1; Hab. 1.1). The prophets' 'words' themselves memorably record a number of highly visual scenes (for example Jer. 1.11–14; Ezek. 1.4–28; Am. 7.1–9; 8.1–3). The prophets are sometimes called to 'enact' the word in very visible, tangible, even sensual ways (for example Ezek. 4.1–5.4; Hos. 1.2–11). Their words, furthermore, are full of figurative language appealing to all the senses: Amos 5.4–7 is an excellent example of a multi-sensory (and very biting) appeal.[29] And the 'apocalyptic' writings, often regarded as having arisen as classical 'prophecy' was on the wane, explicitly mediated the word of God in visionary form (in the OT, see Dan. 7–12; Zech. 1.7–5.8).

The idea of the 'word' being more than audible is also apparent when the prophets speak of resistance to it: 'Keep listening, but do not comprehend; keep looking, but do not understand' (Isa. 6.9). Isaiah 28.1–22 is a very interesting passage in this respect. The appointed leaders of Israel, priests and prophets, have become drunkards (vv. 7, 8). Their words of 'knowledge' have become nothing more than the monosyllabic words one might utter to a baby (vv. 9, 10). The result of this is that 'with stammering lip and with alien tongue [Yahweh] will speak to this people' (v. 11). What does this mean? It is through Yahweh's *acts of judgement* that he will speak to them, as he brings foreign powers to conquer them (vv. 17–22). The appointed channels of his teaching, warning and encouragement have become useless: the 'word of the

---

29 I am grateful to David Schlafer for first pointing out (and enacting!) for me the extraordinary sensory range of Amos's language. See also Claus Westermann, 1990, *The Parables of Jesus in the Light of the Old Testament*, Edinburgh: T & T Clark, for a discussion of the power of OT imagery. Westermann rightly argues that this imagery confirms modern research into metaphor, which demonstrates that metaphor functions not merely as an ornament, but a cognitive, world-shaping linguistic force.

LORD' in that sense will become to them indeed 'precept upon precept, precept upon precept, line upon line, line upon line, here a little, there a little' (v. 13). The literal 'words' of the teachers have become no use to the people; therefore Yahweh will speak to them in actions, through the hands of foreigners.

At first sight it seems very unfair of Yahweh to bring his judgement upon the people on account of the moral failure of his appointed spokesmen. Yet the passage makes clear that the people themselves are not absolved from responsibility. He has spoken to *them* of the way of true 'rest', 'yet they would not hear' (v. 12). And for those who are still willing to attend to him, there is a means of security, a 'sure foundation' even in the midst of the coming crisis: 'One who trusts will not panic' (v. 16). Furthermore, Yahweh has not ceased for ever to relate to them in *words*. Isaiah 40—55 is a lyrical explanation to his people of the disaster of exile through which he has sought to speak to them; now in words he is wooing them back to allegiance to him.

These snapshots from the book of Isaiah suggest three things. First, Yahweh holds his appointed spokesmen specially to account, for they have the power to lead people astray, and to prevent them hearing his life-giving word; yet this does not absolve the people themselves from responsibility. They have heard his word over the years, in the tradition of teaching handed down to them, and his word comes through creation itself (see again Ps. 19). Second, Yahweh is not defeated by the failure of leaders and people to respond to his word; he simply switches from 'speaking' through words to 'speaking' through actions. Third, this 'switch' is seen as a sign of judgement. It is not permanent; he will speak in words to his people again.

All this forms the backdrop for the New Testament's account of God's climactic act of redemption. Using language redolent of the OT concepts of *Torah* and *Hokmah*, John writes that 'the Word became flesh' (John 1.14).[30] Not only does *Torah* come to its fulfilment in him (cf. John 1.17); in Jesus is made manifest the very principle at the heart of creation, the Word through whom all things came into being (John 1.1–3). The appearance of 'the Word' as a human being has important consequences for our construal of the biblical narrative concerning God's self-communication.

First, it constitutes the coming-together of the verbal and the visible in the most integrated way imaginable. God had truly spoken in the

---

30 On the connection of John 1 with the picture of Wisdom in Prov. 8.22–31, see Stevenson and Wright, *Preaching the Incarnation*, ch. 2.

past, but the contrast between his speech 'in many and various ways by the prophets' (Heb. 1.1) and his speech by the Son 'through whom he also created the worlds' (Heb. 1.2) is analogous in many ways to the contrast between the forms of long-distant communication made possible by technology today, and the irreplaceable joy of face-to-face meetings with loved ones. In Jesus, the witness to God of the visible creation and the audible *Torah* come together in perfect harmony. God's most intimate communication with his people in the past had been through the words with which he explained his actions and drew people into partnership with himself. In Jesus he does not turn his back on words, but fleshes them out with actions.

Second, God speaks through Jesus' words and life his word both of judgement and of grace. His mighty works are a means of salvation and belief for those with eyes to see, but for those who are closed to them, they constitute a standing judgement (John 5.19–24). His parables have a similar function (Mark 4.10–12). And Jesus' final great act, his triumphant yielding up of his spirit to God (John 19.30), is both the judgement of 'the world' and its salvation (John 12.31, 32).

Thus the Scriptures ground our preaching ministry not only in the historical narrative of the evolution of God's speech, but also in the grand story of how his self-communication is at the very heart of his work in creating and redeeming the world. This has enormous implications for the theological, ethical and practical reflection on preaching to which we now turn.

Questions for the local church

- What particular patterns from Scripture does the preaching in your church resemble (if any)?
- How could you learn from the unfolding narrative given in this chapter about what authentic contemporary preaching might look like in your situation?

Areas for research

Biblical studies still offers huge potential for research projects. The nature and function of any one of the antecedents of Christian preaching touched on here would repay ample study.

Further reading

William Brosend, 2010, *The Preaching of Jesus: Gospel Proclamation, Then and Now*, Louisville: Westminster John Knox.

Peter K. Stevenson and Stephen I. Wright, 2010, *Preaching the Incarnation*, Louisville: Westminster John Knox.

James W. Thompson, 2001, *Preaching like Paul: Homiletical Wisdom for Today*, Louisville: Westminster John Knox.

6

Continuing the Story: Preaching in the Ongoing Purposes of God

It is the task of theology to gather up the founding story of the Church as Scripture has narrated it for us and interpret it in such a way as to give meaning to the subsequent and present story of the Church and the world. A theology of preaching will therefore take its starting-point from a reading, such as the one I have just given, of the way in which a public ministry of the word of God has evolved through the history Scripture recounts.

As mentioned at the start of Chapter 5, I favour an approach to theology which seeks to develop Christian thinking and perform Christian practice in a way which authentically continues the drama and narrative of God's work whose beginnings are attested in Scripture. In this chapter we will explore how we may think Christianly and theologically about the continuing preaching ministry in the light of Scripture's witness. We will continue to attend to various parts of Scripture as we do so, seeking not to 'proof-text' but to recall (at least implicitly) the unfolding narrative retold in Chapter 5 as the framework for reading individual passages. In the next chapter, we will turn to the outworking of this theology in the ethics of the practice of preaching.

It will be convenient to structure our theological discussion of preaching on a series of questions. Does God still speak? If so, how and where? What role do human agents have in mediating that speech? In what contexts can they be expected?

The continuing speech of God

From our survey of the biblical narrative it is quite clear that when humans speak on behalf of God they do so on the fundamental premise that he has taken the initiative, and spoken first. The 'moments' we identified which may be seen to foreshadow, in various ways, our present preaching ministry – the giving of *Torah*, prophecy, the ministry of Jesus and that of the apostles – are all 'moments' in which God spoke and humans sought to relay to others what he had said. There are indeed reports of people giving their own opinions on important matters without divine authority, but the Bible gives these a ruthlessly negative evaluation (for example 1 Kings 22.1–40; Mark 13.21–22; Acts 13.4–12; 2 Cor. 11.1–15; Rev. 2.19–29).

The question thus arises: Does God still speak? Does he still take the initiative to reveal himself, in a way which calls for human beings not only to hear, but also to relay what he says? What might the trajectory of biblical narrative lead us to say about this? There are two elements which must be held in creative tension.

First, the biblical story in no sense leads us to believe that the God of whom it speaks will one day fall silent. If, for instance, Paul can rejoice that the Thessalonians received his gospel as God's word (1 Thess. 2.13), and if the word of the risen Jesus continues to be revealed to the churches (Rev. 2 – 3), why might we think that at some undefined post-biblical moment such speech would cease? The Bible throughout testifies to a *living* God, and his *word* is 'living and active' (Heb. 4.12).

Second, however, the biblical story also paints the picture of a God who is self-consistent and reliable. He speaks in fresh and pertinent ways to succeeding generations, yet he also calls them to faithfulness to what he has said in the past. Thus the priests regularly gave *Toroth*, instructions and rulings, to address specific situations, but this was not incompatible with respect for a *Torah* which was in some sense permanent and foundational, and which in due course assumed written form. The prophets announced God's messages of warning and encouragement for their times, but they did so on the basis of this foundational *Torah*. Jesus came not to abolish the law and the prophets, but to fulfil them (Matt. 5.17). The apostles, then, with their colleagues and successors, were grounded in what Jesus 'began to do and teach', but this phrase implies that he was continuing to do and to teach things (Acts 1.1). They proclaimed a gospel *concerning Jesus* (Rom. 1.3–4), and handed on his teaching, as the Gospels bear witness. This was not incompatible with a detailed application of this gospel in specific circumstances in which they were conscious, at least at times, of speaking on the direct authority of God (for example 1 Cor. 7.10). Each stage of God's revelation recorded in Scripture, then, builds on that which has gone before, without excluding the possibility of a fresh word being spoken.[1]

The controversial question at this point concerns the nature of any 'fresh words' that might be anticipated from God today and the means of discerning whether they are indeed in accordance with what he has said in the past. Here we evoke a wide range of debates in different parts of the Church, concerning for instance a Catholic understanding of the development of tradition, some Reformed views tying God's present speech very tightly to what he has spoken in Scripture,[2] charismatic understandings of 'prophecy', and radical approaches to Scripture such as some feminist ones which attempt to alter or extend the biblical canon itself.[3] All these debates, and the doctrine of revelation itself, can be followed in more detail elsewhere.[4] Here I will focus, for the sake of clarity and practicality, on how the truth which brings the Scriptural narrative to a climax, that of Jesus Christ as the word of God, can enable us to hold together these essential biblical patterns, of faithfulness to past revelation and openness to a fresh message from God.

At the end of Chapter 5 we saw how in Jesus Christ the audible and visible revelation of God are fused and come to their climax. He not only spoke words which simultaneously enacted judgement and grace; he also, by the very pattern of his life, death and resurrection, *was the ultimate* word of judgement and grace for the world. Christian teaching has rightly interpreted the biblical witness here as pointing to the *finality* of God's revelation in Christ. There is no higher, fuller or more adequate way by which God might in future show himself. Christ is indeed both the agent and the crown of creation (Col. 1.15–20).

The Christ we know, worship and serve is the Christ whose obedient life, recorded in the Gospels, was vindicated by God when he rose from death. There is no higher Christ, no different Christ, from the Jesus of Nazareth who lived in Palestine for thirty-odd years in the first century. Theology has gone astray, and been led into sometimes

---

1 Cf. Keith Ward, 2004, *What the Bible Really Teaches: A Challenge to Fundamentalists*, London: SPCK, p. 23; I. Howard Marshall, 2004, *Beyond the Bible: Moving from Scripture to Theology*, Grand Rapids/Milton Keynes: Baker/Paternoster.

2 For such a view see Peter Adam, 1996, *Speaking God's Words: A Practical Theology of Preaching*, Leicester: InterVarsity Press, especially pp. 27–35, 87–123.

3 For example, as when speaking of the necessity of feminist 'revision' of the Bible: Elisabeth Schüssler-Fiorenza, 1992, *In Memory of Her: A Feminist Theological Reconstruction of Christian Origins*, New York: Crossway, p. 11.

4 Cf. Colin E. Gunton, 1995, *A Brief Theology of Revelation*, Edinburgh: T & T Clark; David Brown, 1999, *Tradition and Imagination: Revelation and Change*, Oxford: Clarendon Press.

dangerous triumphalism, when it has drawn such a contrast between the incarnate and the risen Christ as to suggest that his human humility and sympathy have been abandoned in favour of pomp and distance. Hebrews says the exact opposite (Heb. 2.17–18; 4.15–16; 7.25; 12.1–3). This means that we can never go 'beyond' the story of Jesus' life, from annunciation to ascension, in our understanding of what God is saying. The Christ we know *is* Jesus of Nazareth.

Yet we 'know' him not merely as we 'know', at a distance, a historical figure of whom we are fond. We 'know' him as the *living* Lord. He continued to 'do' and 'teach' things in the early Church, as narrated in Acts. He was glimpsed and heard walking among the churches of Asia (Rev. 2.1). These twin realities, the definitive character of the earthly Jesus for our understanding of God, and his continued life with God, lead me to three claims about the very core of what we are doing if we are to continue to receive and to share God's revelation today.

Christ over Scripture

If the fullness of God was pleased to live in Christ (Col. 1.19), there is no greater or higher calling for a preacher (or anyone else) than to seek to discern and to share, in whatever way, that revelation. If Christ himself was and is the height of God's self-communication, no framework of thought, however biblical, is adequate to comprehend him, nor are any words, even biblical words, adequate to express him. The task of the preacher is seen as being but a subset of the task of humanity itself: to recognize and respond to God in Jesus of Nazareth, and to communicate that which we have seen and heard. Hence the emphasis of important writers about preaching on *the presentation of Christ*, even the *making present of Christ*, in the sermon.[5]

To speak of 'Christ over Scripture' ought, in one sense, not to be controversial. But in another sense it may sound it, and I may need to clarify the claim. I am asserting that although Scripture is indeed adequate for the purpose for which God in his providence has given it (on which more below), in the nature of the case it cannot be 'adequate'

---

5 Significant figures here include Luther, Bonhoeffer, P. T. Forsyth and Barth. For example cf. Dietrich Bonhoeffer, 'The Proclaimed Word', in Richard Lischer (ed.), 2002, *The Company of Preachers: Wisdom on Preaching from Augustine to the Present*, Grand Rapids: Eerdmans, p. 37: 'Because the word is the Christ accepting men, it is full of grace but also full of judgment. Either we will let ourselves be accepted and be forgiven and borne up by Christ, or we remain unaccepted. If we ignore the spoken word of the sermon, we ignore Christ.'

to capture or express the reality of Jesus Christ. In fact, words cannot 'capture' any person or reality, as we saw in Chapter 3. Still less can we expect them to capture the perfect revelation of the eternal God.

Positively, however, the affirmation of 'Christ over Scripture' does not imply that we leave Scripture behind. It implies, rather, that we receive and share the revelation of God today in a full-orbed way that is much richer than just the handing-on or interpreting of *words*, even Scriptural words. It entails three further elements. First, it implies an openness to the *presence of the living Christ* today by his Spirit, and all that he might be communicating by way of encouragement, guidance and warning to his Church and world, not only through specific words of Scripture but through the varied experiences we have as we walk through the world with him. Second, it implies that as God has shown himself in a *person*, so we receive him and share him today in a personal way which includes words but always transcends them. 1 John 1.1–3 gives what is surely a paradigmatic pattern: the writer wants to proclaim not only what he and others have heard, but also what they have seen and touched and experienced. Such 'proclamation' surely includes words, but goes beyond them. Its goal is not just intellectual understanding or even assent, but fellowship together in the Father and the Son (v. 3).

Third, 'Christ over Scripture' implies a *community* of faith in which he is known. Immediately after the resurrection, although Jesus did appear to individuals (Mary Magdalene, John 20.11–18; Simon, Luke 24.34), his most characteristic appearances were among groups (the women, Matt. 28.9; the two on the Emmaus road and at the table, Luke 24.13–32; the eleven in Jerusalem, Luke 24.36–53, John 20.19–25, 26–29; in Galilee, Matt. 28.16–20, John 21.1–23). See also Paul's account of the resurrection appearances in 1 Cor. 15.5–8: Cephas, James and Paul have individual appearances, but also mentioned are 'the twelve', 'five hundred brethren' and 'all the apostles' (whoever Paul exactly meant by 'the twelve' and 'all the apostles'). The famous picture of Acts 2.42 seems to encapsulate the norm of early Christian communal life, through which the presence and power of Christ were revealed: 'And they devoted themselves to the apostles' teaching and fellowship, to the breaking of bread and the prayers.' Acts 4.31 records that after one such gathering, 'when they had prayed, the place in which they were gathered together was shaken; and they were all filled with the Holy Spirit and spoke the word of God with boldness'. Similarly, the manifestation of God today is quintessentially a communal, not a 'solo' affair. Whatever we say about preaching must be seen in this context.

If the heart of our manifestation of Christ is through mutual love (John 13.34–35), solitary revelation is a contradiction in terms.

The Christ of Scripture

We must now go on, however, to claim that though our proclamation is of Christ *over* Scripture, when we speak of Christ it is indeed the Christ *of* Scripture of whom we speak. Nothing inconsistent with the Jesus of Nazareth attested by those who saw and heard him can be allowed to pass for revelation from God today. We are called, like the early Christians, to 'test everything' (1 Thess. 5.20), to 'test the spirits, to see whether they come from God' (1 John 4.1). This implies a yardstick by which to examine claims to 'present' revelation. Classically, for post-biblical generations of Christians this yardstick has been Scripture itself. What understanding of the nature of Scripture enables it to fulfil this role?

I would argue for a historically rooted understanding of Scripture which sees its importance as located in its character as recorded testimony to revelation of God, coming from participants in that revelation who have sought to hand on that testimony faithfully. Scripture is crucial because it is the anciently acknowledged authority on the tale of Yahweh's revelation and its fulfilment in Jesus Christ. I now need to expand and defend this understanding in relation to others.

First, I prefer to define the centrality of Scripture in pragmatic terms, seeing its authority deriving from its closeness to eyewitness testimony of key events (in the case of the NT) and its transmission of ancient traditions as part of a developing understanding of Yahweh (in the case of the OT). I prefer such a conception to simply labelling Scripture the 'word of God'. That terminology has an honourable pedigree, but it is vital to recognize two things about it: that it is a metaphor,[6] and that its application to Scripture as a whole is (of necessity) a post-biblical rather than a biblical act. Too often the phrase 'word of God' as applied to Scripture is taken as short-circuiting the need for careful interpretation, and can lead to readings of Scripture that are flat, crass, and lacking in appreciation of its rich texture and diversity, not to mention of the mysterious fusion of divine providence and human agency that it reflects. Discussions about Scripture as 'the word of God', in turn, easily become arguments about what is essentially a non-biblical proposition, in which Scripture

---

6 See Robert Morgan, 1998, 'The Bible and Christian Theology', in John Barton, (ed.), *The Cambridge Companion to Biblical Interpretation*, Cambridge: Cambridge University Press, pp. 114–28, here p. 116.

is more talked about than actually listened to. Karl Barth developed the notion of the 'three forms' of the word of God (the revelation of God in Christ, Scripture and preaching) in brilliantly sophisticated fashion,[7] but we perhaps do not need this rigorous intellectual elucidation to appreciate how Scripture plays its part in God's providence.

Second, a pragmatic understanding of the nature of Scripture enables us to focus primarily on the essence of its theological witness, rather than becoming mired in debates about its historical origins. This is not to deny the indispensable historical element to that witness, as Bauckham has underlined in the case of the Gospels,[8] and as we shall go on to expand further below. But it means that we receive Scripture as it has been given to us, adopting an essentially trusting attitude to its testimony. We have no other reliable access to the core events of God's revelation, and though we are surely free to question the exact nature or historical status of the ancient stories it contains, our attention is chiefly focused not on such literary and historical debates, but on the truth of God's working in history which in a variety of ways is attested within it. We do not need to claim (or appear to claim) that this revelation was, or is, static, or that all the books or parts of books in the Bible have equal weight, or that any part can be taken on its own. It is enough to say that the Bible is the closest we can get to the history of Yahweh's dealings with Israel, culminating in Christ and spreading out from him to the world.

Third, this pragmatic understanding of the nature of Scripture requires us, nonetheless, to take seriously its clear testimony to the character, words and actions of Jesus.[9] It will not do to proclaim Jesus as Lord, to acknowledge Scripture as our supreme means of access to the record of his life, and then largely to ignore the kind of things he said and the kind of life he led. Too often (in Protestant circles, especially) a proclaimed allegiance to Scripture has effectively elevated the Pauline letters above the Gospels, by focusing on truths which can be affirmed about Jesus' divine status, his saving work and so on, while marginalizing the very narratives which tell us what that divine status in fact looked like and what his saving work in fact entailed.[10] Thus, for

7 Karl Barth, 1975, *Church Dogmatics 1.1, The Doctrine of the Word of God*, 4.1–4, 2nd edn, trans. G. W. Bromiley, Edinburgh: T & T Clark, pp. 88–124.

8 Bauckham, *Jesus and the Eyewitnesses*, see especially pp. 472–508.

9 One conclusion of the sophisticated argument of William Abraham, 2002, *Canon and Criterion in Christian Theology: From the Fathers to Feminism*, Oxford: Oxford University Press, is that debate about the epistemic function of Scripture has consistently muffled an actual hearing of Scripture.

10 I am indebted to my former colleague Jeremy Thomson, especially, for drawing my attention to this point.

example, if we are to take the witness of the Gospels to Jesus seriously, we cannot ignore the socio-economic or political dimensions of Jesus' ministry. To do so is arbitrarily to exclude from consideration data which are clearly embedded in the text, and which an honest reading of the text against its historical background will surely bring out. Similarly, we cannot ignore the ethic of non-violence which Jesus both practised and preached. The fact that certain passages may remain rather obscure, and certain historical details uncertain or unknown, does not absolve us from taking seriously that which is clear.

Fourth, to understand Scripture's character pragmatically is to eschew any absolutized notion of what is 'in' the Bible and what is 'out' of it. It does not matter that there are texts printed in our Bibles which are probably not part of the original book (like Mark 16.9–20), or which are excluded from many Bibles, yet similar at many points to that which is included (like the books of Wisdom and Sirach). The strength and authority of Scripture is not in a kind of verbal precision in which exactly everything is there which 'God wanted' to be there – neither more nor less – but in the unfolding story which runs through its midst like a beating heart. We are not asked to decide exactly why we might, or might not, hear God's word more through Mark 16.1–8 than Mark 16.9–20, or in Proverbs more than Wisdom or Sirach. The existence of different 'canons' of Scripture in different sections of the universal Church need not be a problem when it comes to uniting on the basis of the story that lies at the heart of them all.

Another consequence of not ascribing an unhelpfully 'absolute' status to Scripture (defined, inevitably, by one Church's canon rather than another's) is that the boundary between Scripture and tradition is blurred. This is good, in that it reminds us that the Scriptures and the processes of transmission which gave rise to them are but a stage in the continuing 'tradition' of Yahweh's people since Abraham's time or before. There is no problem about continuing to affirm that the Scriptures occupy a uniquely important place in that chain of tradition; it is they which point to the central period and pivotal events of God's revelation. In this sense, the idea of a *continually* adapting canon is unhelpful.[11] The canon is important precisely because it does fix the testimony at a point in history closest to the events concerned. But recollection of the gradual

---

11 As explored by James A. Sanders, 1987, *From Sacred Story to Sacred Text: Canon as Paradigm*, Philadelphia: Fortress. For views emphasizing the importance of the (ultimately) fixed nature of the canon see Brevard S. Childs, 1979, *Introduction to the Old Testament as Scripture*, Philadelphia: Fortress; Abraham, *Canon and Criterion*.

process by which the 'canons' of both Old and New Testament took shape should warn us against too artificial a demarcation between 'Scripture' and 'tradition'. In fact, as William Abraham argues, the idea of a 'canon' in early Christianity encompassed not only Scripture but a whole network of practices, beliefs, statements of faith, rituals and texts which in combination were to enable people to grow as disciples of Jesus.[12] Thus (for instance) it was the early creeds and 'rule of faith' which gave a necessary sharpness and summary to the witness of the New Testament. They were never meant to stand alone apart from the NT, with its narratives and epistles opening a window into the earliest period of Christian faith. But nor did the NT take shape or become accepted as 'canonical' without being accompanied by such summary creeds, as well as other 'canonical' elements like the practice of the Eucharist, from the very first.[13]

Summarizing this section, we may say that God's revelation today comes through the Christ of Scripture in the following senses. It is Scripture which takes us closest to the life of Jesus, the history of a people which led up to that life and the missionary outpouring to which it gave rise. Scripture focuses on the theological meaning of these events, not allowing us to remain stuck in merely historical concerns. Nevertheless, Scripture gives reliable historical testimony to Jesus, and requires us to take seriously the facts of his earthly life as well as the meaning of his death and resurrection. Finally, Christian tradition, especially that of the earliest period, provides a guide to the interpretation of Scripture which we should not ignore because of a misguided sense that 'Scripture' can be minutely defined and set apart from all other writings as a completely self-enclosed and self-interpreting text.

The Christ of today as foreshadowed by Scripture

My third claim about the ongoing revelation of God is caught in the phrase 'the Christ of today as foreshadowed by Scripture'. In mediaeval times, Scripture was understood to have four 'senses' – literal/historical, moral (giving examples), allegorical/Christological (pointing to Christ) and anagogical/eschatological (speaking of the ultimate future).[14] Applied crudely

---

12 Abraham, *Canon and Criterion*, especially pp. 30–1, 467–8.

13 See for example the confession 'Jesus is Lord' embedded in the NT (Rom. 10.5; 1 Cor. 12.3; Phil. 2.11).

14 See for example Paul Scott Wilson, 2001, *God Sense: Reading the Bible for Preaching*, Nashville: Abingdon.

to texts, this can seem rough and ready to us today, and in fact it was probably never applied in a wooden fashion. But the scheme has much to teach us, not least via the final, 'anagogical' sense.

This 'sense of Scripture' was the way in which it could be heard as speaking of the destiny God had planned for his people and his world. So, for example, the NT idea of a heavenly Jerusalem (Gal. 4.26) or a 'new Jerusalem' (Rev. 21.2) enabled readers to interpret an OT passage such as Zechariah 8, giving a vivid picture of the blessings that will follow on the return of Yahweh to Zion, in terms of the ultimate future rather than the earthly Jerusalem. There were dangers in such readings, if and when they were taken to imply that God had lost his concern for Israel or indeed for the present material conditions of humanity. But they caught an authentic sense that the Bible was an essentially forward-looking as well as backward-looking book. It offered visions and frames of reference within which to imagine how a world under the lordship of Christ would look.

In fact, it was far more common in the early Christian centuries to see the Bible as a lens through which to view the world rather than a set of data to be contemplated in and for themselves.[15] This should be obvious from the free way in which Christian teachers up to the time of the Reformation interwove their comments on biblical texts with comments on the contemporary world.[16] Biblical interpretation was an activity that could never be closed. It was always to be carried out in the context of new circumstances, on which it could shed light, and which might in turn shed light on it and call forth new and powerful significances from it. If Christ – the Christ over Scripture, the Christ of Scripture – remains central to the revelation of God, then it is not only in the past that we must seek him, but in the present, where he lives and is Lord.

All this necessitates that we should read Scripture not just as testimony to who Christ was and is, but as the raw materials through which to create an authentic, imaginative construal of his contemporary significance.

---

15 See Stephen I. Wright, 2004, 'Inhabiting the Story: The Use of the Bible in the Interpretation of History', in Craig Bartholomew et al. (eds), 'Behind' the Text: History and Biblical Interpretation, Carlisle/Grand Rapids: Paternoster/Zondervan, pp. 492–519; C. Clifton Black, 'Augustinian Preaching and the Nurture of Christians', in Roger E. Van Harn (ed.), The Lectionary Commentary: Theological Exegesis for Sunday's Texts (The Third Readings: The Gospels), Grand Rapids: Eerdmans, pp. 603–14.

16 See Stephen I. Wright, 2000, The Voice of Jesus: Studies in the Interpretation of Six Gospel Parables, Carlisle: Paternoster, pp. 62–112.

'Who is Christ for today?' asked Bonhoeffer.[17] We cannot answer this question by allowing the challenge of Christ merely to be equated with the fundamental human challenge as a contemporary philosophy such as existentialism might express it (the route of Rudolf Bultmann).[18] There is some danger, too, in Karl Barth's approach of so emphasizing the transcendence and otherness of the biblical Christ that the careful use of creative imagination in interpreting Scripture is thought unnecessary or even harmful. Rather, the Scriptural witness must become afresh the lens through which, via charitable listening to one another in Christ's body, we learn to see the world as created and redeemed by God, with all that that might entail.[19]

The context for God's continuing speech

If we believe in a living God who continues to speak to his people and his world, and whose speech is mediated by Jesus Christ, at work through his Holy Spirit, the next question is: how, when and where might we expect that speech to come?

The initial answer is easy: by any means, at any time, in any place! Barth saw this with great clarity. 'God can speak through a flute concerto, Russian communism, or a dead dog.'[20] We can earth this truth in the great biblical claims with which we concluded Chapter 5. The creation itself, and its unfolding history, are vehicles for God's speech. But the great climax of this creation and history is Christ. God speaks through his creation, yet we only understand it fully when we see it as fulfilled in Christ. This means that the reason we can expect God to speak through a flute concerto, etc., is that they are a part of his creation. But we only truly understand the significance and goal of that speech if we see it in the light of Christ and allow ourselves to be transformed by him.

Barth took this insight in a strongly ecclesiological direction, arguing that it was the Church's proclamation in preaching and sacrament that constituted 'the promise of future revelation on the basis of the revelation that has already occurred' in Christ.[21] He was reacting against what

---

17 Dietrich Bonhoeffer, 1971, *Letters and Papers from Prison*, London: SCM, p. 279.

18 Bultmann's significance for homiletics is discussed in James F. Kay, 2007, *Preaching and Theology*, St Louis: Chalice Press.

19 On this theme see Garrett Green, 2000, *Theology, Hermeneutics and Imagination: The Crisis of Interpretation at the End of Modernity*, Cambridge: Cambridge University Press.

20 Barth, *Church Dogmatics* 1.1, p. 55.

21 Barth, *Church Dogmatics* 1.1, p. 92.

he saw as human-centred efforts at 'natural theology'. I would prefer to affirm the reality of God's continuing self-revelation through his creation, while also affirming that it is only in and through Christ that its significance is transformatively perceived. In practice this means that we should not conceive of limits to the way God may choose to communicate himself. He can speak, for example, through nature, through events, through the promptings of our hearts, through the texts and quests of different religious faiths. Indeed, it is surely limiting his freedom, grace and power to imagine that he cannot transform a person through Christ without their having heard of him. We are, however, called to make Christ known, and so be faithful to our conviction that it is in him that 'all things hold together' (Col. 1.17), and bring near to people all the possibilities of his transforming love. In this sense, I would echo Barth's agreement with the Reformers that proclamation is 'the *representative* event at the centre of the Church's life' (my emphasis).[22] It points to and, under God, enables that encounter with the self-communicating God in Christ which may take place through many other means.

For those who have come to see Christ as the lynchpin of everything, it is in Christ that they will expect to hear and receive God's revelation most clearly and fully. But what does that mean in practice, given that Christ is not now limited by time and space, and therefore cannot be 'pinned down'?

We have seen that the 'Christ over Scripture' is revealed particularly among and through the community that believes in and follows him. It is right, therefore, to expect to encounter God especially in such a community: not, of course, one which merely bears the name of Christian, but one in which the Christians' distinguishing mark of love is evident (John 13.34–5). In the context of such a community, words which echo and expound the words of Scripture, and imaginatively discern from it the significance of Christ's lordship over all creation today, will carry special weight. That those with a particular gift of wisdom or knowledge (1 Cor. 12.8) or a divine calling as prophet or teacher (1 Cor. 12.28) should be specially entrusted with speaking such words should not be surprising, but Paul makes it clear that the existence of such recognizable gifts in some should by no means preclude the participation of any (1 Cor. 14.26–33). Those who enter the assembly from outside may find themselves caught up into the worship of God, declaring 'God is really among you' (1 Cor. 14.25). And as Barth pointed out, when

22 Barth, *Church Dogmatics* 1.1, p. 70.

God reveals himself, it is not just a matter of hearing a specific instruction or perceiving a specific truth. Far more deeply than that – just as when a human loved one communicates with us – what counts most profoundly is that he has revealed *himself*, that he is relating to us, and that we know the joy of his presence. 'For the point of God's speech is not to occasion specific thoughts or a specific attitude but through the clarity which God gives us, and which induces both these in us, to bind us to Himself.'[23]

This does not mean, however, that a loving fellowship of Christians is the only setting where one might expect to receive God's revelation through Christ. For instance, in a Christian community which continues to bear the name but has lost the love, God may speak through a preacher, or anyone else who is open to God's Spirit, precisely in order to lead people back to the love that had been lost. This would be analogous to the ministry of the Old Testament prophets and Jesus himself, calling the people back to their true allegiance. Moreover, Christian people ought, on the same analogy, to be open to the possibility of a word of God coming from a quite unexpected and/or unauthorized direction. If Jesus could use a Samaritan as an example of true *Torah*-keeping for a Jewish audience (Luke 10.29–37), whom or what might he use to call Christians back to the fundamentals of the good news?

If the gathering of loving Christians is where one might most naturally expect to receive a revelation of God, that does not mean that God's purpose of revelation is narrowly focused, as if he did not wish to show himself to the world. Paul's language in Romans 1.5 is interesting: he believes he is called to bring about 'the obedience of faith for the sake of [Jesus'] name among all the nations' (or 'all the Gentiles'). Paul's aim was not simply to win individual Jews and Gentiles to faith in Christ. It was also to establish Christian communities across the Gentile world as signs and witnesses 'among the nations'. Romans 12.1 – 15.13 shows him, in various ways, explaining to the mixed Jewish-Gentile Christian community how to live a distinctive life in the midst of the not always helpful surroundings of the heart of the Roman Empire. Again, however, it is instructive that the emphasis is on loving one's neighbour (for example 13.8–10) and welcoming one another in the Christian fellowship, despite differences (15.7). If there were occasions of 'public' verbal proclamation, they are not mentioned. Perhaps they happened sometimes, but it appears from these chapters that the word-gifts of prophecy and

---

23 Barth, *Church Dogmatics 1.1*, p. 175.

teaching were exercised in the context of the Christian fellowship (Rom. 12.3–8), while the witness of Christians to the world was to be through loving, peaceable lives, rather than loud public words. A similar emphasis is found in 1 Peter (2.11–25; 3.13–17).

The human task

If God's continuing speech is to be discerned in the ways and contexts that we have just outlined, what does this imply about the human task in relation to it?

It is absolutely clear from our survey of the biblical narrative, and from our theological 'gathering' of that survey in this chapter, that any human attempt in some way to relay the speech of God must only and ever be in response to God's prior revelation. Whether we are thinking of God's 'general' revelation in creation (as in Rom. 1.18) or his 'special' revelation in Christ (Rom. 3.20), it is only because he, as our creator and redeemer, has shown himself to us that we have any claim to be able to manifest him, in speech or in any other way.

Following on from this point, how are we to characterize any such human manifestation of God? The concept of *sacrament* is helpful here.[24] We may leave aside the more technical sense of 'sacrament' as an officially recognized 'means of grace' or ordinance of the Church. In a wider sense, many events, moments, people or things, in the Church and the world, may be seen as 'sacramental'.[25] Naturally, it is possible to overuse this language and thus debase it. Nevertheless, a good theological case can be made for seeing the world itself as sacramental of God's presence, love and power, and Christ himself as the supreme sacrament, the defining centre through which we encounter God.[26] Not only the classically defined 'sacraments' of baptism and Eucharist, therefore, but also Scripture and preaching, may then be seen, in a derived way, as events,

---

24 Gerhard O. Forde writes about the danger of *not* seeing preaching in sacramental terms in 'Preaching the Sacraments', in Mark C. Mattes and Steven D. Paulson (eds), 2007, *The Preached God*, Grand Rapids: Eerdmans, pp. 89–115, here p. 93: 'Instead of *doing* the text with the hearers, preachers at best *explain* it, no doubt with as many clever and appealing illustrations as one can muster . . . The text does not do anything to us to change us or incorporate us into its story; rather the text is changed to fit our story. The Word becomes mere information or description or instruction. Thus instead of being a sacrament, the Word becomes an occasion for us to exercise our powers; it becomes a law, perhaps inevitably a club with which to beat people.'

25 See Harry Blamires, 1963, *The Christian Mind*, London: SPCK, pp. 173–88.

26 See Mary Katherine Hilkert, 1997, *Naming Grace: Preaching and the Sacramental Imagination*, New York: Continuum, drawing on the theology of Karl Rahner.

places, moments through which we encounter God. Crucially, though, they do this not *independently* of Christ, nor of the created universe. Rather, they do this *insofar as* they are signs and pointers to Christ and to his rule over all things.[27]

To conceive of preaching as a sacrament is to guard three truths. First, it saves us from over-presumption or absolutism in claiming that preaching in some sense 'is' the word of God, as baldly stated in Heinrich Bullinger's Second Helvetic Confession of 1562.[28] If we use that phrase, we must do so with exactly the same kind of nuance with which we claim that the bread and wine of the Eucharist 'are' the body and blood of Christ, or that the Bible 'is' the word of God. Hidden in all these expressions classically, I believe, is an innate sense that earthly things may only ever be pointers to divine things – except in the case of the one man in whom heaven and earth were joined, who himself only 'revealed' God in a partly veiled manner on earth. This sacramental or metaphorical sense (which is not the same as denying *reality* to what is claimed) has sometimes been lost in popular understandings both of transubstantiation and of Scriptural inspiration. So congregations and preachers are pointers; we 'are' the body of Christ, yet we are not Christ; we 'speak' the word of God, yet his word is always greater, clearer, more than we can say. All that we have said about the boundedness of human language, community, psychology and personality supports this claim, while the sacramental nature of preaching encourages us to accept rather than rebel against or be depressed by that boundedness.

The second truth guarded by a sacramental understanding of preaching is that God continues to take the initiative and be in control of his own self-revelation. He has given us Scripture, he gathers congregations of disciples, he calls individuals to a particular role in speaking out his word. But none of these realities *guarantees* that he will reveal himself in any particular place, event, time or person. We cannot ensure it by having the most loving or well-led congregation or the clearest, most Scriptural, Spirit-filled preaching. Barth saw this with great clarity; it is remarkable how often his insight has been effaced through his being turned simply into an advocate of a particular kind of preaching, to be listed alongside others. Experience surely

---

27 Cf. John E. Colwell, 2005, *Promise and Presence: An Exploration of Sacramental Theology*, Milton Keynes: Paternoster.

28 Cf. Barth's critique of the claim: '[W]hat this man [i.e. the preacher] can try to say as God's Word in the discharge of preaching cannot be God's own Word as such but only the repetition of his promise' (*Church Dogmatics 1.1*, p. 58).

bears out the claim. God speaks through us, through the life of a Christian community and the words of a preacher, often without our realizing, at least at the time, just whether, how, where and why he is doing so. What really touches a visitor to a church service may well not be the preacher's elegant exegesis, but the unplanned aside, the sudden smile, the glimpse of self-revelation. It may be something that is 'heard' which the preacher never in fact 'said' or even intended to say. Our preaching is always just a 'gesturing' to the Word.[29] *There is more to the 'sign' than the intention of the signer.* This fundamental insight of modern linguistic philosophy, explored in Chapter 3, is confirmed again and again in preaching and is fully embraced by an understanding of preaching as sacramental.

In response to these two dimensions of a sacrament – that it is a pointer, whose efficacy does not depend on human intentionality – we are compelled to ask, thirdly: What then is our human role? How should we describe it?

This is not as difficult a question to answer as we might think. Scripture speaks of created things pointing to the Creator: not in an obvious way, in a fallen world, but really nonetheless (for example especially Ps. 19.1–6; Rom. 1–20). Theological tradition speaks of the 'analogy of being' whereby we may discern the unseen in the seen, the future in the present, the heavenly in the earthly. This should not be misunderstood (as it sometimes has been) as the basis of a 'natural' theology which attempts to *argue* from the lower to the higher, or to make human reason rather than divine revelation the basis of theology. It is simply a recognition that our creaturely signs are not pointers to something or someone *wholly* other, but rather carry within them the reflections, the shadows, the echoes of the reality that is their origin.

This means that our lives and our words – even in our fallen state – are not totally without witness to God in Christ. Our very existence bears testimony – as does all creation – to his power and love. Naturally, in many human communities and individuals the reflection of God's truth is sadly defaced. Yet even a trace of a sense that it is defaced may act as a sign of God for those with eyes to see. How much more, in communities which have been touched by the revealing and transforming grace of Christ, may we expect to see living displays of that truth.

Thus the practice of Christian love is not something so totally alien to our nature that we should despair of ever seeing it much. On the contrary, it is the way we were made; and for those who rediscover it

---

29 R. E. C. Browne, 1976, *The Ministry of the Word*, 2nd edn, London: SCM.

in Christ, it is the most 'natural' thing in the world. God in Christ has given us the means to be real, if always incomplete, revelations of his character and being. If this is true in the Christian community, it is true a fortiori for our *words*, including the words of a preacher. Words can be slippery signs, and they undoubtedly 'work' differently for different speakers and hearers, writers and readers. But like our actions, they nonetheless carry significance, and we bear responsibility for them. To recognize the sacramental nature of preaching, therefore, is to recognize the limitations of our words, but also their extraordinary potential.

Just as, in the last chapter, we saw how the biblical testimony to God's revelation is summed up in the insight that Christ, the fulfilment of *Torah* and *Hokmah*, is at the very heart of creation, so we may sum up our theological assessment of the nature of our human role in preaching with reference to the Scriptural teaching that we are made in the image of God. Although the actual phrase is used quite rarely, the places where it does occur indicate its importance (Gen. 1.26–28; Col. 3.10). So what may this notion teach us about God's revelation and our role in communicating it?

It is surely fundamental. We have seen that if God reveals himself supremely in Christ, this means that he *continues* to show himself, for Christ is alive; and that he shows himself especially in the community of those who seek to follow Jesus. And what is going on in this community? People are 'being renewed in knowledge after the image of the creator' (Col. 3.10). Just as God's plan is to renew the whole cosmos in Christ who is his image (Col. 1.15–20), so within that, he plans to restore the human race so that it fulfils the destiny for which it was created, of being 'in his image'. Human beings are destined to reveal God. Genesis 1 suggests that they are to do so in the two aspects which we highlighted at the end of Chapter 5: the visible and the audible.

An 'image' is a visible reflection or portrayal. Although in one sense all the creation may be said to declare God's glory (Ps. 19.1), it is significant that humanity alone is said in Genesis 1 to be created 'in the image of God'. The background to the phrase lies in the huge statues made by ancient potentates of themselves, to remind subjects – especially far-flung ones – of their rule, and in the fact that the rulers regarded *themselves* as being 'images of God'. This makes the claim of Genesis 1.26–28 stand out in an exciting way.[30] *Human beings*, in all their

---

30 See J. Richard Middleton, 2005, *The Liberating Image: The* Imago Dei *in Genesis 1*, Grand Rapids: Brazos, p. 231. See also Peter K. Stevenson and Stephen I. Wright, 2010, *Preaching the Incarnation*, Louisville: Westminster John Knox, ch. 9.

limitation (in contrast to the opulent rulers), but also all their flesh-and-blood life (in contrast to the stone images!), are called and destined to reflect God. They are the visible manifestation of the invisible God – a destiny which only Jesus Christ has so far fulfilled completely (Col. 1.15). Whatever we say about *words* through which God reveals himself must be seen in the context of this more all-embracing truth, that he is revealed, 'imaged', in our very visible being. The ultimate fulfilment of this destiny is starting to be seen already as together we are renewed in Christ (Col. 3.9).

Within this, however, it is striking that God's main activity in Genesis 1 – indeed, his only activity – is to *speak*. This implies at the very least that for those who are created in God's image, speaking will be a central, possibly a defining activity. This is not to elevate rationality above other dimensions of humanity – body, emotion, spirit, will. The whole person is channelled through speech, as we saw in Chapter 3. We should not underestimate the significance of being the speaking images of a God whose word is so powerful and so central in his outgoing relationship with his creatures.

If Genesis 1 underlines the power of God's speech, Genesis 2 and 3 underline its importance in relating to his world and especially his human creatures. It is through his word that he addresses them, summons them, guides them, chides them. The picture of him 'walking in the garden' where he had placed the man and the woman is more startling in its earthiness and intimacy than is often recognized (Gen. 3.8). But this sets the tone for the Old Testament picture of Yahweh, which in turn sets the tone for the New Testament picture of Jesus.[31] God is a God who comes close to people and relates to them in words. Words make specific and personal that which, in visible form alone, may often be open to misunderstanding. There should be no apology for the use of words, for it is in them especially that we mirror our relational creator.

It is significant that humanity *together* is said to be 'in the image of God'. Speaking is therefore not an individualistic business. It is in mutual relating, listening as well as speaking, using speech as a means to form and cement relationship, that God's image is most clearly seen. This further underlines the significance of Christian *community*. No one person, however gifted or authorized, has a monopoly on 'imaging' God through their speech. In fact, the

---

31 See Stevenson and Wright, *Preaching the Incarnation*, ch. 1.

image of the speaking God is reflected most fully not in preaching itself, but in the way Christians speak the truth to each other in love (Eph. 4.15). Given that our knowledge of the truth is as yet partial (1 Cor. 13.12), that we all still need to 'grow up' (Eph. 4.15), this 'love' must include the humility to learn from the 'truth' that others have learned, and expose our 'truth' to their 'truth'. I take it that this is a key part of the picture of the organic growth of the body of Christ in Ephesians 4.16.

Thus any claim to be speaking the 'word' or 'truth' of God, such as is made in preaching, must be made – if we are to be faithful to the humanness in which God has made us – not in presumptuousness, but in humility, prayer and hope. We are neither claiming to be the sole spokespersons for God in that place, nor to have an immediate access to God's will and purpose that is denied to others. We are, simply, pointers or witnesses to him.[32] In precisely the same way that being 'in the image of God' is different from being God himself, speaking 'God's word' or 'for God' or 'in the name of God' is different from God speaking himself. Yet together we *are* made in the image of God, and in Christ are being renewed in it. A key part of that image is the consciousness of this destiny, the awareness of the glorious responsibility we bear. Thus, though at the moment we rightly say 'we are but broken lights of thee',[33] we may offer our cracked window, our 'brittle crazie glass',[34] in conjunction with that of others, as genuine reflectors of the creator, shining more and more until the day dawns and the morning star rises in our hearts (cf. 2 Pet. 1.16–20).

Questions for the local church

- How does focusing on Jesus help us to understand the purpose and meaning of the Bible?
- In what ways does the church seek to hear God speak through all its members?
- What does it mean for a congregation, and a preacher, to 'speak the truth in love'?

---

32 Cf. Thomas G. Long, 2005, *The Witness of Preaching*, 2nd edn, Louisville: Westminster John Knox.

33 Alfred Lord Tennyson, *In Memoriam*, 1.19.

34 George Herbert, 'The Windows'.

Areas for research

It continues to be important to work on the theology of preaching, not least when the very idea of preaching is so contested. Implications for preaching of the theology of some of the giants of the twentieth century – Karl Barth, Rudolf Bultmann, Karl Rahner – are still being worked through. It would also be intriguing to do an empirical study on the means through which congregation members believe that they hear God speaking to them, and relate this to a theology of preaching such as that outlined in this chapter or elsewhere.

Further reading

James F. Kay, *Preaching and Theology,* 2007, St Louis: Chalice Press.
Michael Pasquarello III, 2006, *Christian Preaching: A Trinitarian Theology of Proclamation*, Grand Rapids: Baker Academic.
William H. Willimon, 2006, *Conversations with Barth on Preaching*, Nashville: Abingdon.

7

Ethical Guidance for Preaching

In the last chapter I explored a theology of preaching whose implication for the human dimension of the task was that we are called, along with all who are in Christ, to be the image of God in our community life and in the shared speech with which we relate to one another. As preachers we simply represents this shared speech in a public way. In this chapter I will unfold what I believe this means for an ethic of preaching, an authentically Christian approach to the ministry of the word.

The preacher as listener

If it is the case that as creatures and children we can have no pretension to *initiate* genuine God-speech that is both loving and true, but can only repeat, echo and imitate that which God himself has already said or is saying, then it follows that the preacher's first task is to be a listener to God. If, in addition, it is the case that only *together* in human community are we destined to bear God's image, and that *together* in Christ we are 'being renewed in knowledge after the image of the creator' (Col. 3.10), we are called also to be listeners to others, and especially those within the body of Christ.

We will listen for God in those places and in that manner that are suggested by our account of how God has revealed himself. We will hear him first and above all in Christ: the Christ who is alive, who speaks through his Spirit, who is more than Scripture and over Scripture, yet is also the Christ *of* Scripture, those books where through humility and prayer the Church has discerned that he is especially and normatively to be found. But at the same time, in Christ we discern that God's creation itself, the world of nature and of history, are also vehicles of God's revelation, so we shall not neglect to look and listen for his word there too.

To claim that God in Christ both continues to speak by his Spirit and continues to speak through his creation (which, of course, is imbued and enlivened with his Spirit) will sound risky to those who wish to guard the preacher's words – and the Church – by tying 'the word of God' in a strict sense to Scripture itself. Yet, as we have seen, a living Christ and a creation of which Christ is Lord forbid us from thus narrowing the field within which we may listen out for God's word. This does not mean that we may presume to discern in events or culture or nature a 'word' from God that is inconsistent with the trajectory of Scripture.[1] It is rather that a respect for the dynamism of the word of the living God forbids us from *confining* that word to Scripture or thinking that careful Bible study, principled exegesis and prayer will somehow guarantee the faithfulness or appropriateness of our message, or that it will be a means of encounter with God or teaching from God.

Listening *only* in Scripture for 'the word of God' may sound a safe option, but in fact it is not. Significantly different readings of Scripture as a whole are offered by different Christian groups. When we get down to individual passages, a glance at the commentaries or a discussion with Church members will quickly reveal that even on matters of some importance, the implications of the text are received in a wide range of ways. 'Refuge in Scripture' may end up, therefore, being a mask for refuge in the preacher's own construals – delivered as if they were the authoritative guide to the authoritative word.

Openness to the Spirit who speaks in the present, and to the creation too as a vehicle for God's speech, may seem to make our discernment of God's word less secure and certain, but in fact it acts as a bulwark. Scripture is our central, definitive channel for this word, but it is not the only one. Another difficulty with the view that confines God's word simply to Scripture is that it offers no help with drawing out Scripture's import for our own times, which in the nature of the case cannot be found within the pages of Scripture itself. To recognize that there are other channels for God's revelation is to allow the impact of Scripture to be felt in an authoritative way, as its witness is confirmed, clarified and applied through God's speech through his Spirit and his world.

Another vital check on our preaching is the calling to listen to others, especially those within the Christian community. This is far more than a merely pragmatic matter, as if this were just a good way to 'communicate better' or 'make the gospel relevant'. It is the ethical consequence of the shared character of our calling to bear the image of God and echo his voice in the world. As we have seen, this is perfectly compatible with the calling and gifting of some individuals to be special 'voicers' of the word of God. But such spokespeople are called not just to listen

---

1 For this idea of a 'trajectory' see I. Howard Marshall, 2004, *Beyond the Bible: Moving from Scripture to Theology*, Grand Rapids/Milton Keynes: Baker/Paternoster.

to God in the silence of meditation or Bible study, nor only in the careful discernment of God's ways in the world, but also among God's people themselves (cf. 1 Cor. 14). In all these ways the preacher must listen out for the voice of God, as he or she prays: 'Lord, speak to me, that I may speak / In living echoes of thy tone.'[2]

The preacher as gospeller

If we as preachers are fundamentally creatures, called to echo the tones of the creator, what may we further say about the kind of voice we should be listening out for, the kind of tones we can expect to hear?

The key reality here is the gospel itself. The gospel is the proclamation of God's good news for the world, and it concerns Jesus Christ. It cannot be reduced to a formula, or simply summed up in a guaranteed form of words. It is God's own pronouncement and decree, and as such belongs to God himself. It cannot be domesticated any more than any of his words can be. But as we read the Scriptural testimony to the gospel, we discover that, amazingly, it is precisely this good news to which all his other words point.

We may say, therefore, that it is both illogical and unethical for a preacher to preach anything but 'good news'. There are countless ways to 'preach the gospel', for different occasions and groups, and these will be modified as the gospel is unfolded for each new generation. We shall look at some of the classic varieties of the sermon in Chapter 8. But the essential gospel character of God's revelation, and therefore of our attempts to echo it, have certain implications which must apply to *all* our preaching. Especially, it is important to hold together certain realities that at first glance may be seen as incompatible or even as opposites.

First, to preach the Gospel is to announce *what God has done in Christ*, in fulfilment of his promises, but also to relate it to the contemporary world. If we preach a vaguely comforting but timeless message about (say) God's present care, we are not preaching the good news, which is unambiguously tied in the New Testament to the Christ-event. Equally, if we preach a historically sound message about what God did in Christ, but demonstrate no sense of what God in the living Christ can do and is doing now, we are not preaching the good news, whose climax is not the death of Christ but his exaltation to the Father's right hand as living, present, Lord.

---

2 The first line of a hymn by Frances Ridley Havergal.

Thus all preaching must hold together these two poles of the decisive past action of God in Christ, and the claim that action makes upon us in the present. Fundamentally, that claim is simply that we should accept that past action for what it was and live out its consequences. But a preacher who is unable to discern or to communicate any particular ways in which those consequences are being or should be played out today will be a poor guide and gospeller to the world.

Too often Christian preaching has suffered from a dichotomy. The 'liberal' tendency has emphasized the present reality and possibility of human transformation – not denying Christ, but always in danger of relegating him to a timeless principle, and downplaying the uniqueness of his historical life, death and resurrection. Meanwhile, the 'conservative' tendency has emphasized the uniqueness of his historical life, death and resurrection, but has sometimes downplayed his power in the present by speaking of the impact of his work in purely inward and individualistic terms. A gospel that is faithful to the living Lord of Scripture will speak both of the historical story of Jesus and of how his transforming power remains for us not only as individuals, but as communities, and for the world itself.

Second, the gospel is both *good news* in the profoundest, most heart-warming sense, and a *challenge* to the most fundamental and radical reorientation of life. To drive a wedge between these two is to separate what God has joined. Both Jewish and Roman backgrounds of the word 'gospel' emphasize this, and it is confirmed in the way both Jesus and his early followers announce God's 'gospel'.

In Judaism, 'gospel' carries echoes of Isaiah 40–66. The 'good news' is Yahweh's royal proclamation that his people's sins are put behind them, and behind him, and that he is coming in power to give them a new start. This is a breathtaking, intoxicating hope. But it is also a profoundly, disturbingly world-shattering hope. There is no room left for the dreary, despairing settling-down which would seem the only option if the future were unchangeable and purposeless. The good news is an announcement demanding a response. The same is true of Roman imperial decrees: the birth of the emperor Augustus may indeed have been 'good news' for the whole earth, but this is not merely a benevolent reassurance (that people might or might not have found credible) that the emperor was the guarantor of worldwide peace. Such peace was *dependent* on submission to the imperial rule and system.[3]

---

3 On the Roman imperial background to the announcement of good news in Christ, see Marcus J. Borg and J. Dominic Crossan, 2008, *The First Christmas: What the Gospels Really Teach about Jesus's Birth*, London: SPCK, pp. 159–61.

When Jesus goes public in Galilee proclaiming God's gospel, it is de-monstrably 'good news' for all who find themselves restored in mind, body and spirit, welcomed back into the community of God's people, and joyfully encountering God himself in Jesus. But this is the gospel of a 'kingdom', a divine empire, a real state of affairs which demands a transformed attitude and praxis in all spheres of life. It demands 're-pentance' (Mark 1.14). Jesus brings to fulfilment the hope announced through the 'gospel' of second Isaiah (Luke 4.16–21; cf. Isa. 61.1–4). It is intoxicating in its joy, and uncompromising in the new perspectives and actions it calls for. None is excluded by God, but only by their own hardness of heart.

So it is with the gospel *concerning* Jesus proclaimed by the apostles and their colleagues. It is good news of God's eternal love (cf. John 3.16; Rom. 5.8; 8.31–9) but as the New Testament amply testifies, it is quite possible to remain in a state of resistance to it. It calls for re-cognition – not a merely passive response, but faith or faithfulness like that of Abraham, active trust in God that demonstrates one's right re-lationship with him as a true member of his family (Rom. 4). God in his mercy has overlooked past transgressions, but now commands all people to repent. Jesus is not only Saviour, but the one through whom and by whose faithfulness to Yahweh the world will be judged (Acts 17.30–1).

So if the sum of God's words is 'gospel', and our words are to echo God's, all our preaching will have the two-sided character of 'gospel' as both genuine good news, and news which demands a response. Some-times preaching has failed to hold these two sides together as Scripture does. The sharp Lutheran theological division of 'law' and 'gospel', for example, can push *Torah* away from gospel in an unscriptural fashion (though as Paul Scott Wilson has shown, this was not Luther's own approach to *preaching*).[4] There is good news in *Torah* – it is given as a gracious gift to guide God's people, by the one who has redeemed them (Exod. 20.2; Ps. 119). And the gospel is, in important ways, the summa-tion of the law. Jesus' disciples are commanded to go and make more disciples, teaching them to observe everything Jesus has commanded them (Matt. 28.20). This closeness between *Torah* and gospel explains the tension seen in Paul's writing between different statements about the 'law'. It is good, yet on its own it is insufficient, because a fuller

---

4 Paul Scott Wilson, 2004, *Preaching and Homiletical Theory*, St Louis: Chalice Press, pp. 74–5, and see his whole discussion of the 'law-gospel' tradition on pp. 74–86.

revelation of God has now appeared in the gospel. Therefore preaching which echoes God's word cannot neatly divide up these 'words' of God, law and gospel, for the one is truly fulfilled in the other.

It is also quite possible to get the weighting of good news and challenge wrong even without a doctrinaire law/gospel division. Any sermon may fall into a trap of proclaiming a merely reassuring 'gospel' without the challenge, or a merely challenging 'gospel' without the reassurance. Some may genuinely try to do both, yet fall short, as when the good news of Jesus is followed by various unrelated or purely humanly inspired exhortations or demands. Hence the power of Eugene Lowry's proposal that having allowed the congregation to *experience* the gospel, a preacher should simply 'anticipate the consequences'.[5] The 'so what' flows out of the gospel itself; it is not a mere add-on. Paul Scott Wilson's schema of 'trouble and grace' in the sermon is also a helpful check to ensure that the preacher's 'gospel' is really 'gospel'.[6]

Thus it is a part of the basic ethic of preaching that it is genuine good news which echoes that of God. This responsibility may be expounded further in terms of the preacher's calling to be an *interpreter*, especially of the Scriptures and of the world around.

The preacher as interpreter of Scripture and world

The role of interpreter is not one imposed upon the preacher as it were artificially, from outside. As we saw in Chapter 3, all people are interpreters of the world around by virtue of being born into it. From the earliest linguistic or even pre-linguistic stage, we are seeking to make sense of the data presented to us from outside and from our own inward self-awareness.

'New' data constantly force revisions of our construals of the world, usually in small ways, but occasionally in major ones.[7] Such major changes of worldview can be very traumatic, yet may also be liberating. The child who has utterly depended on her mother will be devastated if her mother dies. But the adult who has always suffered from low self-esteem may discover an extraordinary joy when that deeply rooted

---

5 Eugene L. Lowry, 2001, *The Homiletical Plot: The Sermon as Narrative Art Form*, expanded edn, Louisville: Westminster John Knox, pp. 80–8.

6 Paul Scott Wilson, 1999, *The Four Pages of the Sermon: A Guide to Biblical Preaching*, Nashville: Abingdon, pp. 91–100.

7 Cf. John W. Wright, 2007, *Telling God's Story: Narrative Preaching for Christian Formation*, Downers Grove, IL: InterVarsity Press Academic, pp. 25–45.

estimate of himself is overturned through a new human relationship or the discovery of faith in Jesus.

The gospel concerning Jesus Christ is the greatest new 'datum' to emerge in human history. Some, of course, were more or less prepared for it (for example Simeon and Anna in Luke 2.25–38). Thankfully, many aspects of cultures and societies have been influenced by it since the time of Jesus, and this means that for many, receiving it need not be a traumatic event; indeed, children may grow up in its atmosphere and accept it for themselves in a very natural way. Sometimes cultures and societies which have never heard of the gospel receive it gladly and immediately as if it were just what they had been waiting for all along. But it remains true that for many, not least in the materialistic West, the gospel comes to our ears as a strange sound, one that upends many of our presuppositions and deepest beliefs about the world.

The preacher therefore finds himself or herself in the position of helping people to see how the gospel in all its strangeness does not lead to a fundamental schizophrenia in worldview, and therefore in personality, but actually enables us to make sense of the world in a way that no other key can manage. As a new 'datum', for many it will certainly disrupt, challenge and transform, but it is also the means to genuine integration of outlook. Such an outlook will always be fragmented and incomplete until the time when we 'know as we are known' (1 Cor. 13.13); puzzling pieces of 'data' will continue to remain puzzling, despite the light the gospel sheds. Christian people are putting together the data of the world and the datum of the gospel all the time, in the ongoing quest to 'make sense'. The preacher finds himself or herself in the middle of this quest, serving others in the common journey of understanding.

The act of interpretation in preaching is earthed in the tangible data of the Bible and the world. The Bible is a gift of God to the Church, a key component of the data which are part of the heritage of any who join God's family. We need to make sense of it, but not as an end in itself: we seek to understand it not for its own sake, but as a key to construing the gospel's transforming impact on the world. Similarly, the world around is a gift of God into which we enter by conception and birth. We need to make sense of it, yet again not for its own sake, but because that is one of the tasks its creator has bequeathed to us.[8]

To speak of Scripture as a means of 'making sense' of the world is immediately to highlight the ethical nature of our task of interpretation.

---

8 Cf. Garrett Green, 2000, *Theology, Hermeneutics and Imagination: The Crisis of Interpretation at the end of Modernity*, Cambridge: Cambridge University Press.

To believe in the authority of Scripture as God's sufficient provision for guiding us in the ways of salvation and holiness is, by definition, to believe that there is no *separate* authority for discerning the patterns by which Scripture forms an interpretative grid over the world. We must simply do this guided by the Holy Spirit, attentive to Christian tradition, and using our God-given reason. It is clear that such a process is open to all kinds of uncertainty and variety. No one 'method' exists for 'how to do it'.[9] But it should be clear that there is huge potential for getting it *ethically* wrong. We may misrepresent passages of Scripture in order to advance a personal hobby-horse. We may draw false analogies between the Bible and today. The making of metaphors has often been seen as an oratorical skill, but in preaching especially, it is more than this: it is a moral challenge. If we do not see the 'two in one', as metaphor forces us to – one thing in the light of the other, the Bible through the lens of the world, the world through the lens of the Bible – we are reneging on our call to let Scripture be heard as a voice that continues to be authoritative today. Yet it is quite possible for this two-in-one vision to be simplistically skewed. Examples could be multiplied: regarding Acts as a template to be placed neatly over our present church life, either to affirm it or to critique it; regarding Old Testament instructions as speaking directly to contemporary circumstances; regarding Revelation as a timetable incorporating current and future events in detail. Such oversimplifications invite scrutiny of an interpreter's motives.

Thus the interpretation of Scripture demands the ethical respect for the text that historical and literary angles of approach can open up.[10] But it also demands the theological wisdom and integrity to discern how Scripture makes sense of the world. Historical and literary study of the text 'in itself' cannot and does not claim to take this further step. Indeed, it is a part of its own integrity that it does not. It requires that

---

9 Here I am following Hans-Georg Gadamer's opposition to 'method': Hans-Georg Gadamer, 2004, *Truth and Method*, 2nd edn, trans. J. Weinsheimer and D. G. Marshall, London and New York: Continuum.

10 Of course, there are kinds of historical and literary approach which do not fulfil this ethical criterion, as when the texts are squeezed to fit a particular philosophy of history (as in some nineteenth-century accounts of the development of Israelite religion) or are so consciously read through a particular 'lens' (whether political, economic, gender-related or anything else) that the end result is that one sees more of the lens than of the text. I agree with John Barton that the ideal of critical biblical study in modern times (whether it is labelled 'historical' or 'literary') is to pay genuine respect to the text, allowing it to be heard, rather than just to say what we want it to say: John Barton, 2007, *The Nature of Biblical Criticism*, Louisville: Westminster John Knox. But I want to go further than Barton in arguing for the crucial place of a 'theological' reading of Scripture in the Church.

we fix our gaze on the text itself in its own setting. But as is increasingly recognized,[11] allowing the Bible to exercise its authority over the Church (and through the Church, the world) demands that we affirm the theological context in which it has been given to us, and bring authentically theological approaches to bear upon its interpretation, rather than simply borrowing those of the historians or the literary critics. What might such theological approaches be?

First, we can recognize that the Bible has been shaped and received by the Church as *canon*, not as a mere collection of individual books, and thus explore what it means to read it with integrity as a canon. Among other things, this would entail exploring the interconnections between biblical books, and the overarching narrative which links them. This is to be done without descending to simplistic harmonization or reading the Bible 'in the flat', ignoring the differences in time, content and relative 'weight' between its parts.[12] Second, we need to be open about the *traditions* within which we have learned to read Scripture: to appreciate that which they have highlighted in the Bible, but also to be critical of that which they have suppressed. Third, we need genuinely to rediscover what it is to read the Bible *in community*, so that the connections drawn by one person between Bible and world – especially the preacher – are tested out in company with others, so that eccentric readings are guarded against, and a healthy variety of insights into the Bible's pertinence is allowed to emerge. Fourth, we need to re-imagine and re-present the *impact* of the words of Scripture, so that it is heard not as a dead letter but a living word. Fifth, we need to acknowledge the fundamental posture of faith and personal outlook with which we approach Scripture: not to apologize for such presuppositions (for everyone has them, whether they are from faith or non-faith), but to be honest concerning our perspective, and humble about the insights which might emerge from those who do not share it. Finally, an interpretation of the world in the light of Scripture calls for careful attention to the world itself in its rich complexity. This is not a 'non-theological' task, for it depends upon our perception, by faith, of the significance of the world as created, redeemed and ultimately to be renewed by God.[13] We should not treat Scripture as if it gives us *both* all the 'data' we need to know

---

11 The most comprehensive recent guide to such 'theological' reading of Scripture is Kevin J. Vanhoozer (ed.), 2005, *Dictionary for Theological Interpretation of the Bible*, Grand Rapids/London: Baker/SPCK.

12 See Craig G. Bartholomew et al. (eds), 2006, *Canon and Biblical Interpretation*, Scripture and Hermeneutics Series 7, Carlisle: Paternoster.

13 Cf. Green, *Theology, Hermeneutics and Imagination*.

and the framework for interpreting them. Most of the data in fact come from our observation of the world; Scripture provides the normative framework for making sense of them.

These theological approaches point to a reflective and authentic linking of Scripture and world, which is not tied in an unhealthy way to purely academic biblical study or unthinking fundamentalism or narrow allegiance to a particular tradition or the whims or prejudices of the preacher. They can thus enable the preacher to fulfil the task of helping the congregation to 'make sense' of the world in the light of their faith, especially by demonstrating the ways in which Scripture may address us today.[14] Such 'sense-making' will always be provisional. It must, of course, be the hearers who make the clinching connections in their own minds and lives. But even those connections that are made, by us or our hearers, will always be subject to revision. To say that our grasp of truth is partial is not to commit ourselves to the dreary path of endless relativism. Knowledge and understanding do genuinely increase. But if that *is* the case, we must also affirm that our present knowledge and understanding are in perpetual need of refinement. One of the basic ethical demands of being an interpreter is that one should be a constant learner.

The preacher as speaker of truth to power

The final way in which we may characterize the ethical demand on a preacher is as speaker of truth to power. This is a reality which has been helpfully explored by Charles Campbell.[15]

The idea of the preacher as interpreter of Scripture and world might, on its own, be construed in an over-intellectual way, as if the central appeal of preaching was to the mind. However, words are more than intellectual tools. They fulfil important *functions* in social interaction and political life, understood in the broadest sense: they not only *say* things, they *do* things. Thus a preacher's words (like anyone else's) do not leave a situation unchanged. The ethical question is whether we can plan that change in a way that leads to positive results.

---

14 Cf. Stephen I. Wright, 2004, 'Inhabiting the Story: The Use of the Bible in the Interpretation of History', in Craig Bartholomew et al. (eds), *'Behind' the Text: History and Biblical Interpretation*, Carlisle/Grand Rapids: Paternoster/Zondervan, pp. 492–519; Paul Scott Wilson, 2001, *God Sense: Reading the Bible for Preaching*, Nashville: Abingdon.

15 See Charles L. Campbell, 2002, *The Word before the Powers: An Ethic of Preaching*, Louisville: Westminster John Knox.

In an important sense, our task is not to plan for particular results from preaching. A belief in the sovereign freedom of God, as outlined in Chapter 6, surely forbids this, highlighting it as potential manipulation. We have been given a story to tell, a gospel to proclaim, and our task is no more (and no less) than to share it, and leave the results to God.[16] This is a corollary of the belief that it is God alone who can bring about genuine transformation in people's lives, as well as of the more pragmatic recognition that to plan 'results' of one's words for a whole group of people would be an utter impossibility.

What then of the idea that all sermons should have a 'function' as well as a 'focus'?[17] Long, and others, argue for the importance of some kind of *aim* in the preacher's mind for each act of preaching, even while we recognize that God can and will do far more things, and quite different things, than what we envisage. The idea of a sermon 'function' is not necessarily incompatible with a belief in God's free sovereignty. In fact, to recognize the performative *potential* of our words (without predicting what they will *actually* do) is surely one of the ethical requirements of preaching. It is bound up with our taking responsibility for what we say. Just as in daily conversation, we weigh up potential words for their effect on those around us (the more so, the more weighty the topic), so a sensitive preacher will weigh up what her words might *do*, and can turn this into a degree of active planning.

'Speaking truth to power' is a phrase that encapsulates well the overarching function of the speech of preaching. It evokes the ministry of the prophets, of Jesus and the apostles. Theirs was not tame, conformist speaking, but discourse which consciously stood against the structures of thought and speech with which people had become comfortable. The immediate response, characteristically, was rejection: the victory of truth, however, became seen in the longer term. Campbell articulates the task in terms of the vulnerability and relationality of words, pitted against the spiritual and political power-structures of the world. He points out how the actions and reactions of individuals and systems are so often *violent*, while *words* have the power to counter violence, to present an alternative vision, to reach out to others instead of squashing or harming them.[18] War itself is the glaring instance. Wars

16 Campbell warns against the attempt to plan preaching too carefully as an experience for the hearers in an earlier book: Charles L. Campbell, 1997, *Preaching Jesus: New Directions for Homiletics in Hans Frei's Postliberal Theology*, Grand Rapids: Eerdmans.

17 Thomas G. Long, 2005, *The Witness of Preaching*, 2nd edn, Westminster John Knox, pp. 99–116.

18 Campbell, *Word before the Powers*, especially pp. 70–71, 79.

are waged with bombs, bullets, missiles and tanks; but peace treaties are made with words. Paul envisaged his ministry, and by implication that of the whole Church, as one of reconciliation, bringing near to people the peacemaking Christ (2 Cor. 5.18–21). And this is a vocation that brings suffering: for strangely, people do not want to know him (2 Cor. 6.1–10).

The gospel itself is the power of God for salvation (Rom. 1.16), and it is interesting that in this verse Paul stresses that it is for *all* who believe, both 'Jew and Greek'. A strong theme of his letter – indeed, perhaps its main aim – is to show how Jew and Gentile can be *united* in Christ, on the same footing with him. 'The gospel' is, as we have seen, a greater reality than any human words can capture. Its most powerful channel and advocate is a united Christian community.[19] But within such a community, the *words* with which it is articulated carry their own power.

The ethical demand this places upon the preacher is considerable. We have already seen that the sum total of a preacher's message, if it is authentically Christian, is 'gospel'. Therefore, fundamental to the task of weighing up the power our words will carry is discerning whether the character of the gospel of Christ runs through them like a wick through candlewax. More specifically, and in the light of Campbell's argument, we must ask: What is this 'truth' that must challenge 'power'? The perpetual danger is that our *words* come out tainted by the very anti-Christian, anti-human characteristics that belong to the powers we are seeking to resist. It is sadly possible for words, like deeds, to get violent, in overt or subtler ways. In that case, even if we speak of the gospel of peace, our words will not carry 'truth', because the force of what we say contradicts the meaning of our words.

'Truth', as a quality recognized supremely in Christ (John 14.6), names an ethical virtue as much as it names a metaphysical reality. No doubt the Greek *alētheia* ('truth') in the New Testament carried some overtones of Greek philosophical ideas of truth as something abstract. But for early Christians, and others of Jewish background, it would also have carried strong overtones of the LXX, the Greek translation of the Hebrew Bible, in which it can translate the word *emeth*, 'faithfulness', for example in Ps. 85.10 (84.11 LXX): 'Steadfast love and faithfulness (*emeth / alētheia*) will meet; righteousness and peace will kiss each other' (nrsv). Christ is pictured in Revelation 19.11 as a rider who is

---

19 Cf. Lesslie Newbigin, 1989, *The Gospel in a Pluralist Society*, London: SPCK, p. 234.

called Faithful and True (*pistos kai alēthinos*), a parallelism demonstrating the close link between the concepts.

The truth the preacher speaks must therefore be much more than a 'correct' form of words. We are called to be true to the Truth, the one who was genuinely faithful to God and who expressed God's loving faithfulness to humanity. We cannot expect our words to be vehicles for bringing Christ near to people otherwise. Summed up in the idea of 'truth' is not only the historical reality of the story of Jesus, nor only the Christian teaching developed by early Christians about him, but the *manner* of his being, speaking and acting in the world. This, as the gospels tell us, was both completely courageous in standing up to the powers of 'untruth', and completely loving and non-violent towards people in that resistance.[20] Moreover, the 'truth' about ourselves is also bound up with this. We cannot represent the one called Faithful and True if we are not allowing his truth to expose the reality of who we are – in our imperfections, but also our God-given personality, gifts and situation. This does not imply that preaching should always entail profound self-exposure. Jesus himself, after all, was highly secretive about the deepest aspects of his identity and calling (for example Mark 1.34, 44). Still less does it imply that it is an arena for self-publicity. It does, however, imply that the kind of self-knowledge (and knowledge of others) seen in Chapter 4 to be essential to all effective communication is no less essential for the preacher. 'Truth' demands honesty about oneself; it demands that others see the impact of the truth of Christ upon one's self-perception.

The truth of Christ and the love of Christ meet together, and if we work through the implications of 'speaking truth in love' in preaching, as in our conversations, we will see that a rigorous – even ascetic – self-denial and concern for 'the other' is bound up in them.[21] The response we get to such genuinely truthful speech will be unpredictable, and if we are being faithful to Christ (and his prophets and apostles) we can expect hostility sooner or later. For truth demands that we cannot keep silence about evil and oppression and injustice; and though we do not expect to have hardened perpetrators of these things in our regular congregations, the words with which a preacher

20 The whip of cords Jesus took in the temple might be taken as an exception to this (John 2.15); however, it appears to have been the sheep and oxen he was driving with it.

21 For a radical statement of this point see John McClure, 2001, *Other-wise Preaching: A Postmodern Ethic for Homiletics*, St Louis: Chalice Press.

addresses their flock have a habit of going further, when they are genuinely addressing truth to power. Conversely, if we believe that the very context of our preaching within a congregation is inhibiting this calling, is this a cue that we should be taking our message to the streets?[22]

What then of Long's notion that each sermon should have a specific 'function'? Can we be any more specific than saying that each sermon should unleash truth against power? There is a tension here between recognizing the inevitable force of our words, for good or ill, and therefore seeking to harness them responsibly in the right direction, and acknowledging with Paul that the source of the gospel's own power is not 'eloquent words of wisdom' but 'Jesus Christ and him crucified' (1 Cor. 1.17–2.5). In the tradition of Paul, Augustine, though he had learned much from classical rhetoric and applied it to preaching, subordinated rhetoric to truthfulness.[23]

Long is surely right that just as we must be clear about the focus of what we are saying, so as not to cause confusion, so we must think carefully about the effect our words will have, and plan accordingly. But we must set this human planning in the context of our faith that through our words, with all their limitations and unpredictable effects, God in Christ can and will meet people in his own truth and truthfulness in a multitude of unplanned and unplannable ways.

These four characteristics, therefore, mark out the ethical challenge for a preacher that arises from the theology of preaching developed in the previous two chapters. The preacher is to be a listener, a gospeller, an interpreter of Scripture and world, and a speaker of truth to power. We now turn to some of the main types of preaching practice with a view to assessing their potential as ways of responding to this challenge.

Questions for the local church

- In what ways are preachers listening to God, sharing the gospel, interpreting the Bible and the world, and speaking truth to power?
- How might preachers work at these dimensions of the task?
- Is preaching being carried out in an ethical manner?

22 Cf. Stuart Blythe, 2009, 'Open-Air Preaching as Radical Street Performance', unpublished PhD thesis, University of Edinburgh.
23 On this see Wright, *Telling God's Story*, pp. 159–63.

Areas for research

Ethics is always a sensitive research topic. Nevertheless, investigations into the way in which listeners feel about sermons – not just about their content, but what they 'do' to people as pieces of communication – can be extremely valuable and revealing.

The subject of our calling to be interpreters, of text and world, continues to be a very fruitful area of exploration.

Further reading

Charles L. Campbell, 2002, *The Word before the Powers: An Ethic of Preaching*, Louisville: Westminster John Knox.

David J. Schlafer and Timothy F. Sedgwick, 2007, *Preaching What we Practice: Proclamation and Moral Discernment*, Harrisburg, PA: Morehouse Publishing.

Leonora Tubbs Tisdale, 1997, *Preaching as Local Theology and Folk Art*, Minneapolis: Fortress Press.

8

Patterns and Practices for Preaching

Having sought to gather up the narrative of Scripture in an outline theology of preaching, and explored its ethical implications for the preacher, in this chapter we will examine some of the key preaching 'practices' of the Church, with a view to discerning their potential as ethical expressions of contemporary preaching.[1] I will call these practices the liturgical sermon, the teaching sermon, the evangelistic sermon and the street sermon.[2] Having outlined these practices I will discuss them with reference to the ethical characteristics outlined in the last chapter.

All categorizations of types of preaching are of necessity an attempt to make tidy what is inherently untidy. Readers may immediately be able to think of sermons which fall into more than one category. Nor do I claim either originality or traditional authority for this typology; it seems to me simply a convenient way to gather the various varieties of preaching into family groups for the purpose of evaluation. My focus in this categorization is not the actual form or structure of the sermon but its ethos, setting and aim.[3] A great variety of forms and structures may serve well each of the types.

---

1 On the epistemic potential of examples of good practice, their power to contribute to knowledge and understanding as well as be normative guides to what we do, see Richard R. Osmer, 2008, *Practical Theology: An Introduction*, Grand Rapids: Eerdmans, pp. 153–60, drawing especially on the work of Elaine Graham.

2 I used a slightly more extensive typology in Geoffrey Stevenson and Stephen Wright, 2008, *Preaching with Humanity: A Practical Guide for Today's Church*, London: Church House Publishing, pp. 12–28. There I also included brief snapshots of actual examples of the different kinds of preaching. Here I am attempting to categorize the main practices of preaching with fewer headings, which means that a broader range is included within each. I did not include the street sermon in that volume; indeed, the one reference to such preaching was a disparaging one (p. 1). The evaluation of the categories in that book was on the basis of their respective value in respect of the missional, pastoral and educational ministries of the Church.

3 In contrast to *Preaching with Humanity*, pp. 12–28, where for practical purposes I mixed up ethos and form.

The liturgical sermon

'The liturgical sermon' may be defined here as a sermon whose main aim is subordinated to that of the service of worship within which it takes place. It has a long history, going back to the early Christian homilies in the small gatherings of believers. Today this conception of the sermon is standard in Roman Catholic and Orthodox churches,[4] as well as many Anglican ones.[5] But in the wake of the 'Liturgical Movement' of the mid twentieth century, it has also influenced many of the Free Churches.[6]

The key feature of the liturgical sermon is that it is oriented towards the worship of God rather than the edification or persuasion of human beings. This is not to imply that the other types may not also be worshipful, nor that the liturgical sermon may not also be edifying and persuasive to the congregation. Rather, it is to do with the shared perception that the sermon is but one stage – an important stage, to be sure – in a larger drama. Each of those stages may play its part in encouraging the genuine worship of those present, and building them up in the faith. And importantly, conceiving of preaching as a 'liturgical' act often goes hand-in-hand with conceiving it, and the other parts of the service, as *sacramental* acts. This is not just a question of whether the sacraments of Baptism or Eucharist are celebrated in the service, though in these churches the Eucharist regularly is. It is rather that all parts of the service, including the sermon, are seen, quite consciously, as incomplete in themselves, pointers to the reality of God beyond us. Not only is each incomplete in itself, but all put together are but a sign of a greater reality. Thus songs of praise may be heard as echoes of (and a rehearsal for) the praises of heaven. The gathered congregation may be seen as a token of God's will to gather all people into his kingdom. And the preached word, whatever it is, can be seen as signalling God's entire act of self-communication to humankind. In concert, all the various elements of the service point to the presence and purpose of God. Meanings multiply as God's people come together to worship him, and thus to know themselves and their world again in the light of their creator and redeemer.

---

4 See Duncan Macpherson, 'Preaching in the Roman Catholic Ecclesial Context', in Geoffrey Stevenson (ed.), 2010, *The Future of Preaching*, London: SCM, p. 27–33.

5 An important Anglican study was that of Reginald H. Fuller, 1957, *Liturgical Preaching*, London: SCM.

6 For a Baptist advocate of a form of liturgical preaching, see Neville Clark, 1991, *Preaching in Context: Word, Worship and the People of God*, Bury St Edmunds: Kevin Mayhew.

The liturgical sermon will therefore often inspire echoes in the rest of the worship, and connections may be deliberately planned. Especially, it is normally closely linked to the use of a lectionary as a pattern for regular reading of Scripture. It aims not so much for an extended examination or explanation of a text or texts, as for focusing on a facet of the gospel to be found in them, as it relates to the contemporary life of the Church and the world.[7] This aspect of the gospel is offered as an inspiration and challenge to the congregation as they regularly draw near to receive the bread and wine, so that their reception of the elements may be matched by an informed and renewed faith in Christ, thus becoming a genuinely nourishing start to another week of discipleship. Preaching on other special occasions such as weddings, funerals or ordinations can also be seen as 'liturgical' preaching.

The teaching sermon

The teaching sermon is one which may stand more or less alone apart from an act of worship, although in practice it is often linked to one. Rather than being seen as an integral part of the worship, it makes an extensive attempt to teach some aspect of the Christian faith and its outworking in life. In his book on liturgical preaching, Reginald H. Fuller recognized the importance of the teaching function of preaching, but proposed that the place for 'teaching' sermons was not in the main weekly Eucharistic celebration, but at another time (within the Anglican ethos of his time – the late 1950s – he said that Evening Prayer was the best place for it): 'The aim of the sermon is proclamation and the response of faith, whereas the aim of teaching is to secure understanding of the doctrinal, ethical and devotional implications involved in that response of faith.'[8] In Free Church tradition, as in Anglican Morning and Evening Prayer, the sermon often comes nearly at the conclusion of the service, when the act of worship is more or less complete. Fuller's book shows that there is no contradiction or incompatibility entailed in having liturgical sermons and teaching sermons in the same church. They simply fulfil different functions and are fitting at different times.

In some Evangelical churches the notion of a sermon or preaching is more or less synonymous with 'teaching', and this 'teaching' is

---

7 See Fuller, *Liturgical Preaching*; Ian Paton, 2004, 'Preaching in Worship', in Geoffrey Hunter et al. (eds), *A Preacher's Companion: Essays from the College of Preachers*, Oxford: Bible Reading Fellowship.

8 Fuller, *Liturgical Preaching*, p. 53.

essentially 'teaching of the Bible'. But a teaching ministry is a fundamental part of the life of the whole Church (cf. Matt. 28.19), and extends much wider than sermons. Also, though the Bible will naturally be a core element of a teaching sermon, theological reflection on it and discernment of how it reframes our view of the world are, as we have seen, properly integral to the process of interpretation.

Two variations on 'the teaching sermon' should be mentioned. The first is the teaching *service*,[9] in which an entire act of worship has a strong didactic thread. This has been common in many Free Churches and is a favoured mode of all-age worship in Anglican churches. In effect, what happens is that the 'sermon' is broken up into different sections and a range of different activities, so that the whole service is designed to communicate a dimension of God's truth.

The second is the revival of the catechumenate, of an extended *course* of instruction, especially for those who are new to the faith. Osmer cites this as an example of 'good practice', rooted in ancient tradition, in the contemporary American Church.[10] In the UK, courses such as Emmaus fulfil such a function, as does the Roman Catholic practice of 'mystagogical' preaching, the regular instruction of the newly baptized in the period after Easter.[11] Whereas in the 'teaching service' the teaching is extended through a whole act of worship, in these courses of instruction it is extended through a number of occasions over several weeks.

The evangelistic sermon

The evangelistic sermon is directed towards the announcement of the gospel to unbelievers with the hope of winning them to faith. The days of large evangelistic 'rallies' or meetings seem to have faded somewhat in the UK; certainly we have seen in the twenty-first century nothing on the scale of the Billy Graham crusades of the latter half of the twentieth. But evangelistic preaching continues as churches hold special guest services and, in a more informal setting, run courses such as Alpha®. Often, major festivals such as Christmas are taken as opportunities for evangelistic preaching.

Evangelistic sermons are best defined here according to their intended audience. They are different from liturgical or teaching sermons in

9 Cf. Margaret Withers, 2010, 'Preaching for All: Inclusivity and the Future of Preaching in All-age Worship', in Stevenson (ed.), *Future of Preaching*.

10 *Practical Theology*, p. 153.

11 Macpherson, 'Preaching in the Roman Catholic Ecclesial Context', p. 30–1.

being consciously aimed at those who are not (yet) believers. As with the other types considered in this chapter, there is no one structure or form that is 'proper' to them. In some traditions they will regularly conclude with an appeal for people to make a response of faith, perhaps visibly signalled in some way, for example by standing, coming to the front or asking for prayer. But the presence and manner of such an appeal will often depend on the theology of the sermon. Those who especially emphasize the sovereignty of God will tend to be restrained, while those who especially emphasize the need for human response will wish to make clear opportunity for such response.

Evangelistic sermons in modern times are heirs to the 'revivalist' tradition of Finney, Moody and others in the nineteenth century.[12] In some places they may incorporate an invitation to receive healing or a new experience of the Holy Spirit. The emphasis is on the constant and immediate challenge to receive and respond to God's blessings, whatever stage of spiritual growth one has reached. In Pentecostal churches, and especially in the African–American tradition, 'response' is visible not just at the end of a sermon, but throughout it, in the vocal pattern of call-and-response that is set up between preachers and hearers.

We may include with the evangelistic sermon the apologetic sermon, whose aim is to give a reasoned defence of Christian faith (or some aspect of it), especially with sceptics or doubters in mind.

The street sermon

A final example of preaching practice which it is right to consider here is the open-air or 'street' sermon. The fortunes of this form of preaching have waxed and waned over the centuries. While there are examples of poor practice here,[13] as there are with all the other kinds of sermon just considered, it is healthy to remember the open-air ministry of Jesus and the apostles, and of important figures and movements in the story of preaching ever since, as we saw in Chapter 1. The friars, Wesley and Whitefield, the nineteenth-century revivalists, Spurgeon: all had huge influence, taking the gospel beyond the walls of a church building. Recently, writers such as Stanley Saunders and Charles Campbell,[14] and

---

12 See Stevenson and Wright, *Preaching with Humanity*, pp. 22–4.
13 Cf. Stevenson and Wright, *Preaching with Humanity*, p. 1.
14 Stanley P. Saunders and Charles L. Campbell, 2000, *The Word on the Street: Performing the Scriptures in an Urban Context*, Grand Rapids: Eerdmans.

Stuart Blythe,[15] have advocated a renewal of this practice, in which Christian preachers – not necessarily alone, but in company with others, for example a drama group – take the message of Christ physically into the 'market-place' of competing ideas and consumer concerns. Such preaching is of course 'evangelistic', but is strikingly different from all the other practices considered here (including 'evangelistic preaching') in being conducted outside the safety of the gathering of believers, directly exposed to whatever the world may – metaphorically or literally – hurl at it.

Assessing the types

We will now examine these four contemporary preaching 'practices' in the light of the outline ethic of preaching developed in the previous chapter. We will ask to what extent each of them allows scope for the elements of that ethic to be expressed. How does each enable a mode of preaching that entails listening to God, gospelling, interpreting, and speaking truth to power?

Listening

In that a preacher in any one of these four preaching practices may listen more – or less – to God, it is obvious that no one of them has an inherent pre-eminence in this respect. However, some of them encourage the practice of listening more than others. In liturgical preaching, the teaching *service* and the call-and-response of some evangelistic/revivalist preaching, the preacher can be very consciously reminded of the presence of God by the elements of the worship and the contributions of different members (for example, through the words of a song, or the way in which someone reads a Scripture passage, enacts a drama, or affirms a point made with an 'Amen'). These may be means by which God catches the preacher's attention and enables him or her to speak not just what is thought but what is heard.

Other forms of preaching which put a premium on the preparedness and dominance of the preacher – particularly in teaching, evangelism and street preaching – may appear, for this reason, to downplay the role of the preacher as listener. This need not at all be the case: not only because of

---

15 Stuart Blythe, 2009, 'Open-Air Preaching as Radical Street Performance', unpublished PhD thesis, University of Edinburgh.

the preacher's careful listening beforehand (in a variety of ways), but also because the preacher – like any effective communicator – will be seeking to pick up the 'vibes' of response from the hearers, and adjust aspects of their speech accordingly.[16] However, it may be that those engaging in these more heavily monological preaching practices have at least often given the *impression* of not being 'listening' preachers, and the reaction against such forms is therefore a healthy reminder to all that the preacher is called first and foremost to be a listener to God along with everyone else.

Gospelling

I have argued above that *any* claim to be discovering or speaking God's word of truth must be tested by asking: is this an authentically *gospel* word? Does it in some way reflect, echo, point back to, the great good news of God announced in and through Jesus Christ? If this is so, it follows that any and all of the four preaching practices considered in this chapter both can and should be vehicles of the gospel.

It is a common misunderstanding to think that only preaching which is specifically 'evangelistic', directed to non-believers (and probably including an appeal for response) – whether in church or on the 'street' – can be called 'gospel' preaching. In the New Testament, it seems that 'gospel' is something that believers go on needing to hear.[17] In fact, the proclamation of the gospel is the main aim of 'liturgical preaching'.[18] The 'teaching sermon', if it is faithful to Scripture and Christian tradition, will communicate the gospel, for it is the gospel which gives Scripture its dynamic and holds it together.

If a vital element of the communication of the gospel is the way in which the message is expressed, it is very possible for 'evangelistic' preaching to fall short of being real 'gospel', and conversely for the other practices to approximate 'gospel' very closely. The 'evangelistic' preacher who is hectoring or manipulative will not be *experienced* as a good-news preacher, whatever their fine words about the grace of God. But the 'teaching' preacher whose words, manner and very being are shaped to give heart and hope to the hearers may communicate the gospel, in both its aspects of comfort and challenge, without a word of direct 'appeal' being spoken. The 'liturgical' preacher would usually

---

16 Cf. Chapter 3 above.
17 Cf. Rom. 1.15.
18 See Fuller, *Liturgical Preaching*, pp. 12, 22, 53.

feel no need of a direct appeal, for the liturgy itself provides the pattern within which the hearer can make a response.[19]

'Street' preaching may, in a striking way, present the demand of the gospel along with its invitation. In its very intrusion on to 'public space' it calls for a response, even though the actual response will regularly be one of indifference. In this sense, it may encourage a more definite presentation of the gospel's challenge than preaching which takes place in church, for in the safe environment of 'church', preacher and congregation may collude in the sense that they are insulated from that challenge. Conversely, the negative reaction to some kinds of 'street preaching' among both Christian believers and unbelievers may be precisely because it does not come over as 'good news' at all. The justice of God is undoubtedly part of the good news, but sermons which simply proclaim that all should repent 'because the end is nigh' do little to commend Christ, and potentially much to harm his cause.

Faithful interpretation

We saw in the last chapter that a third ethical challenge for the preacher is that of being a faithful interpreter of the Scriptures and the world. Once more, all the practices of preaching allow for the fulfilment of this role with the kind of ethical care that we described. As we have seen, we are by nature interpretative beings. As preachers we do not start this process, but as soon as we open our mouths we enable people to take it a stage further. In this sense, a fairly short liturgical sermon which tersely brings together a text from the day's readings and an event from the week's news may be as usefully interpretative as a longer teaching sermon which explores the meaning and contemporary significance of Scripture much more explicitly.

The teaching sermon is the *locus classicus* for the act of interpretation, simply because it allows for the greater development of ideas and therefore the removal of possible misunderstandings and the achievement of sharper clarity. The other preaching practices, however, have an important role to play. Evangelistic preaching takes place at what is potentially a turning-point in many people's lives, a crisis in which one way of seeing the world and oneself is about to be displaced by a different interpretation. This calls for great skill and sensitivity on the

19 An interesting exploration of this point has been made by Angela P. Watts, 2008, 'A Theological Reflection upon the Principle and Practice of "Preaching for a Decision"', unpublished MTh dissertation, London: Spurgeon's College, University of Wales.

part of the one guiding the interpretation. Street preaching might take as a starting-point some building, object or event familiar to everyone, perhaps even in view: the sermon can then become an invitation to think of it in the light of the Christ revealed in the Scriptures.

Speaking truth to power

It is in our fourth ethical demand, speaking truth to power, that street preaching especially comes into its own.[20] In the public 'square', there is a sense of a direct confrontation of the gospel with the invisible 'powers' that hold sway over people's lives, whether those be the lure of consumer goods, the poison of idolatrous philosophies or many other forces. This confrontation may or may not become visible in active hostility to the preacher. However, the preacher feels in this arena more than any the keen vulnerability of embodying, for a careless and often hate-filled world, the message of a forgiving, loving Saviour. All we have to offer is the word of God's truth.

Yet once more, we should not neglect the potential of the other preaching practices to express this ethical requirement. The fact that preaching takes place in a church building does not mean that the powers of the world are automatically excluded. On the contrary, those who come to church are as caught up in the spiritual struggle as anyone else. It is in the community which carries the name of Christ that, as in Jesus' company of disciples on the road to Jerusalem, vital lessons about the meaning of discipleship are learned, and misconceptions addressed. We should not be surprised that churches can be scenes of conflict, for we are communities of learners. Within this setting, the preacher is called to address the underlying spiritual forces which are at work, reminding people that our real conflict is not with 'flesh and blood' but with principalities and powers (Eph. 6.12).

Preaching within the church setting can in fact contribute powerfully to the occasion being one both of liberation in itself for those who attend, and also of equipment of them for being good soldiers of Christ in their daily lives. The gathering of people in the name of Christ is a scene where he especially promised his presence (Matt. 18.20). Liturgical preaching is part of a drama in which the parts reinforce each other as means of building Christian identity and renewing Christian assurance. The teaching sermon can do far more than simply impart

---

20 See Saunders and Campbell, *Word on the Street*; Blythe, 'Open-Air Preaching'.

information; it evokes memories, reinforces faith and shapes the hearers' sense of their place in the grand story of God. These are not just cognitive effects; they are transformational, working on the deepest levels of spiritual self-perception, catching up mind, body, emotion and will. The evangelistic sermon can seek to put its finger with special care and challenge on those points of human life which are acting as barriers to a full-hearted openness to the coming of God's kingdom in power.

A short case study: Alpha®

We can see that all these classic practices of the Church, with their long pedigree and continued contemporary vitality, may be vehicles for an authentic ethical expression of preaching today. Each of them, as we have seen, embraces quite a broad range of actual practices. None should be taken as straitjackets. I have discussed them here as a prelude to the final section of the book in which we turn to the 'pragmatic' task of practical theology as it relates to preaching, the exploration of actual ways in which the Church and the preacher may carry out their task on the basis of the way it has been described, interpreted and theologically understood. There may be developments of each in different, perhaps surprising directions in years to come. They are not types or paradigms set in stone, but examples of 'good practice' which may shape both our theological understanding of what preaching is about, and the way in which we carry it out.

By way of conclusion to this chapter we will look at a short case study, that of the Alpha® course. This is a widely used evangelistic course which recognizes two basic realities of contemporary life. First, most unchurched or unbelieving people need more than a single sermon to understand the gospel and be moved to respond to it. Second, many people appreciate the hospitable atmosphere of a meal and the informal setting of a group in which they can feel relaxed and free to ask questions. Yet there is a considerable quantity of 'teaching', and the need to make a response to the gospel is kept to the fore, particularly in the 'Holy Spirit weekend' which comes at the centre of the course.

Alpha® is but one instrument for the work of God in the world today, but its format brings together in an interesting way the examples of preaching practice we have considered in this chapter.

Worship is at the heart of the course, as seen in the 'Holy Spirit weekend' at the centre, and in that sense the 'preaching' does not stand alone, but is seen as part of an ongoing experience in which the presence of God is sought and acknowledged. Christians are encouraged to attend so that the leader is not alone in seeking and acknowledging God's presence. There is also strong 'teaching' content, whether or not everyone agrees with just what that content should be; indeed, a doyen of conservative evangelicalism, the main tradition guarding the 'teaching sermon', was recently cited as commending Alpha as a model of contemporary catechesis.[21] In this way, it can be extremely helpful for believers as well as non-believers.

Evangelism is clearly also at the heart of the course, with specific opportunity given to make a response, but not without plenty of interaction throughout, allowing the course (ideally) to feel a 'safe' space. Finally, although it does not take place exactly 'on the street' like street preaching, Alpha takes place away from formal church gatherings, and has been very effective in settings such as prisons. It deliberately seeks engagement with people on more 'neutral' ground than in a church service, and to address the specific questions and circumstances of their lives. It can be seen, therefore, as a very specific instance of preaching practice today, which combines elements of four traditional models and as it does so expresses the importance of preaching as listening, as gospelling, as interpreting and as speaking truth to power.

Questions for the local church

- Which of these practices of preaching is most familiar to you? What do you think you could learn by listening to, or practising, less familiar ones?
- In your experience, how effective are these practices at fulfilling the ethical demands of preaching?

Areas for research

The actual practice of preaching is far more varied than the simple categorization in this chapter suggests. An analytical survey of the types of preaching practised in a local area or a denomination or a group of churches of different types would yield fascinating results which would take forward the process of productive theological reflection on the preaching task.

Further reading

Ronald J. Allen, 1996, *The Teaching Sermon*, Nashville: Abingdon.

---

21 J. I. Packer, 2010, in *Alpha News* 49 (March–June), p. 15.

Stephen Vincent DeLeers, 2004, *Written Text Become Living Word: The Vision and Practice of Sunday Preaching*, Collegeville MN: Liturgical Press.

Stanley P. Saunders and Charles L. Campbell, 2000, *The Word on the Street: Performing the Scriptures in an Urban Context*, Grand Rapids: Eerdmans.

PART 4

Introduction

The fourth and final stage of the process of practical theology is called by Osmer 'The Pragmatic Task – Servant Leadership'.[1] Thus far we have described the activity of preaching, interpreted it in terms of various analytical categories, and sought to discern what is going on by means of a normative theological framework. The final task is not a mere addendum to these, but emerges naturally out of it, as we ask 'How might we respond in ways that are faithful and effective?'[2] In describing this task as 'servant leadership', Osmer is proposing that the practical theologian (whether minister, lecturer, writer or whoever) should act as a servant of the Church in helping others to draw out practical implications of the understanding of the situation or activity that has been reached. That is what I will attempt to do in this part of the book, with respect to preaching.[3]

What consequences for our regular practice of preaching emerge from the theological understanding of the event we have been discussing? One very important truth must be highlighted again at this point. All that we have said so far suggests that the question 'how to preach' is fundamentally an *ethical* question before it is a technical one – although the employment of *technē*, skill, is also entitled. The practice of preaching must flow out of the place we believe it has in the purposes of God, and the ethical ramifications of that. This means that handbooks of preaching that focus simply on the skills it requires will inevitably skew the nature of preaching from the start.

Osmer's deceptively simple yet careful question, 'How might we respond in ways that are faithful and effective?', gives us another preliminary clue as to the nature of our task in this part. 'Faithful and

---

1 Richard R. Osmer, *Practical Theology: An Introduction*, Grand Rapids: Eerdmans, pp. 175–218.

2 Osmer, *Practical Theology*, p. 10.

3 Just as the Bishop of Rome has been seen traditionally as the 'servant of the servants of God', so the teacher of preaching may be seen as a 'servant of the servants of the Word'.

effective': but effectiveness plays second fiddle to faithfulness. This may help us strike the balance between an approach to preaching which ignores the pragmatic matters of technique altogether – as if *all* we needed was faithfulness to God and to his Word – and an approach which forgets the mysterious divine dimension, thinking that various kinds of human techniques can produce desired results on their own.[4] The very word 'effectiveness' is a problematic one in the discussion and evaluation of preaching, so bound up is it with modern humanist pragmatism. We cannot deny that 'effectiveness' is good, and a goal to be aimed for, but we must recognize that when viewed in its divine dimensions the 'effectiveness' of preaching is ultimately impossible to quantify.

With these clues in place, we shall explore the practical outworkings of our discussion of preaching in two parts. There are an attitude and tasks for the Church, both as a whole and in specific congregations, and there are an attitude and tasks for the preacher.

The discussion in Part 3 has set preaching in the wide context of the speech of God and his gift of speech to all humanity. The Church, as the foretaste of this new humanity, is called to echo and express the speech of God in truth and love, in its voicing of God to the world, and in all the mutual relationships which it encompasses. Within this, the preacher exercises a special role as voicer of the gospel in, to and on behalf of the Christian community. It is therefore a travesty of our Christian calling to shunt off the ministry of preaching into a specialized compartment, or to leave the preacher, after an initial period of training, to 'get on with it' because that is their 'job' and they have, supposedly, the 'expertise'. It is a ministry that the whole Church must own, support and, in one sense, share in. This still leaves wide open the manner and mode in which preaching takes place; but again, discussions about this should be the preserve of the Church as a whole, not just preachers or a *cabal* of practical theologians.

This is true on the level of the congregation as well as on the level of the wider Church. If an essential aspect of theology is its local character,[5] and the word of God to be discerned is no mere vague generality

---

4 See André Resner Jr, 1999, *Preacher and Cross: Person and Message in Theology and Rhetoric*, Grand Rapids: Eerdmans; Michael Pasquarello III, 2006, *Christian Preaching: A Trinitarian Theology of Proclamation*, Grand Rapids: Baker Academic, especially pp. 19–31, in which he argues for a properly theological approach to preaching rather than the pragmatic one seen, for example, in Rick Warren's 'purpose-driven' model.

5 See Leonora Tubbs Tisdale, 1997, *Preaching as Local Theology and Folk Art*, Minneapolis: Fortress.

but something rooted in the universal and yet intended to guide the life of *these* people, it is vital that congregations work together with their preachers in the discernment of the word and the exploration of how it may best be expressed. A local congregation which truly owns its preaching ministry will be one which supports its preachers and enters into the ministry, whether as listener or, in some way, as active participant, in such a way as to make the event a dynamic and genuinely two-way moment – whatever exact form it may take. This should not mean that the congregation *controls* the preaching ministry – in the sense that they refuse to hear an unpalatable message and, *in extremis*, might remove the preacher. It means, rather, that they support the preacher, who is a Christian of no greater status than themselves, in the work of listening to God and articulating his word, which brings all – the preacher included – under the sound of both judgement and grace. I shall explore the attitude and tasks of the Church with reference to its being a *missionary* body.

There are also, of course, an attitude and tasks for the preacher himself or herself. Even in this final 'pragmatic' part of the book, we must stress the priority of the attitude over the tasks, for only a healthy apprehension of the divine, mysterious quality of what we are engaged in will give us a proper sense of proportion and focus in the execution of the tasks. The practical business of preparing, delivering and reflecting on a weekly – or more frequent – sermon is important to consider, and it arises naturally from such a healthy posture. We will point out how certain sermon structures may helpfully serve the ethical requirements for preaching we have identified, within one or more of the four preaching practices discussed – or others yet to be invented. We will also suggest habits of life which will sustain a preacher and potentially – in the providence of God – enable him or her to take their place in the procession of influential (though not always famous) ministers of the word with whom we began in Chapter 1.

9

Tasks for the Church

The missionary task of the whole Church

Recent decades have seen a welcome revival in the Church's self-understanding as a *missionary* body. There has been a gradual – if slow and often stunted – recovery of consciousness that we are truer to our identity when we are dynamic, flexible, on the move, open to change, people with a purpose, taking into the world the good news of the kingdom in deed and word, than when we stay static, resistant to change and preoccupied with the perpetuation of institutions or outmoded traditions.[1]

How should preaching relate to the 'missionary' task of the Church, thus conceived and executed? This is a contested question. On the one hand, we have historical testimony to the role played by preaching in many stages of the Church's missionary expansion and its influence on individuals and society. A line can easily be traced from the apostles, via the Fathers, the friars, the reformers and the revivalists, right up to noted preachers of the present and recent past. Some contemporary advocates of preaching point to this great tradition as a continued inspiration for the present: not simply harking back to a 'golden age', but quite fairly implying that the burden of proof should surely lie with those who question the place of preaching in the Church's mission today.

On the other hand, those who do question this place have on their side the vital point that a truly missionary church is always open to development, not being bound by the forms of the past. They could also, quite fairly, say that though there may indeed be a 'great tradition' of preaching, that tradition has been far from homogeneous. Preaching has had many different shapes and settings. Further, it has not always advanced the gospel or promoted love for God and neighbour. Thus, it is argued, a mission-conscious Church, inspired

---

1 See the classic work of David Bosch, 1991, *Transforming Mission: Paradigm Shifts in Theology of Mission*, New York: Orbis Books.

by the Spirit, must be alert to the needs of the present as much as to the inheritance of the past. No one form of preaching has achieved 'canonical' status; perhaps, then, the missionary urgency of the times is such that preaching must 'morph' into something that may be – initially at least – quite unrecognizable as 'preaching'?

Four representatives of such a view may be cited briefly. In Britain, David Norrington argues that preaching as we have known it has been much too imbued with an authoritarian ethos associated with the hierarchical power-structures of Christendom, and thus no longer has a place in the mission of a chastened, post-Christendom church.[2] Building partly on Norrington's argument, Stuart Murray advocates 'interactive' preaching,[3] saying that this is educationally and culturally the appropriate way to approach the task today. In the United States, John McClure has sought to preserve the outward form of preaching while radically subverting its traditional authoritarian associations. The preacher is called to give attention to the voices of the 'other' and one practical expression of this is the emergence of the sermon from a 'roundtable pulpit', a discussion group which shapes the preacher's thinking.[4] More drastically, Doug Pagitt writes off traditional preaching as 'speaching', an event that in its very nature does violence to the hearers. Nonetheless, the title of his book is not *Preaching Buried* but *Preaching Re-Imagined*.[5]

Is there in fact a way in which preaching can be 're-imagined' such that it accords with the Church's renewed missionary consciousness? If we affirm the validity of that consciousness (which not all do),[6] we ought to affirm the questions raised by all these authors, for they are raised in response to genuine missionary thinking. For whereas until quite recently the close connection between 'preaching' and 'mission' was widely taken for granted, it is the very 'missionary' impulse which is now causing some to question the appropriateness of preaching.

---

2 David C. Norrington, 1996, *To Preach or Not to Preach?*, Carlisle: Paternoster.

3 Stuart Murray, 1999, 'Interactive Preaching', in *Evangel* 72 (Summer 1999), pp. 53–7.

4 John McClure, 2001, *Other-wise Preaching*, St Louis: Chalice Press; 1996, *The Roundtable Pulpit: Where Preaching and Leadership Meet*, Nashville: Abingdon.

5 Doug Pagitt, 2005, *Preaching Re-Imagined: The Role of the Sermon in Communities of Faith*, Grand Rapids: Zondervan.

6 For example, those who believe that the very idea of 'mission' is too bound up with 'Christian' abuses of the past such as anti-Jewishness. This is simply pushing the argument of Murray et al. a stage further back, such that not only preaching, but 'mission' itself is seen as irredeemably tainted. In response one could argue that just as 'preaching' might be re-imagined without its authoritarian associations, so whether one still believes in 'mission' has much to do with how one defines it (or redefines it). The whole discussion illustrates the power of specific words to have a hold over our imaginations, for good or ill.

ALIVE TO THE WORD

However, while affirming the importance of the question such writers are posing, we ought not simply to jump into accepting any of their answers. This, I suggest, is for the very same 'missionary' reasoning which propels their question. If preaching is to be alert to its mission context, surely no single prescription for either re-imagining or removing preaching will be valid across the board. Central to contemporary mission insight is the need for contextualization. There is no 'one size fits all' approach to mission, just as preachers have always known that there is no 'one size fits all' sermon. So there cannot be a 'one size fits all' approach to replacing or reconceiving the sermon. The immediate context must shape the way our mission is expressed – or not – in our preaching. In this respect, of the four writers just mentioned I find McClure the most persuasive, for he shows us that it is not the outward form of a sermon which is really the issue, but rather the extent of respect for the 'otherness' of its various hearers – the 'other' for whom those in Christian mission are always primarily concerned, as they seek not to be served but to serve.

Thus rather than attempting some sort of universal answer to the question 'How should preaching adapt to fit into the Church's missionary task today', it will be much more useful – and true to the spirit of localized mission – to offer a few examples of how in specific cases it might or might not need to do so.

Few readers are likely to object to the proposition, for a start, that authoritarian preaching does not serve to advance the kingdom of God. (This, surely, has always been the case; the prevailing mood may have highlighted it but certainly did not come up with the idea.) But this does not exclude 'authoritative' preaching where the 'authority' is that not conferred by rank or office but by character, experience, knowledge and faith. Likewise, preaching that fosters sectarian or interreligious animosity runs clearly counter to the mission of Christ. But this does not exclude careful exploration of traditional Christian teachings or winsome advocacy of Jesus.

Similarly, if in any place there is preaching which simply props up an institution, confirms a community's prejudices, sees itself as the only true means of mission, or bores people to death, such preaching deserves only to die and be buried. If, however, there is preaching which interprets the times for God's people engaged in his mission, affirms the whole gamut of their activities as a potential agent of it, encourages and inspires them in their task, and speaks good news to the hearts of any who hear, such preaching deserves to flourish and grow. Moreover, as believers in God's power to redeem and transform, let us remember that preachers and congregations who have been active in maintaining the first kind may in time become those who practise the second.

The Church seeks to advance God's mission today by all sorts of means in addition to traditional manifestations of the Church's identity. Different settings call for different forms for Christian speech. A discussion group in a pub is a very different environment from a big celebration in a church. Of course, in the former preaching will be 're-imagined' or, more likely, removed altogether. In the latter it will still often be a pivotal and very helpful part of the occasion. A half-way house on which the jury is still out is 'café church', which seeks to mingle elements of a traditional service with elements of informality. A hybrid is not always healthy; if you are going to have a 'talk' in any normal sense, then it is probably unhelpful to speaker and hearers to encourage people to go and fill up with coffee and doughnuts while it is proceeding. However, if it is the kind of group where focused, informal discussion will be productive, this may surely often be a better way of truly engaging with people – including the 'others' whom such settings seek to attract – than a formal address. But again, a missionary spirit precludes generalization.

One assumption that needs to be challenged is that small-group discussion and informality is inevitably more attractive and less threatening to newcomers than an address in a formal setting. It depends entirely on the people concerned. Many, indeed, will value the former kind of arena and will soon feel at home there. Others may find it very off-putting to be invited to an informal gathering where they hardly know anyone and are expected to be forthcoming in discussion before they have had opportunity to learn whom they can trust and to what extent. For such people, taking part in a formal occasion where they are free to listen to an address and then reflect on it in their own time and space, with others or not as they wish, is a far more helpful way to be introduced to the way and people of Christ. A vital element, of course, in making it helpful will be the sermon itself. Browbeating and hectoring will drive people away. But an inviting approach that truly respects the hearers' freedom may be at the same time deeply challenging and deeply heartwarming. All this suggests that even within a local church, only a *range* of missionary patterns can begin to deal adequately with the variety of the population in their situations and needs.

Thus preaching evolves and adapts naturally in response to a genuine missionary impulse. It may change – in some settings, almost beyond recognition – but one cannot predict or prescribe how. Calls that 'preaching must change' because a shifting culture means a different missionary context do not therefore take us very far, and adopting new off-the-peg solutions is no more satisfactory than adopting old off-the-peg ones. Hence the importance of readers doing their own practical theological reflection by asking what *their* missionary situation demands by way of preaching.

The complexity of this picture, in which preaching rightly develops in different ways in different places, is well illustrated and informed by the story of changing media of communication.[7] Christian preaching arose in predominantly oral cultures where a good storyteller like Jesus could gather an open-air crowd in Galilee, and a good debater like Paul could hold his own in the forum at Athens. The dynamic of preaching subtly changes, though, when the written text of Scripture becomes a key element. A public oral address will always be more intellectually challenging when it is commenting on a written text, which the hearers may or may not know well. This would have been especially so in the ancient world when literacy levels were much lower than they are today. Conversely, the words of the text would have been heard (and often memorized) far more carefully by those for whom the oral medium was their only access to it, and the words of the preacher would often have been fastened on all the more eagerly as the main means of Christian education (or sometimes any education at all). It is not surprising, then, that within a culture of developing Christian literacy, the words of preachers came to be written down and, in many cases, circulated. That is, the spoken word was not fetishized above the written, but each fed into the other. Many biblical commentaries of the Fathers (and later teachers) started out as sermons, while many texts of 'sermons' preserved from the past show signs of having been edited for the edification of a wider readership in their published form.[8]

The invention of printing permitted both more sophisticated forms of Bible-based preaching (the preacher could easily have his own vernacular text of Scripture to prepare and preach from) and, in due course, more accountability (the listeners, too, had Bibles – at home if not in church). But as this era coincided with an age of intense controversy, it is not surprising that preaching, both Protestant and Catholic, could assume a strongly doctrinal (and often frankly partisan) caste. Mission

7 See Jolyon P. Mitchell, 1999, *Visually Speaking: Radio and the Renaissance of Preaching*, Edinburgh: T & T Clark; Andrew Walker, 1996, *Telling the Story*, London: SPCK; Shane Hipps, 2005, *The Hidden Power of Electronic Culture: How Media Shapes Faith, the Gospel and Church*, El Cajon, CA: Youth Specialities.
8 See for example Edwards' discussion of Bernard of Clairvaux in O. C. Edwards Jr, 2004, *A History of Preaching*, vol. 1, Grand Rapids: Eerdmans, pp. 185–97.

is conceived not just as reaching out with the gospel to unbelievers, or to humanity in general, but as correcting that which is perceived as wrong belief.

The story of the modern 'missionary' movement – beginning with the Catholic missionaries of the sixteenth century – despite its many episodes of heroism and genuinely Christian achievements, has also been, unfortunately, the story of competition between various versions of Christianity. A key tool in the process has been preaching in which the preacher is a channel for the propagation of certain interpretations of the Bible for which his Christian grouping stands. In the case of the multiplying Protestant groups, this became a question of advancing the case for a particular interpretation of the Bible, to which all the various groups had access, in competition with interpretations offered by other Protestants as well as Catholics. In the case of Catholic preaching, it was more a question of continuing to assert the authority of the Church to interpret, on the basis of its tradition, the Bible to which, by and large, its members did *not* have access. Indeed, this assertion needed now to be more forceful precisely because of the way in which alternative readings were multiplying.

It could be argued, then, that the consequence of preaching's relationship to mission in post-Reformation times has been ambivalent. On the one hand, it has taken advantage of the invention of printing to open up the Scriptures in far greater depth and to a far wider audience than was previously possible; at its best it harnessed this fresh possibility to foster a love of truth with mind, heart and spirit. On the other hand, it has fostered a renewed authoritarianism and sectarianism, both Protestant and Catholic.

It is this negative side of preaching, particularly, to which writers such as Murray, Norrington and Pagitt have responded. One could say that the coincidence of the Reformation and the invention of printing has, in subsequent centuries, unleashed further the potential of preaching for harm as well as good, just as it unleashed the ambivalent potential of Christian mission. Perhaps, then, it is right to see the apparently quite 'pragmatic' issue of changing media of communication as central to the rediscovery of an appropriate relationship between preaching and mission today.

Six hundred years since printing was invented, and in the wake of many other cultural developments related to communication, it is indeed important to assess the trajectory preaching has followed and redirect it as needed for the right missionary ends. Now that the vast majority of congregation members (whether Catholic or Protestant) either own or have ready access to Bibles, not to mention many sources of help in understanding and applying them apart from preaching, the educational 'mission' of the preacher is not what it was in the earlier post-Reformation years.[9] Moreover, now that we can honestly face the disunity that has followed in the wake of the Reformation, we recognize the harm that can be done by over-dogmatic interpretations of the Bible, and more Christians from all the main denominations are now open to genuine learning from those of other traditions.

In this climate, it is interesting that various thinkers have been advocating a return to the attempt to listen to the Bible as a challenging and disturbing text, so as to echo and replicate it in its strangeness, as a text that upsets our traditions as much as it may confirm them.[10] The Reformers may have believed that 'the reformed Church always needs to be reformed' but in practice preaching has often served to validate that which was 'reformed' in a previous generation, rather than motivate the ongoing 'reform' that is needed in every generation.

Therefore it is anachronistic to think of preaching as necessarily a primary means of educating people in biblical truth; and to use preaching as a means of solidifying division in the Church is to perpetuate a discredited past. What, however, might preaching be within the context of a mission that is sensitive to the current dynamics of communication?

Walter Ong has referred to our era as one of 'secondary orality'.[11] With the advent of various electronic media, the nature and forms of written 'text' and oral 'speech' have become confusingly intermingled. After the era of print in which 'writtenness' reigned, along with all its implications of order, predictability, logic and fixity, we have entered an era in which orality has come to the fore again: not, now, as in the era of the largely pre-literate world of 'primary orality', but with all the resources of written and printed texts of the last few hundred years at our disposal to play with. 'Play' is an appropriate word here. For one of the main characteristics of this era is the subversion of those very notions of order, fixity and so on that have been associated with writing and the printed word. This is evident on the most everyday level in our culture, as we 'talk' to people freely by sending 'text' messages (an

---

9 See Stephen I. Wright, 2010, 'The Future Use of the Bible in the Future of Preaching', in Geoffrey Stevenson (ed.), *The Future of Preaching*, London: SCM, pp. 84–100.

10 See John W. Wright, 2007, *Telling God's Story: Narrative Preaching for Christian Formation*, Downers Grove, IL: InterVarsity Press Academic, and the many works of Walter Brueggemann.

11 Walter J. Ong, 2002, *Orality and Literacy*, 2nd edn, London: Routledge, p. 10.

informal, 'oral' kind of 'writing') or engaging in live 'chat' online through typing on a keyboard. The boundary between the freedom and spontaneity of oral speech, on the one hand, and the formality and preparedness of writing, on the other, has been breached. On the philosophical level, Jacques Derrida has argued that (contrary to modernist claims and assumptions) writing in fact gives even more scope for fluidity in interpretation than speech.[12] The fixed appearance of the printed word (enhanced by tools like dictionaries) is now seen as an illusion.

This situation means that preaching which mimics the forms of textual and literary order (as much preaching has done in modern times) is increasingly seen as culturally inappropriate.[13] Why read a learned discourse in a literary style when most people would now be able to read it themselves, and would gain much more from it by being able to do so in their own time, looking backwards and forwards to gain in understanding, and so on? (And, indeed, converse with the writer on her blog?) Our cultural expectation is that oral communication will be more engaging and immediate. We can go to the books, and online resources, if and when we want to; a live speaker can largely assume that. In most settings, speech is a time for encounter, not for high-flown discourse that just replicates what would be better put in writing. Mission-minded thinking about preaching should have no problem with this. After all, the 'literate' modernist approach was a natural 'missionary' response to changing culture too; our problems only arise when we set such an approach in stone, imagining it to be timelessly fitting.

Another way of conceiving of our present communication preferences is as the return of the image, repressed by the modern age of the printed word. Interestingly, in his analysis of postmodernism, the architect Charles Jencks specifically identifies modernity with the ascendancy of Protestantism, the (austere?) religion of the word.[14] He sees in 'postmodern' art and culture a sense of liberation from the constraints of order which that era entailed, as it were a return of the 'Catholic' emphasis on image, visible sign, sacrament and embodiment. Historically this may be a sweeping judgement, as the interplay of religious and wider 'cultural' forces is always complex. But in its symbolizing of a mood, Jencks' analysis is surely right. Electronic media, again, have

---

12 Jacques Derrida, 1988, *Of Grammatology*, corrected ed., trans. G. C. Spivak, Baltimore: Johns Hopkins University Press.

13 See Richard A. Jensen, 1994, *Thinking in Story: Preaching in a Post-Literate Age*, Lima, OH: CSS Publications.

14 Charles Jencks, 1996, *What is Post-Modernism?* 4th edn, London: Academy Editions, pp. 21–40.

played an enormous part in the return of the image. Any individual – including public speakers – with access to the internet and the right computer software has access to, and can pass on to others, any of an infinite range of images – photographic, artistic, manipulated, still or moving, quiet or with sound. And this is the way in which we are accustomed to receive and share much of our communication.

On the one hand, the immediacy of images may make communication much more vivid, moving and evocative than that which is limited to words alone. On the other hand, their openness to varied interpretation may make it more confusing,[15] while at the same time – unless used with care – more open to manipulative tactics than words alone. Thus a sermon which uses a picture of a starving child near its beginning, in order to remind people of the needs of the world into which Christ came, may thereby make its initial point powerfully and helpfully. But a sermon which uses that picture towards its end, as part of a challenge to obey Jesus' teaching today through generous giving, will probably be manipulating the hearers unhelpfully, seeking to take away the freedom which is a non-negotiable part of our responses to God and to other people.

Present-day preaching evinces various creative responses to this complex character of our communication. For some, the affirmation or rediscovery of sign, symbol and sacrament as vital elements of worship alongside preaching holds 'word' and 'image' in healthy balance. Andrew Walker argues along these lines, with the hope that the 'word' or the 'story' will be made *visible* again.[16] For others, the sensitive use of multi-media technology is seen as an important way of enhancing preaching. For yet others, it is storytelling, drama, narrative-shaped sermons,[17] the use of vivid word-pictures or direct interaction with the congregation that will enable preaching to be a true moment of encounter appropriate to an age of 'secondary orality' and the return of the image.

Such responses take seriously the critiques of much 'modernist' preaching from the 'print' era. They also demonstrate that just to assert that 'preaching has had its day' is much too simplistic. In some ways, in fact, preaching seems to be returning to styles and forms which it

15 Cf. Jean Baudrillard, 1983, *Simulations*, trans. Paul Foss, Paul Patton and Philip Bleitchman, New York: Semiotext.

16 Walker, *Telling the Story*.

17 See Roger Standing, 2004, *Finding the Plot: Preaching in Narrative Style*, Milton Keynes: Paternoster; Richard Littledale, 2007, *Stale Bread: Refreshing a Preaching Ministry*, Edinburgh: St Andrew Press.

possessed in the era of 'primary orality' before the arrival of print. For example, it is now more common to hear sermons which arise naturally out of a biblical passage – whether they consist of a verse-by-verse exposition or a shorter homily or perhaps a narrative rendering – than those which follow an elaborate format of subdivisions or points, a structure derived from the classical disciplines of dialectic and rhetoric.[18] The latter format became popular in the late Middle Ages, gained further impetus from some post-Reformation doctrinal preaching, then from later preaching theorists such as John Broadus.[19] (The familiar 'three-point sermon' is a simplified version.) Immediacy and naturalness are now much more likely to be the watchwords, as they surely were in the preaching of Jesus and many who followed him in the early Christian era.[20] One might say that we are learning again to be 'missionary' preachers as our first forebears were.

There can surely be no doubt that despite the unprecedented wealth of 'information' of all kinds – reliable and otherwise – there is increasing poverty of knowledge of the Christian story, Scriptures and traditions, often even among those who attend church regularly. This might be thought to challenge my statement that today's missionary context of communication requires preaching to be concerned with encounter rather than education. I would argue to the contrary. In a culture where (despite all the changes) people do still gather, and do still debate and discuss, and do still listen to lectures and speeches, and where there is exponential growth in demand for continuing education of all kinds, there are many excellent opportunities for Christian learning. In such a culture, there are educational resources and potential available which will never be available in the normal church setting where sermons happen. What is uniquely available in the church setting is the orientation and atmosphere of Christian worship. In that setting, preaching is essentially an appetite-whetter. Yes, the fundamentals of the Gospel must

---

18 My MTh student Gary Jenkins has shown that in Evangelical Anglicanism, for instance, the influence of Charles Simeon and John Stott leads to a kind of preaching ordered according to the sequence of a biblical text rather than an elaborate rhetorical schema; though Stott's expository preaching certainly adopted a more ordered rhetorical form than that of Martyn Lloyd-Jones. Gary Jenkins, 2010, 'The Influence of Simeon and Stott on Evangelical Anglican Preaching in the Church of England', unpublished MTh dissertation, London: Spurgeon's College/University of Wales.

19 John Broadus, 1874, *A Treatise on the Preparation and Delivery of Sermons*, London: Hamilton Adams.

20 Maybe, indeed, we can see precedent for the revival of the image in preaching in Paul's words to the Galatians: 'Who has bewitched you, before whose eyes Jesus Christ *was publicly portrayed as crucified*?' (Gal. 3.1).

be taught and re-taught. Yes, congregations must be introduced to the contours of our great story and regularly reminded of them; they must be helped to handle the Scriptures that bear witness to them. But above all, they must be led towards an encounter with Jesus, the subject and object of the gospel and the central character of the story: an encounter which will propel them on a journey of lifelong discipleship, learning his way via all sorts of means and people, not just as an intellectual pursuit but as a way of life. With all the adjustments that preaching rightly makes in response to the missionary demands of the time, as God-directed utterance within worship it continues to fulfil a unique role.

A church which is aware of its missionary task is called to be alert to the times as well as the old, old story which has made it who and what it is. A part of this alertness will be to the changes in society and culture – including patterns of communication – which may call for a change in attitudes to and forms of preaching. Those committed to a preaching ministry need have no fear of such alertness. Upon examination, they will surely find that it arises from the same impulse which propelled them to preach in the first place: the impulse to extend the kingdom of God into the world in word and action, celebrating and continuing the ministry of Christ. In this great missionary enterprise, no form of preaching is sacrosanct; the idea of 'preaching' itself should not become a mere mantra, or sacred cow that cannot be touched.[21] The ordinary preacher in his or her week-by-week task should not overestimate its place in the great scheme of things. For many, an encounter with a friendly Christian in a shelter for the homeless, an informal discussion in a pub, or an online home-study course may turn out to be far more significant means of meeting the Lord and growing in grace. But nor, by any means, should the preacher underestimate what they do. Anyone who through the words they speak can be for a group of people on a regular basis a gateway to encounter with God, a glimpse of Christ, a stimulus to faith and to deeper discipleship, is performing an incalculable service in God's mission. And they need and deserve all the encouragement from the wider Church, in its leadership, structures, and local fellowships, that they can get.

The local level

If preaching is a task belonging to the whole Church, this must be expressed not only in grand statements about the Church's mission, but

---

21 See Jeremy Thomson, 1996, *Preaching as Dialogue: Is the Sermon a Sacred Cow?*, Cambridge: Grove.

also in the concrete realities of local church life. In practice this means shared decision-making about the worship, outreach and educational ministries of the Church and a readiness by congregations to engage in active partnership with the preachers for their encouragement and the sharper discernment of God's word by all.

In Chapter 2 we noted the important contribution preaching makes to worship. This context can both save preaching from self-importance and enable it to play a pivotal role in the formation of Christian consciousness. If this is to work in practice, it depends on co-operation among all those responsible for organizing services. Dissonances in corporate worship may partly be caused by the failure to 'fit' preaching appropriately into the whole. If the preaching is not allowed to have any serious effect on the kind of songs that are sung or the kind of prayers that are prayed, worshippers readily suffer confusion (at least unconsciously) and a splitting of consciousness. This is not to advocate the rigid adoption of a 'theme' for a whole service: such services, in fact, are in danger of narrowing the richness of the gospel and replacing a mood of spiritual expectation with a mood of didacticism. But if the theology of the sermon and that of other parts of the service are markedly at odds, it scarcely encourages worshippers to sing and pray with the mind as well as the spirit (1 Cor. 14.1). In the longer term, a compartmentalizing of the sermon and other parts of the service may contribute subtly to a weakening of the identity of that part of the body of Christ.

The context of worship may make things more difficult for the preacher. Worship that is trivial, banal or self-serving provides an inhospitable atmosphere for the word of God to be proclaimed. Sometimes the whole setting may imply that the preaching is devalued. For example, if the Eucharist dominates too much over preaching, there remains the perpetual danger of a superstitious faith, a faith which is indeed 'acted out' and may be deeply felt, but is not *informed* in a way which can lead to mature discipleship. In such a setting, the sermon becomes a more difficult time for both preacher and congregation because of the (probably unspoken) sense that is of secondary importance.

If preaching, on the other hand, dominates over everything else, including the Eucharist, there remains the perpetual danger that the preacher's office and person, or the sermon itself, may be allowed to exceed their station, and human activity, human words, shape consciousness more deeply than the regular enacted reminder of God's work in Christ. Maybe some Christian hostility to preaching in recent years is a reaction to a kind of preaching which has transgressed its natural boundaries. To those who complain that preaching is the prime instance of the inordinate 'wordiness' of Christianity, we might respond that the central traditions of Christian worship have always sought to balance word with action in the drama of the Eucharist. Preaching interprets the Eucharist; the Eucharist dramatizes the good news that is preached and assists the worshippers to take it to their hearts.

The local church's ministries of outreach and education may also entail preaching, and it should be a matter of responsible shared decision-making, sensitive to local needs, as to what part preaching plays in these. For example, in some churches, regular or occasional special services with an evangelistic sermon may be right. In other places, evangelistic activity may be focused on an Alpha® course. Elsewhere, it will be far less formal, and take the form of open discussions in neutral venues. Similarly, the vital task of teaching and nurturing people in the faith needs to be seen in a co-ordinated way. Teaching sermons on particular occasions can dovetail with study groups or midweek classes. One value of a teaching sermon is that its context within a service reminds the church, at least subliminally, that learning and study for the Christian (as for the Jewish tradition) is a spiritual activity, and indeed that only within the context of submissive reverence towards God can we be saved from intellectual pride. On the other hand, in some congregations it may be much better to have all 'teaching' carried out in an informal, interactive setting. This need be no less prayerful than a service, while allowing participation, an essential element of learning for many.

There is now a body of literature concerning ways in which preachers and congregations may co-operate so that preaching truly becomes a shared enterprise.[22] If such a venture is to succeed, it is fundamental that the congregation should 'own' the event of preaching, not seeing it as the preserve of the preacher alone, and that the church together should initiate the co-operation, rather than leaving it to the preacher to persuade others to enter into partnership with him or her. Such partnership will often entail a culture shift, in both its initiation and its execution. A sense of the preacher as the resident 'expert' or

---

22 See for example David J. Schlafer, 2004, *Playing with Fire: Preaching Work as Kindling Art*, Cambridge, MA: Cowley; Roger E. Van Harn, 2005, *Preacher, Can You Hear Us Listening?*, Grand Rapids: Eerdmans; McClure, *Roundtable Pulpit*; Geoffrey Stevenson and Stephen Wright, 2008, *Preaching with Humanity: A Practical Guide for Today's Church*, London: Church House Publishing, pp. 108–15.

authority-figure dies hard, even in contemporary culture. Yet a dethroning of this perception could go a great distance towards disarming the critics of preaching.

This kind of co-operation is predicated not on the idea that 'the preacher needs support', still less on some secular ideal of democratizing the word of God, but on the conviction that the Spirit who leads us into all the truth is given to all believers in Jesus. If God's truth is to be discerned in Scripture and his way followed in the world, this cannot but be a shared enterprise. The preacher has a special responsibility within this, for seeking to hear and articulate what God is saying. But she or he needs the insights of God's people, not just in order to make 'relevant application' but in order to be saved from idiosyncrasy and grasp God's truth more richly.

The effectiveness of all kinds of informal absorption by the preacher of others' insight, especially through regular pastoral work, should not be underplayed. Yet there are several forms that more intentional co-operation might take. For example, David Schlafer has demonstrated, in his writing and practice, the effectiveness of 'preaching discernment groups' in which the 'conversation' of the sermon is, as it were, prolonged.[23] A group meets at some point in the following week to discuss it, not in order to pick it apart, but as a spiritual act of continuing to listen to the voice of God. This forms a healthy context for the development of the preacher's skills, but that is a secondary aim, not the primary one. It may also be combined with opportunities for preacher and hearers to meet before the preaching occasion so that, for instance, different insights into the passage of Scripture may be gleaned. The preacher, as appointed spokesperson, takes responsibility for the way in which such insights are, or are not, incorporated into the sermon. But the hearing of them will have given him or her a richer sense of how the Bible is *already* connecting with people, before the sermon ever begins.

Leonora Tubbs Tisdale outlines a thorough process of 'congregational exegesis' which will enable a preacher to gain a far more in-depth grasp of the outlook and values of hearers than is possible through casual osmosis alone.[24] This may sound over-analytical or intrusive, but in fact is simply a matter of attending more deeply in order to communicate more deeply. It is also rooted in a healthy concept of 'local

---

23 Schlafer, *Playing with Fire*, pp. 133–48.

24 Leonore Tubbs Tisdale, 1997, *Preaching as Local Theology and Folk Art*, Minneapolis: Fortress, pp. 64–89.

theology' which recognizes that God's word needs to be earthed in different ways in different places. Congregations who are made aware of what the preacher is doing should appreciate the care that this shows. There are many other possibilities for co-operation, of different kinds: questionnaires, interviews, keeping 'diaries' as listeners,[25] and so on. Preachers may work closely with drama groups or those with other skills, such as technological ones. And preachers may share with other preachers, for instance in regular discussion of forthcoming lectionary readings.

The key, once more, is that there should be no thoughtless buying-in to an off-the-peg way of instigating such co-operation. As the people of God seek to discern the word of God in their local situation, contributing to the articulation of it by the preacher, they need to find a shared means of doing that which fits them. The benefits, potentially, are enormous, both in raising Christian people's sense of shared responsibility for discovering and doing the will of God, and in relieving a preacher's sense of loneliness in the task.

Questions for the local church

- In what way does preaching, of one kind or another, fit into the mission of your local church? How is it related to other activities?
- How can your church be doing its part to foster and encourage the ministry of those who may be called to preach in the future?
- What processes would help preachers and congregation to work together so that preaching becomes a more deeply shared event?

Areas for research

The ways in which particular groups of people respond to God's message as culture and technology change will continue to be a vital area of investigation for those concerned with Christian mission. A range of co-operative ventures between congregation and preacher in seeking to deepen shared listening to God's word might also be the subject of illuminating research projects.

---

25 Roger E. Van Harn, 1992, *Pew Rights: For People who Listen to Sermons*, Grand Rapids: Eerdmans, pp. 155–9.

Further reading

Michael J. Quicke, 2003, *360-degree Preaching: Hearing, Speaking and Living the Word*, Grand Rapids/Carlisle: Baker/Paternoster.

David J. Schlafer, 2004, *Playing with Fire: Preaching Work as Kindling Art*, Cambridge, MA: Cowley.

Geoffrey Stevenson (ed.), 2010, *The Future of Preaching*, London: SCM.

10

Tasks for the Preacher

The immediate temptation in this final chapter is to try to round things off in thoroughly pragmatic vein with 'ten top tips for the preacher' or some such. Such is the pragmatist culture that so often reigns, even in the Church, with a plethora of how-to books available, that such a move almost feels like a 'default position' when writing about preaching. But of course it would fly in the face of all that I have been trying to achieve in this book. Rather, I aim here simply to 'anticipate the consequences'[1] of our discussion so far for preachers, not to establish rules or prescribe remedies. These consequences fall into two halves: the preacher's ongoing disposition, and the process of sermon preparation, delivery and reflection.

The preacher's ongoing disposition

If my theological understanding of preaching as developed in Part 3 carries weight, it should be clear that the preacher's first task is to do nothing at all, except gladly to recognize that God is a communicative God who has spoken to us fully and gloriously in Jesus Christ and continues to speak by his Spirit, the Spirit of Jesus. The preacher can relax. God is in charge. However much we may try to 'get God right', to speak words which echo his, God's speech is never going to be within our control. He is going to say things to people which were not what we intended or, very likely, ever dreamed of. This realization provides the essentially relaxed disposition of prayer, in which we acknowledge our total dependence on God. We are renewed in this sense through intentional periods set aside for coming before God, but it is a disposition that we can carry round with us the whole time.

---

1 I borrow this term from the final stage of Lowry's famous 'homiletical plot': Eugene L. Lowry, 2001, *The Homiletical Plot: The Sermon as Narrative Art Form*, expanded edn, Louisville: Westminster John Knox, pp. 80–8.

The effect of this realization – paradoxically, perhaps – is not to de-motivate us or rob us of a sense of our human responsibility, but rather to energize us and enable us to embrace our task the more gladly. Once we realize that speaking the word of God is (surprise, surprise?!) the work of God, the pressure is off and we are free to do our part as signs, pointers and sacraments, listening to God, echoing his gospel, making sense of his word and world, speaking his truth to the power-structures of the world. We are free to work with others in discerning God's word for now. We are free to exploit the God-given potential of language, media and rhetoric, explored in Chapter 3, in the service of being sacra-ments of the word. We are free to develop the identity-forming power of shared speech, explored in Chapter 4, to help form communities, not defensive and exclusive ones, but ones in which the truth is shared in love. We are free to use our personalities, in process of being made whole (Chapter 4 again), in discerning and proclaiming God's word. As we do so we will be preaching not as an end in itself but in service to the mission of the Church (Chapter 9), in the various contexts in which that mission is carried out (Chapter 2).

The process of sermon preparation, delivery and reflection

Preparation

Within this overarching atmosphere of prayerful trust in God and glad use of the gifts he has given us in the context in which he has placed us, the process of preparation will surely begin by assessing the kind of pat-tern or practice of preaching that is called for on a particular occasion (Chapter 8). This is not to say that all occasions will neatly fit into one of those practices identified there – as I made clear. But it is to make the perhaps obvious, yet crucial point, that the answer to the questions of what to say and how to say it must be profoundly conditioned not only by our prayerful listening to God but also by our grasp of the con-text. Our God is a God who communicates in specific terms, times and places, with specific people; our communication can do no less.

The distinction between 'what to say' and 'how to say it', although never watertight, is nonetheless a very useful one. Craddock explains it well.[2] It enables us to preserve the sense that before we ever get down to 'writing a sermon', we are called to listen to God and what his word might be for this occasion. This listening will involve careful listening

---

2 Fred B. Craddock, 1985, *Preaching*, Nashville: Abingdon.

to the text(s) of Scripture for the occasion (whether chosen for us or by us), the congregation, the world around and our own hearts. In and through a combination of all these modes of listening we can expect to hear the Spirit speak.[3]

The form of a speech or piece of writing is never 'neutral', and will always in some way shape understanding of the content. So it is that when we move from 'what to say' to 'how to say it', there should be an organic connection between them. Hence the emphasis among some of the most distinguished modern preachers on allowing the biblical text to shape one's sermon as well as provide its essential content. This is true not only for the 'new homiletic' practitioners in North America – for example, Fred Craddock's advocacy of reproducing for the congregation the preacher's own journey of discovery with the text,[4] and Thomas Long's exploration of how the literary forms of the Bible may shape preaching on those texts[5] – but also, in a different way, for the brand of 'expository' preaching practised by John Stott in the UK.[6] A sermon that takes a form or shape that is quite alien to the message it seeks to communicate will usually end up as a poor act of communication.

The preacher's task, therefore, is to plan the communication of the message in a form and structure that will allow that message to achieve its work in as wide a range of hearers as possible.[7] We must reiterate that the effect of the message is always beyond the preacher's control; but our calling is to imitate a God whose communication has been anything but careless.

The structure of the sermon will be influenced not only by considerations of the text, the occasion and the congregation, but also of the preacher's background, personality and preferred style – all of which may show themselves in unconscious ways, and which it is therefore helpful to seek to raise to consciousness as much as possible. As with the 'patterns and practices' of preaching considered in Chapter 8, it is

---

3 See David J. Schlafer, 1992, *Surviving the Sermon: A Guide for Those Who Have to Listen*, Cambridge, MA: Cowley, pp. 39–58.

4 Fred B. Craddock, 2001, *As One without Authority*, 2nd edn, St Louis, Chalice Press.

5 Thomas G. Long, *Preaching and the Literary Forms of the Bible*, Philadelphia: Fortress; 2005, 'The Use of Scripture in Contemporary Preaching', in David Day et al. (eds), *A Reader on Preaching: Making Connections*, Aldershot: Ashgate, pp. 34–42.

6 I am indebted to Gary Jenkins for his highlighting of this point in Gary Jenkins, 2010, 'The Influence of Simeon and Stott on Evangelical Anglican Preaching in the Church of England', unpublished MTh dissertation, London: Spurgeon's College/University of Wales.

7 See Geoffrey Stevenson and Stephen Wright, 2008, *Preaching with Humanity: A Practical Guide for Today's Church*, London: Church House Publishing, pp. 72–7.

impossible to fit possible sermon structures into neat categories, simply because the demands of the occasion and the creativity of the preacher produce an almost infinite variety. It is important not to lose sight of the essential simplicity and yet mysterious wonder of the task in the midst of a plethora of options for sermon structure. I am deeply attracted by the straightforwardness of George Herbert's advice in the seventeenth century:

> The Parsons Method in handling of a text consists of two parts; first, a plain and evident declaration of the meaning of the text; and secondly, some choice Observations drawn out of the whole text, as it lyes entire, and unbroken in the Scripture it self. This he thinks naturall, and sweet, and grave. Whereas the other way of crumbling a text into small parts, as, the Parson speaking, or spoken to, the subject, and object, and the like, hath neither in it sweetnesse, nor gravity, nor variety, since the words apart are not Scripture, but a dictionary, and may be considered alike in all the Scripture.[8]

I quote Herbert not by way of discouraging creativity or decrying the many helpful approaches to sermon structure available,[9] but by way of reminder that at the heart of preaching is the simple act of one person opening up a biblical text for others. What follows is neither an exhaustive list nor a thorough evaluation of different structures, but rather an attempt to clarify some commonly used terms and concepts which can often be used loosely and therefore confusingly. It will be seen that these terms do not necessarily refer to mutually exclusive types of structure.

First, there is the 'expository' approach, in which the Bible itself may provide the structure for the sermon. This may happen in various ways. It may take the form of a quite informal, verse-by-verse commentary on the text (as seems to have happened often in the early Church). In modern times, Martyn Lloyd-Jones would preach through books of the Bible, sometimes taking a whole sermon to preach on a single verse. John Stott, on the other hand, while also concerned with preaching the whole of Scripture and preaching sermon series, gave a more ordered and systematic treatment of texts, not getting so immersed in details as to fail

---

8 George Herbert, *A Priest to the Temple*, VII, in F. E. Hutchinson (ed.), 1941, *The Works of George Herbert*, Oxford: Clarendon Press, pp. 234–5.

9 See for example Kenton C. Anderson, 2006, *Choosing to Preach: A Comprehensive Introduction to Sermon Options and Structures*, St Louis: Chalice Press.

to allow the overall message of a passage or book to appear.[10] In this respect Stott has been shown to be in the line of a great Anglican Evangelical of the nineteenth century, Charles Simeon.[11] But it is important to note that 'exposition' may take many forms. At its root, the ideal of exposition is not an ideal *structure* so much as an expression of what an ideal *posture towards* Scripture by the preacher should be. In this sense, many preachers would want to see themselves as 'expounding' Scripture, while not thinking of themselves as limited by this to a particular form. For example, David Day in his well-used *Preaching Workbook* affirms his desire to be an expository preacher,[12] but here and in his subsequent book[13] explores a wide range of creative approaches to preaching which all remain rooted in the expositor's desire for faithfulness to the text.

Second, there is 'deductive' preaching in which a proposition is stated, then broken down into sub-propositions, and deductions drawn from it for Christian belief and behaviour.[14] It is often, wrongly and confusingly, treated as being equivalent to an 'expository' approach. It is possible to expound Scripture without starting with a proposition and sub-propositions from which one then deduces conclusions. Similarly, it is possible to take a 'deductive' approach without really expounding Scripture (one might simply be expounding one's own 'take' on the Bible or doctrine, without any close engagement with the text). A deductive approach has the advantage of clarity, while carrying the risk of imposing over-neat systematization upon a text or a complex issue.

Third, there is the 'inductive' approach advocated by Craddock.[15] Craddock argued that to start a sermon by asserting a proposition is to assume a readiness on the part of the hearers to accept the preacher's authority that is no longer widely present. Craddock's book appeared initially in 1971 and this point, at least, is even more true now than it was then. The inductive strategy of starting at a place of human experience shared by preacher and congregation, leading the hearers into a discovery of how a biblical text addresses such an experience, and thus replicating the preacher's own journey of discovery, can powerfully cross

---

10 See his rationale for his approach in John R. W. Stott, 1982, *I Believe in Preaching*, London: Hodder & Stoughton.

11 See Jenkins, 'The Influence of Simeon and Stott'.

12 David Day, 1998, *A Preaching Workbook*, London, SPCK, p. 15.

13 David Day, 2005, *Embodying the Word: A Preacher's Guide*, London: SPCK.

14 See John Broadus, 1874, *A Treatise on the Preparation and Delivery of Sermons*, London: Hamilton Adams.

15 Craddock, *As One without Authority*; 2001, *The Cherry Log Sermons*, Louisville: Westminster John Knox.

the distance between preacher and hearer. It places the preacher firmly as a listener to God and a learner from Christ alongside the congregation. It can also lead to a satisfying journey in which the depiction of human experience at the beginning poses a question which is pursued until the disclosure of the key biblical truth at the end. In this way it does not run the same risk as deductive preaching that a single proposition or idea may get dissipated in the mass of detail into which it is broken down.

In practice, however, it may often be helpful to reach the key biblical truth somewhat before the end of the sermon, allowing an element of deduction to follow on from it. It depends on the occasion and the particular function the preacher seeks to achieve in the sermon. For example, a teaching sermon may often helpfully have a stronger element of deduction than other kinds; but that is not to say that teaching cannot be done inductively (educationalists would certainly agree!) or that deduction is not appropriate in other kinds of preaching practice.

Fourth, David Buttrick argued that humans have a common structure of consciousness which responds in a certain way to speech such as a sermon.[16] He therefore advocated that a sermon should consist of a series of carefully planned 'moves'. Each of these is to be clear in itself and also connect fluently to those around it. The aim of this chain of moves is not so much the expounding of truth or ideas as a symbolic disclosure of 'understandings of God, of God's mysterious purposes, and of unseen wonders of grace in human lives'.[17] The notion of a 'move' captures the enacted nature of preaching much better than the more cerebral notion of a 'point'. While this idea of 'moves' is a helpful way of thinking about sermon structure, many remain unconvinced that human consciousness (and concentration) can be described in such a generalized fashion, and therefore prescribed for in the detail that Buttrick offers.[18] Nevertheless, Buttrick takes very seriously the way in which people *actually* hear a sermon, and offers a model for thinking about this that must be taken equally seriously.

A fifth way of envisaging how a sermon should unfold uses the category of *narrative*. Various different possibilities are covered by the term 'narrative preaching'. In his book *The Homiletical Plot*, first published in 1980,[19] Eugene Lowry made a strong case that narrative should

---

16 David Buttrick, 1987, *Homiletic: Moves and Structures*, Philadelphia: Fortress.

17 Buttrick, *Homiletic*, p. 41.

18 See further the brief critique of Buttrick in Paul Scott Wilson, 2004, *Preaching and Homiletical Theory*, St Louis: Chalice Press, pp. 16–17.

19 Lowry, *Homiletical Plot*; 1997, *The Sermon: Dancing the Edge of Mystery*, Nashville: Abingdon.

provide the basic 'deep structure' of a sermon. Not only is this congruent with the widespread use of narrative in Scripture; it reflects the perennial appeal of narrative to hearers and readers. Suspense, character, plot, scene-setting, resolution, the invitation to imagine oneself in a particular world – all such structural features of narrative and more can feature in preaching. Lowry himself set out a classic five-stage narrative pattern that has become known as the 'Lowry Loop' (later adapted to four stages).[20] This continues to be a fruitful starting-point for thinking how particular sermons may take a congregation on a journey in which appetite is whetted, real difficulties honestly faced, and a satisfaction attained which nonetheless leaves hearers thinking about how the journey might be taken further.

Yet Lowry's proposal can be critiqued, along lines similar to the critique of Buttrick. Is narrative really such an all-embracing way of interpreting and communicating experience? Do hearers really respond to narratives in the stereotyped fashion which might seem to emerge from Lowry's schema?[21] And even if we did, would not the very pattern quickly become predictable and boring – one of the very things it was designed to counter?

Just as Buttrick's 'moves' can certainly not be ignored in discussing sermon structure, neither can Lowry's belief that in some way these can be explicitly planned as *narrative* 'moves'. Both yield much insight into what is going on in a speech-journey in time.[22] In addition to Lowry's 'loop', a range of other possibilities for narrative preaching have been explored, including the patterning of the sermon on a narrative text of Scripture,[23] and the use of different 'voices' or standpoints by the preacher, including first-person narrative.[24] John W. Wright develops a 'homiletical rhetoric of turning' designed to allow the often shocking

---

20 See his *The Sermon* and the expanded edition of *Homiletical Plot*.

21 Lowry himself has continued to modify and refine his initial proposal. For recent assessments of his idea of 'the homiletical plot' as it has developed, and faced criticism, see the essays in Mike Graves and David Schlafer (eds), 2008, *What's the Shape of Narrative Preaching?*, St Louis: Chalice Press, especially those by Richard L. Eslinger, 'Tracking the Homiletical Plot', pp. 69–86, and Thomas G. Long, 'Out of the Loop: The Changing Practice of Preaching', pp. 115–30.

22 On the theme of the sermon as an event in time see Eugene Lowry, 1985, *Doing Time in the Pulpit: The Relationship between Narrative and Preaching*, Nashville: Abingdon.

23 For example Eugene L. Lowry, *How to Preach a Parable: Designs for Narrative Sermons*, Nashville: Abingdon.

24 For example Roger Standing, 2004, *Finding the Plot: Preaching in Narrative Style*, Milton Keynes: Paternoster; Richard Littledale, 2007, *Stale Bread: Refreshing a Preaching Ministry*, Edinburgh: St Andrew Press.

force of the biblical narrative to be felt.[25] Charles Cosgrove and Dow Edgerton explore an approach of 'incarnational translation' in which biblical stories, and texts of other genres, are rendered in an idiom appropriate to the hearers.[26] All such strategies potentially appeal to the full human being in a more rounded way – to emotions, imagination and will as well as mind – than more linear structures: that is the nature of story. 'Truth embodied in a tale can enter in by lowly doors.'[27]

A sixth approach makes the involvement of the listeners a more overt part of the sermon. This is the stream of 'black preaching' in which the preacher regularly seeks and receives affirmation from the hearers as the sermon proceeds.[28] The presence of such affirmation is taken as assurance that the speech of the preacher is being rhetorically effective; the absence of it as undermining such assurance. Narrative plays a significant part in this kind of preaching also. There is a strong sense of a shared story binding preacher and congregation together, often deriving from the experience of oppression. This shared story is, as it were, enacted in preaching as the preacher seeks a dynamic and imaginative way of immersing the congregation in the biblical narratives.[29]

From one angle, this seems the most efficient means of ensuring the effectiveness of one's rhetoric as a preacher: genuine interaction. What could be better than hearing through the 'Amens' and 'Hallelujahs' of the listeners that they are attending, emotionally engaged, and agreeing? It is, however, important to guard against the possibility that habits of overt agreement may lead to unhealthy patterns of submission, manipulation and collusion. The element of genuine relationship, in which the honesty and freedom of both speaker and hearers are respected and honoured, needs to be preserved.

Still under the heading of interactive structures, others put a more fundamental question-mark against the idea of the monologue sermon. Various Christian groups have always placed a high value on the shared

---

25 John W. Wright, 2007, *Telling God's Story: Narrative Preaching for Christian Formation*, Downers Grove, IL: InterVarsity Press Academic, pp. 77–104.

26 Charles H. Cosgrove and W. Dow Edgerton, 2007, *In Other Words: Incarnational Translation for Preaching*, Grand Rapids: Eerdmans.

27 Alfred Lord Tennyson, *In Memoriam*, XXXVI, 7–8.

28 See Henry H. Mitchell, 1991, *Black Preaching: The Recovery of a Powerful Art*, Nashville: Abingdon.

29 On the connection between African-American preaching tradition and narrative approaches to preaching see William McClain, 2008, 'African American Contexts of Narrative Preaching', in Graves and Schlafer (eds), *What's the Shape of Narrative Preaching?*, pp. 55–66.

nature of the task of listening for and responding to the word of God.[30] In contemporary Church life, many forms of worship embraced by the loosely defined 'emerging Church' – including, for example, some of those in the 'Fresh Expressions' movement in the UK – entail an informal, interactive approach to 'preaching' which, it may be argued, stretches the definition of 'preaching' to breaking point or beyond.[31] This may involve a kind of dialogue led by a 'preacher' but left open-ended for others' contributions,[32] or group discussion, or some other form of attempt to discern and understand God's word in which the active participation of as many as possible is sought. Insofar as such activities tend consciously to displace a 'sermon' of other kinds, it is important to consider them as potential examples of good 'preaching' structure. They are an authentic attempt to take as many as possible on the journey of hearing the word of God. They encourage the preacher, as well as everyone else, to be a genuine listener. Interactive preaching can allow the congregation's experiences of the world to mesh with the preacher's more specialized understanding of the text – as well as providing insights into the text itself from a range of perspectives.[33] It may even (surprisingly, perhaps) be hospitable to 'speaking truth to power'. There may be no authoritative declarations here 'from the front', but it may be precisely in the interactions, as individuals are given permission to voice what is in their heart, that those barriers to the power of God's kingdom are owned, exposed and allowed, in the supportive ambience of grace, to come tumbling down.

Seventh, and finally, we consider briefly the incorporation of elements other than the spoken word into the sermon. The possibilities are endless, not least when technological facilities are available.[34] But the need for some kind of planned structure is as great in this kind of sermon as in any other. The mere use of pictures, objects, film clips and so on does not guarantee that the hearers will be taken on a journey that helpfully enables them to encounter God. Indeed, the introduction

---

30 Stuart Murray and others have highlighted the corporate nature of 'preaching' in the Anabaptist tradition, for example. See Stuart Murray, 'Interactive Preaching', *Evangel* 72, 2010, 'Preaching and Liturgy: An Anglican Perspective', pp. 53–7.

31 Cf. Roger Spiller, in Geoffrey Stevenson (ed.), 2010, *The Future of Preaching*, London: SCM, pp. 34–41, here p. 37.

32 Murray, 'Interactive Preaching'.

33 See Tim Stratford, 1998, *Interactive Preaching: Opening the Word then Listening*, Cambridge: Grove.

34 For helpful discussion of a range of ideas, including the use of Powerpoint®, see Day, *Embodying the Word*. See also Stevenson and Wright, *Preaching with Humanity*, pp. 105–7.

of other media needs careful management, since, as we have seen, the visual has much greater potential than the oral/aural both for touching people deeply and for sending ambiguous signals. It heightens the sense of preaching's ethical requirements, which must be the fundamental undergirding of whatever structure we adopt: the honesty, self-giving and attention, discussed in Chapter 3 as being basic to all rhetoric; and those which are peculiar to Christian preaching, listening, gospelling, interpreting and truth-speaking, discussed in Chapter 7.

In reviewing these approaches to planning the rhetorical journey of the sermon, we can see that there are no short-cuts or easy solutions to the discovery of a structure which will be engaging and persuasive for a whole range of hearers without being manipulative. Clearly, mutual knowledge and trust between speaker and hearers are very important factors. This does not disqualify the 'visitor' from the task of speaking, nor make satisfactory speaking to large groups impossible, but it does demonstrate the measure of the challenge.

Delivery

Learning to deliver a sermon is much more than a matter of technique, important though that is.[35] Indeed, 'delivery' is all too pedestrian a metaphor for what we are doing; 'performance' is much more satisfactory.[36] For in preaching, we are not merely handing over a package. We are actively relating with others face-to-face, sharing with them the truth which we have encountered on a deep level, in such a way that they may encounter it too. And that truth is personal – in fact, a Person. It is ultimately not through our words alone, but our whole person that that truth will be revealed.

We will have prepared a sermon, but simply to 'read out' what we have prepared is a travesty of preaching. We have prepared not simply a *script*, but *ourselves*, and what we now share we share *as from ourselves*, putting heart and soul into the task. The proper care and use of the voice is vital, but more fundamentality it is the 'voice' of our personality, given to God, which must come through.[37] Being true to our

---

35 For a discussion of what it means in practice to deliver a sermon with one's whole human personality, see Stevenson and Wright, *Preaching with Humanity*, pp. 82–107.

36 See Jana Childers, 2008, 'Recovering Performance', in Paul Scott Wilson (ed.), *The New Interpreter's Handbook of Preaching*, Nashville: Abingdon, pp. 213–15.

37 See David J. Schlafer, 1995, *Your Way with God's Word: Discovering Your Distinctive Preaching Voice*, Cambridge, MA: Cowley.

uniqueness as individuals – learning from others yet ultimately answerable to God alone – is an essential part of what it means to be holy, set apart for God and by God. Whether we use a full script or short notes or no notes at all; whether we use monologue, dialogue or wider interaction; these are secondary matters compared to the requirement that our hearers see that what we say comes from deep within us.

Some may depart from what they have prepared more than others. But again, the extent of such departure is not the main issue here, which is our calling to bring together our preparation and our sensitivity to the moment of speech in an outgoing act of gospel communication. This seems to me to require *both* thorough preparation (and for all but those with exceptional memories, this probably means the writing of a full script) *and* complete readiness to respond to the immediacy of the situation, if necessary by varying, adding to or subtracting from what has been prepared.[38] Preparation, surely, is a part of the self-giving creativity fundamental to the ethics of rhetoric. But the readiness for spontaneity is an outworking of the honesty and attention that are equally fundamental to such ethics. People must get at least a glimpse of the truth of you or me as preachers as we are *now*, not just veiled through a script we prepared a day or two before. And they must sense that we are attending to *them*, to their hungers and needs, to their responses, not just to our script or our notes. The delivery of a sermon can thus become a profound and central example of the fulfilment of our human calling as those destined to bear the image of God: of speaking truth in love.

Reflection

If preaching is seen in the properly corporate context which we outlined in Chapters 6 and 7, we will not regard the end of the sermon as the end of the event. All preachers know how significant, from various angles, are those moments, hours and days following a sermon in which we may receive some form of feedback from hearers, as well as entertaining a mixture of feelings about the event ourselves. It is vital that we recognize the ways in which people are responding, positively or negatively, to what we are saying. Structured forms of ongoing discussion such as

---

38 On this topic I remain very grateful for stimulating exchanges with my former PhD student Dr Daniel Sheard. See Daniel W. Sheard, 2005, 'Preaching in the Hear and Now: Justification, Development, and Assessment of 'Parabolic Engagement' Pedagogy in French-speaking Missionary Settings', unpublished PhD thesis, University of Wales.

those mentioned in Chapter 9 play a valuable role here. But attention to the hearers, whenever and however one encounters them, is vital. This is not primarily in order to seek affirmation for ourselves (though it is important to receive that gratefully when it is given) but to observe what the living God, in his sovereign freedom, is saying to people; and also to pick up any ways in which our sacramental pointing to him has become a barrier for some rather than a channel. Such feedback will usually *not* best be garnered by putting people on the spot, with a question like 'What did you think of my sermon?', which may often elicit either a bland or a confused response. Human response to communication is complex and people will often not find it easy to put into words what a particular sermon has meant to them. But if we are getting to know our hearers over a period of time, as individuals and as congregations, and make ourselves open to them, we will find that we gradually become more attuned to how and what they are hearing from God, and how we might serve them better in that process.

We thus return to the question of a preacher's ongoing disposition. A recognition that speaking the word of God is the work of God liberates us, after preaching, from taking personal offence at negative comments which may be made (even if said or meant offensively), as well as from taking pride in positive ones. We rejoice in the way in which God can use us, while gradually learning more and more about being a helpful pointer to him.

If we are to develop as preachers, some kind of review process is very valuable.[39] It would be impossible, of course, to do the kind of thorough review of preaching suggested by the pattern of this book for every sermon! But from time to time an intentional assessment of how one's preaching is going is useful, and I hope that the 'practical theology' model outlined here, focused in the questions at the end of the chapters, will be one helpful way of doing that. But my deeper concern is that something like the process outlined here will become, as it were, part of the bloodstream of every church and preacher, as they allow their practice to emerge from a continually renewed sense of what they are doing and why, as human beings bearing the image of God, caught up in the purpose of God, and alive to the word of God for the world within a loving community that embodies it.

---

39 See Charles Chadwick and Phillip Tovey, 2001, *Developing Reflective Practice for Preachers*, Cambridge: Grove; Keith Beech-Grüneberg and Phillip Tovey, 2007, *Evaluating the Use of the Bible in Preaching*, Cambridge: Grove.

Questions for the local church

- As a preacher, what is your pattern of preparation and how might it be enriched?
- Are there particular skills of delivery that you could work on to aid the process of communicating God's word in your true 'voice'?
- What kind of review process would it be helpful to initiate so that the preaching in the church is kept fresh?

Areas for research

The ways in which different kinds of hearers respond to different kinds of sermon structure would be an interesting topic to investigate. It would also be valuable to survey different approaches to sermon preparation and delivery and correlate these to preachers' denominations, traditions or personalities.

Further reading

Kenton C. Anderson, 2006, *Choosing to Preach: A Comprehensive Introduction to Sermon Options and Structures*, Grand Rapids: Zondervan.

David Day, 2005, *Embodying the Word: A Preacher's Guide*, London: SPCK.

Richard L. Eslinger, 2002, *The Web of Preaching: New Options in Homiletic Method*, Nashville: Abingdon.

Paul Scott Wilson, 2003, *Preaching and Homiletical Theory*, St Louis: Chalice Press.

Bibliography

Abraham, William J., 2002, *Canon and Criterion in Christian Theology: From the Fathers to Feminism*, Oxford: Oxford University Press.

Adam, Peter, 1996, *Speaking God's Words: A Practical Theology of Preaching*, Leicester: InterVarsity Press.

Anderson, Kenton C., 2006, *Choosing to Preach: A Comprehensive Introduction to Sermon Options and Structures*, St Louis: Chalice Press.

Augustine, 1977, *On Christian Doctrine*, trans. D. W. Robertson, Indianapolis: Bobbs-Merrill Educational Publishing.

Barr, James, 1961, *The Semantics of Biblical Language*, London: SCM.

Barth, Karl, 1975, *Church Dogmatics*, 1.1, *The Doctrine of the Word of God*, 2nd edn, trans. G. W. Bromiley, Edinburgh: T & T Clark.

Bartholomew, Craig G., 2005, 'Biblical Theology', in Vanhoozer, Kevin J. (ed.), *Dictionary for Theological Interpretation of the Bible*, Grand Rapids/London: Baker/SPCK, pp. 84–90.

Bartholomew, Craig and Goheen, Michael, 2006, *The Drama of Scripture: Finding our Place in the Biblical Story*, London: SPCK.

Bartholomew, Craig G. et al. (eds), 2006, *Canon and Biblical Interpretation*, Scripture and Hermeneutics Series 7, Carlisle: Paternoster.

Barton, John, 2007, *The Nature of Biblical Criticism*, Louisville: Westminster John Knox.

Bauckham, Richard, 2006, *Jesus and the Eyewitnesses: The Gospels as Eyewitness Testimony*, Grand Rapids: Eerdmans.

Baudrillard, Jean, 1983, *Simulations*, trans. Paul Foss, Paul Patton and Philip Bleitchman, New York: Semiotext.

Beech-Grüneberg, Keith, and Tovey, Phillip, 2007, *Evaluating the Use of the Bible in Preaching*, Cambridge: Grove.

Berger, Peter L. and Luckmann, Thomas, 1971, *The Social Construction of Reality*, Harmondsworth: Penguin.

Berne, Eric, 1964, *Games People Play: The Psychology of Human Relationships*, Harmondsworth: Penguin.

Black, C. Clifton, 2001, 'Augustinian Preaching and the Nurture of Christians', in Van Harn, Roger E. (ed.), *The Lectionary Commentary: Theological Exegesis for Sunday's Texts (The Third Readings: The Gospels)*, Grand Rapids: Eerdmans, pp. 603–14.

Blamires, Harry, 1963, *The Christian Mind*, London: SPCK.

Blythe, Stuart, 2009, 'Open-Air Preaching as Radical Street Performance', unpublished PhD thesis, University of Edinburgh.

Bonhoeffer, Dietrich, 2002, 'The Proclaimed Word', in Lischer, Richard (ed.), *The Company of Preachers: Wisdom on Preaching from Augustine to the Present*, Grand Rapids: Eerdmans, pp. 31–7.

Bonhoeffer, Dietrich, 1971, *Letters and Papers from Prison*, London: SCM.

Booth, Wayne C., 2004, *The Rhetoric of Rhetoric: The Quest for Effective Communication*, Malden, MA and Oxford: Blackwell.

Borg, Marcus J. and Crossan, J. Dominic, 2008, *The First Christmas: What the Gospels Really Teach about Jesus's Birth*, London: SPCK.

Bosch, David, 1991, *Transforming Mission: Paradigm Shifts in Theology of Mission*, New York: Orbis Books.

Boyd-Macmillan, Ronald, 2009, 'The Transforming Sermon: A Study of the Preaching of St. Augustine, with Special Reference to the *Sermones ad populum*, and the Transformation Theory of James Loder', unpublished PhD thesis, University of Aberdeen.

Broadus, John, 1874, *A Treatise on the Preparation and Delivery of Sermons*, London: Hamilton Adams.

Brosend, William, 2010, *The Preaching of Jesus: Gospel Proclamation, Then and Now*, Louisville: Westminster John Knox.

Brown, David, 1999, *Tradition and Imagination: Revelation and Change*, Oxford: Clarendon Press.

Brown, Rosalind, 2009, *Can Words Express the Wonder? Preaching in the Church Today*, Norwich: Canterbury Press.

Browne, R. E. C., 1976, *The Ministry of the Word*, 2nd edn, London: SCM.

Brueggemann, Walter, 1989, *Finally Comes the Poet*, Minneapolis: Fortress Press.

Brueggemann, Walter, 2003, *An Introduction to the Old Testament: The Canon and Christian Imagination*, Louisville: Westminster John Knox.

Butler, Angela, 1999, *Personality and Communicating the Gospel*, Cambridge: Grove.

Buttrick, David, 1987, *Homiletic: Moves and Structures*, Philadelphia: Fortress.

Campbell, Charles L., 1997, *Preaching Jesus: New Directions for Homiletics in Hans Frei's Postliberal Theology*, Grand Rapids: Eerdmans.

Campbell, Charles L., 2002, *The Word before the Powers: An Ethic of Preaching*, Louisville: Westminster John Knox.

Chadwick, Charles and Tovey, Phillip, 2001, *Developing Reflective Practice for Preachers*, Cambridge: Grove.

Childers, Jana, 2008, 'Recovering Performance', in Wilson, Paul Scott (ed.), *The New Interpreter's Handbook of Preaching*, Nashville: Abingdon, pp. 213–15.

Childs, Brevard S., 1979, *Introduction to the Old Testament as Scripture*, Philadelphia: Fortress.

Clark, Neville, 1991, *Preaching in Context: Word, Worship and the People of God*, Bury St Edmunds: Kevin Mayhew.

Clark, Timothy, 1999, 'Literature and the Crisis in the Concept of the University', in Fuller, David and Waugh, Patricia (eds), *The Arts and Sciences of Criticism*, Oxford: Oxford University Press, pp. 217–37.

Colwell, John E., 2001, *Living the Christian Story: The Distinctiveness of Christian Ethics*, Edinburgh and New York: T & T Clark.

Colwell, John E., 2005, *Promise and Presence: An Exploration of Sacramental Theology*, Milton Keynes: Paternoster.

Cosgrove, Charles H. and Edgerton, W. Dow, 2007, *In Other Words: Incarnational Translation for Preaching*, Grand Rapids: Eerdmans.

Craddock, Fred B., 1985, *Preaching*, Nashville: Abingdon.

Craddock, Fred B., 2001, *As One without Authority*, 2nd edn, St Louis, Chalice Press.

Craddock, Fred B., 2001, *The Cherry Log Sermons*, Louisville: Westminster John Knox.

Cross, F. L. (ed.), 1958, *The Oxford Dictionary of the Christian Church*, London: Oxford University Press.

Dawn, Maggi, 1997, 'You have to change to stay the same', in Cray, Graham et al., *The Post-Evangelical Debate*, London: SPCK, pp. 35–56.

Day, David, 1998, *A Preaching Workbook*, London: SPCK.

Day, David, 2005, *Embodying the Word: A Preacher's Guide*, London: SPCK.

Derrida, Jacques, 1988, *Of Grammatology*, corrected edn, trans. G. C. Spivak, Baltimore: Johns Hopkins University Press.

Dodd, C. H., 1936, *The Apostolic Preaching and its Developments*, London: Hodder & Stoughton.

Edwards, O. C., 2004, *A History of Preaching*, 2 vols, Grand Rapids: Eerdmans.

Ellis, Christopher J., 2004, *Gathering: A Theology and Spirituality of Worship in Free Church Tradition*, London: SCM.

Eslinger, Richard L., 2008, 'Tracking the Homiletical Plot', in Graves, Mike and Schlafer, David (eds), *What's the Shape of Narrative Preaching?*, St Louis: Chalice Press, pp. 69–86.

Eusebius, 1975, *Oration in Honour of Constantine on the Thirtieth Anniversary of his Reign*, in Wiles, Maurice and Santer, Mark (eds), *Documents in Early Christian Thought*, Cambridge: Cambridge University Press.

Forde, Gerhard O., 2007, 'Preaching the Sacraments', in Mattes, Mark C. and Paulson, Steven D. (eds), *The Preached God*, Grand Rapids: Eerdmans, pp. 89–115.

France, R. T., 2007, *The Gospel of Matthew*, The New International Commentary on the New Testament, Grand Rapids: Eerdmans.

Francis, Leslie J., 2005, *Faith and Psychology: Personality, Religion and the Individual*, London: Darton, Longman & Todd.

Francis, Leslie J. and Village, Andrew, 2008, *Preaching with all our Souls: A Study in Hermeneutics and Psychological Type*, London: Continuum.

Fuller, Reginald H., 1957, *Liturgical Preaching*, London: SCM.

Gadamer, Hans-Georg, 2004, *Truth and Method*, 2nd edn, trans. Weinsheimer, J. and Marshall, D. G., London and New York: Continuum.

Gibbs, Eddie and Bolger, Ryan, 2006, *Emerging Churches: Creating Christian Communities in Postmodern Cultures*, London: SPCK.

Goldsmith, Malcolm and Wharton, Martin, 1993, *Knowing Me, Knowing You: Exploring Personality Type and Temperament*, London: SPCK.

Graves, Mike, 1997, *The Sermon as Symphony: Preaching the Literary Forms of the New Testament*, Valley Forge, PA: Judson Press.

Graves, Mike, 2006, *The Fully Alive Preacher: Recovering from Homiletical Burnout*, Louisville: Westminster John Knox.

Graves, Mike and Schlafer, David (eds), 2008, *What's the Shape of Narrative Preaching?*, St Louis: Chalice Press.

Green, Garrett, 2000, *Theology, Hermeneutics and Imagination: The Crisis of Interpretation at the end of Modernity*, Cambridge: Cambridge University Press.

Gunton, Colin E., 1995, *A Brief Theology of Revelation*, Edinburgh: T & T Clark.

Härtner, Achim and Eschmann, Holger, 2004, *Learning to Preach Today: A Guide for Communicators and Listeners*, Sheffield: Cliff College.

Hilkert, Mary Katherine, 1997, *Naming Grace: Preaching and the Sacramental Imagination*, New York: Continuum.

Hipps, Shane, 2005, *The Hidden Power of Electronic Culture: How Media Shapes Faith, the Gospel and Church*, El Cajon, CA: Youth Specialities.

Hipps, Shane, 2009, *Flickering Pixels: How Technology Shapes your Faith*, Grand Rapids: Zondervan.

Hustler, Jonathan, 2009, *Making the Words Acceptable: the Shape of the Sermon in Christian History*, London: Epworth.

Hutchinson, F. E. (ed.), 1941, *The Works of George Herbert*, Oxford: Clarendon Press.

Jencks, Charles, 1996, *What is Post-Modernism?*, 4th edn, London: Academy Editions.

Jenkins, Gary, 2010, 'The Influence of Simeon and Stott on Evangelical Anglican Preaching in the Church of England', unpublished MTh dissertation, London: Spurgeon's College/University of Wales.

Jensen, Richard A., *Thinking in Story: Preaching in a Post-Literate Age*, Lima, OH: CSS Publications.

Kay, James F., 2007, *Preaching and Theology*, St Louis: Chalice Press.

Lalleman, Hetty, 2004, *Celebrating the Law?: Rethinking Old Testament Ethics*, Carlisle: Paternoster.

Littledale, Richard, 2007, *Stale Bread: Refreshing a Preaching Ministry*, Edinburgh: St Andrew Press.

Long, Thomas G. and Tisdale, Leonora Tubbs (eds), 2008, *Teaching Preaching as a Christian Practice*, Louisville: Westminster John Knox.

Long, Thomas G., 1989, *Preaching and the Literary Forms of the Bible*, Philadelphia: Fortress.

Long, Thomas G., 2005, 'The Use of Scripture in Contemporary Preaching', in Day, David et al. (eds), *A Reader on Preaching: Making Connections*, Aldershot: Ashgate, pp. 34–42.

Long, Thomas G., 2005, *The Witness of Preaching*, 2nd edn, Louisville: Westminster John Knox.

Long, Thomas G., 2008, 'Out of the Loop: The Changing Practice of Preaching', in Graves, Mike and Schlafer, David (eds), *What's the Shape of Narrative Preaching?*, St Louis: Chalice Press, pp. 115–30.

Lowry, Eugene L., 1985, *Doing Time in the Pulpit: The Relationship between Narrative and Preaching*, Nashville: Abingdon.

Lowry, Eugene L., 1989, *How to Preach a Parable: Designs for Narrative Sermons*, Nashville: Abingdon.

Lowry, Eugene L., 1997, *The Sermon: Dancing the Edge of Mystery*, Nashville: Abingdon.

Lowry, Eugene L., 2001, *The Homiletical Plot: The Sermon as Narrative Art Form*, expanded edn, Louisville: Westminster John Knox.

Maclaren, Duncan, 2004, *Mission Implausible: Restoring Credibility to the Church*, Carlisle: Paternoster.

Macpherson, Duncan, 2010, 'Preaching in the Roman Catholic Ecclesial Context', in Stevenson, Geoffrey (ed.), *The Future of Preaching*, London: SCM, pp. 27–33.

Marshall, I. Howard, 2004, *Beyond the Bible: Moving from Scripture to Theology*, Grand Rapids/Milton Keynes: Baker/Paternoster.

Martyn, J. Louis, 1997, *Galatians*, Anchor Bible 33A, New York: Doubleday.

McClain, William, 2008, 'African American Contexts of Narrative Preaching', in Graves, Mike and Schlafer, David (eds), *What's the Shape of Narrative Preaching?*, St Louis: Chalice Press, pp. 55–66.

McClure, John, 1996, *The Roundtable Pulpit: Where Preaching and Leadership Meet*, Nashville: Abingdon.

McClure, John, 2001, *Other-wise Preaching: A Postmodern Ethic for Homiletics*, St Louis: Chalice Press.

McGuinness, Julia, 2009, *Growing Spiritually with the Myers-Briggs Model*, London: SPCK.

Middleton, J. Richard, 2005, *The Liberating Image: The* Imago Dei *in Genesis 1*, Grand Rapids: Brazos.

Milavec, Aaron A., 1989, 'A Fresh Analysis of the Parable of the Wicked Husbandmen in the Light of Jewish-Catholic Dialogue', in Thoma, Clemens and Wyschogrod, Michael (eds), *Parable and Story in Judaism and Christianity*, New York: Paulist Press, pp. 81–117.

Mitchell, Henry H., 1991, *Black Preaching: The Recovery of a Powerful Art*, Nashville: Abingdon.

Mitchell, Jolyon P., 1999, *Visually Speaking: Radio and the Renaissance of Preaching*, Edinburgh: T & T Clark.

Morgan, Robert, 1998, 'The Bible and Christian Theology', in Barton, John (ed.), *The Cambridge Companion to Biblical Interpretation*, Cambridge: Cambridge University Press, pp. 114–28.

Murray, Stuart, 'Interactive Preaching', *Evangel* 72 (Summer 1999), pp. 53–7.

Murray, Stuart, 2000, *Biblical Interpretation in the Anabaptist Tradition*, Kitchener, Ontario: Pandora Press.

Newbigin, Lesslie, 1989, *The Gospel in a Pluralist Society*, London: SPCK.

Niebuhr, H. Richard, 1951, *Christ and Culture*, New York: Harper & Row.

Norén, Carol M., 1992, 'The Word of God in Worship: Preaching in Relationship to Liturgy', in Jones, Cheslyn et al. (eds), *The Study of Liturgy*, rev. edn, London: SPCK.

Norrington, David C., 1996, *To Preach or Not to Preach?*, Carlisle: Paternoster.

O'Day, Gail R., 1993, 'Toward a Biblical Theology of Preaching', in O'Day, Gail R. and Long, Thomas G. (eds), *Listening to the Word: Studies in Honour of Fred B. Craddock*, Nashville: Abingdon, pp. 17–32.

Old, Hughes Oliphant, 1998, *The Reading and Preaching of the Scriptures in the Worship of the Christian Church*, 6 vols, vol. 1: *The Biblical Period*, Grand Rapids: Eerdmans.

Ong, Walter J., 2002, *Orality and Literacy*, 2nd edn, London: Routledge.

Osmer, Richard R., 2008, *Practical Theology: An Introduction*, Grand Rapids: Eerdmans.

Pagitt, Doug, 2005, *Preaching Re-Imagined: The Role of the Sermon in Communities of Faith*, Grand Rapids: Zondervan.

Pasquarello III, Michael, 2005, *Sacred Rhetoric: Preaching as a Theological and Pastoral Practice of the Church*, Grand Rapids: Eerdmans.

Pasquarello III, Michael, 2006, *Christian Preaching: A Trinitarian Theology of Proclamation*, Grand Rapids: Baker Academic.

Paton, Ian, 2004, 'Preaching in Worship', in Hunter, Geoffrey et al. (eds), *A Preacher's Companion: Essays from the College of Preachers*, Oxford: Bible Reading Fellowship.

Pitt, Trevor, 2010, 'The Conversation of Preaching and Theology', in Stevenson, Geoffrey (ed.), *The Future of Preaching*, London: SCM, pp. 65–83.

Postman, Neil, 2006, *Amusing Ourselves to Death: Public Discourse in the Age of Showbusiness*, 2nd edn, London: Penguin.

Quicke, Michael J., 2005, 'The Scriptures in Preaching', in Ballard, Paul and Holmes, Stephen R. (eds), *The Bible in Pastoral Practice*, London: Darton, Longman & Todd, pp. 241–57.

Quicke, Michael J., 2003, *360-Degree Preaching: Hearing, Speaking and Living the Word*, Grand Rapids: Baker.

Quicke, Michael J., 2006, *360-Degree Leadership: Preaching to Transform Congregations*, Grand Rapids: Baker.

Resner Jr, André, 1999, *Preacher and Cross: Person and Message in Theology and Rhetoric*, Grand Rapids: Eerdmans.

Ricks, Christopher (ed.), 1969, *The Poems of Tennyson*, London: Longman.

Rogers, Andrew, 2007, 'Reading Scripture in Congregations: Towards an Ordinary Hermeneutics', in Walker, Andrew and Bretherton, Luke (eds), 2007, *Remembering our Future: Explorations in Deep Church*, Milton Keynes: Paternoster, pp. 81–107.

Rowe, Arthur, 1999, 'Preaching and Teaching', *Evangel* 17.2, pp. 48–50.

Sanders, James A., 1987, *From Sacred Story to Sacred Text: Canon as Paradigm*, Philadelphia: Fortress.

Saunders, Stanley P. and Campbell, Charles L., 2000, *The Word on the Street: Performing the Scriptures in an Urban Context*, Grand Rapids: Eerdmans.

de Saussure, Ferdinand, 1977, *Course in General Linguistics*, trans. Baskin, Wade, Glasgow: Fontana.

Schlafer, David J., 1992, *Surviving the Sermon: A Guide for those who have to Listen*, Cambridge, MA: Cowley.

Schlafer, David J., 1995, *Your Way with God's Word: Discovering Your Distinctive Preaching Voice*, Cambridge, MA: Cowley.

Schlafer, David J., 2004, *Playing with Fire: Preaching Work as Kindling Art*, Cambridge, MA: Cowley.

Schüssler-Fiorenza, Elisabeth, 1992, *In Memory of Her: A Feminist Theological Reconstruction of Christian Origins*, New York: Crossway.

Selby, Peter, 2009, *Grace and Mortgage: The Language of Grace and the Debt of the World*, 2nd edn, London: Darton, Longman & Todd.

Sheard, Daniel W., 2005, 'Preaching in the Hear and Now: Justification, Development, and Assessment of 'Parabolic Engagement' Pedagogy in French-Speaking Missionary Settings', unpublished PhD thesis, University of Wales.

Smyth, Charles, 1940, *The Art of Preaching: Preaching in the Church of England 747–1939*, London: SPCK.

Spiller, Roger, 2010, 'Preaching and Liturgy: An Anglican Perspective', in Stevenson, Geoffrey (ed.), 2010, *The Future of Preaching*, London: SCM, pp. 34–41.

Stackhouse, Ian G., 2004, *The Gospel-Driven Church: Retrieving Classical Ministry for Contemporary Revivalism*, Milton Keynes: Paternoster.

Standing, Roger, 2004, *Finding the Plot: Preaching in Narrative Style*, Milton Keynes: Paternoster.

Standing, Roger, 2010, 'Mediated Preaching: Homiletics in Contemporary British Culture', in Stevenson, Geoffrey (ed.), *The Future of Preaching*, London: SCM, pp. 9–26.

Stanton, Nicky, 2004, *Mastering Communication*, 4th edn, London: Palgrave Macmillan.

Stern, Philip, 1993, 'Torah', in Metzger, Bruce M. and Coogan, Michael D. (eds), *The Oxford Companion to the Bible*, Oxford: Oxford University Press, pp. 747–8.

Stevenson, Geoffrey and Wright, Stephen, 2008, *Preaching with Humanity: A Practical Guide for Today's Church*, London: Church House Publishing.

Stevenson, Peter K., 2007, 'The Preacher as Poet', *Ministry Today* 41, pp. 29–38.

Stevenson, Peter K. and Wright, Stephen I., 2010, *Preaching the Incarnation*, Louisville: Westminster John Knox.

Stott, John R. W., 1982, *I Believe in Preaching*, London: Hodder & Stoughton.

Stratford, Tim, 1998, *Interactive Preaching: Opening the Word then Listening*, Cambridge: Grove.

Tannen, Deborah, 1998, *The Argument Culture: Changing the Way we Argue and Debate*, London: Virago.

Thomson, Jeremy, 1996, *Preaching as Dialogue: Is the Sermon a Sacred Cow?*, Cambridge: Grove.

Tisdale, Leonora Tubbs, 1997, *Preaching as Local Theology and Folk Art*, Minneapolis: Fortress.

Tomlinson, Dave, 2008, *Re-enchanting Christianity: Faith in an Emerging Culture*, Norwich: Canterbury Press.

Van Dyk, Leanne, 2009, 'The Church's Proclamation as a Participation in God's Mission', in Treier, Daniel J. and Lauber, David (eds), *Trinitarian Theology for the Church: Scripture, Community, Worship*, Downers Grove, IL/Nottingham: InterVarsity Press Academic/Apollos, pp. 225–36.

Van Harn, Roger E., 1992, *Pew Rights: For People who Listen to Sermons*, Grand Rapids: Eerdmans.

Van Harn, Roger E., 2005, *Preacher, Can You Hear Us Listening?*, Grand Rapids: Eerdmans.

Van Seters, Arthur (ed.), 1988, *Preaching as a Social Act: Theology and Practice*, Nashville: Abingdon.

Vanhoozer, Kevin J., 1998, *Is there a Meaning in this Text?: The Bible, the Reader and the Morality of Literary Knowledge*, Leicester: Apollos.

Vanhoozer, Kevin J. (ed.), 2005, *Dictionary for Theological Interpretation of the Bible*, Grand Rapids/London: Baker/SPCK.

Village, Andrew, 2007, *The Bible and Lay People: An Empirical Approach to Ordinary Hermeneutics*, Aldershot: Ashgate.

Walker, Andrew, 1996, *Telling the Story*, London: SPCK.

Walker, Andrew and Bretherton, Luke (eds), 2007, *Remembering our Future: Explorations in Deep Church*, Milton Keynes: Paternoster.

Walton, Heather and Durber, Susan (eds), 1994, *Silence in Heaven: A Book of Women's Preaching*, London: SCM.

Walton, Roger, 2003, 'Using the Bible and Christian Tradition in Theological Reflection', *British Journal of Theological Education* 13.2, pp. 133–51.

Ward, Keith, 2004, *What the Bible Really Teaches: A Challenge to Fundamentalists*, London: SPCK.

Watts, Angela P., 2008, 'A Theological Reflection upon the Principle and Practice of Preaching for a Decision', unpublished MTh dissertation, London: Spurgeon's College/University of Wales.

Webb, Joseph M., 2001, *Preaching without Notes*, Nashville: Abingdon.

Webb, Joseph M., 2008, 'Without Notes', in Wilson, Paul Scott (ed.), *The New Interpreter's Handbook of Preaching*, Nashville: Abingdon, pp. 429–31.

Webber, Robert E., 2008, *Ancient-Future Worship: Proclaiming and Enacting God's Narrative*, Grand Rapids: Baker.

Wells, Samuel, 2004, *Improvisation: The Drama of Christian Ethics*, London: SPCK.

Westermann, Claus, 1990, *The Parables of Jesus in the Light of the Old Testament*, Edinburgh: T & T Clark.

Whybray, R. N., 1993, 'Prophets – Ancient Israel', in Metzger, Bruce M. and Coogan, Michael D. (eds), *The Oxford Companion to the Bible*, Oxford: Oxford University Press, pp. 620–2.

Wilson, Paul Scott, 2001, *God Sense: Reading the Bible for Preaching*, Nashville: Abingdon.

Wilson, Paul Scott, 2004, *Preaching and Homiletical Theory*, St Louis: Chalice Press.

Wilson, Paul Scott, 1999, *The Four Pages of the Sermon: A Guide to Biblical Preaching*, Nashville: Abingdon.

Withers, Margaret, 2010, 'Preaching for All: Inclusivity and the Future of Preaching in All-age Worship', in Stevenson, Geoffrey (ed.), *The Future of Preaching*, London: SCM, pp. 115–29.

Wolff, Hans Walter, 1977, *Joel and Amos*, Hermeneia – A Critical and Historical Commentary on the Bible, Philadelphia: Fortress.

Woods, John D., 2008, 'Bearing Witness: The Homiletic Theory and Practice of Thomas G. Long', unpublished DMin thesis, University of Wales, Lampeter.

Wright, John W., 2007, *Telling God's Story: Narrative Preaching for Christian Formation*, Downers Grove, IL: InterVarsity Press Academic.

Wright, N. T., 1991, 'How Can the Bible be Authoritative', http://www.ntwrightpage.com/Wright_Bible_Authoritative.htm, originally published in *Vox Evangelica* 21, pp. 7–32.

Wright, N. T., 1996, *Jesus and the Victory of God*, London: SPCK.

Wright, Stephen I., 2000, *The Voice of Jesus: Studies in the Interpretation of Six Gospel Parables*, Carlisle: Paternoster.

Wright, Stephen I., 2004, 'Inhabiting the Story: The Use of the Bible in the Interpretation of History', in Bartholomew, Craig, et al. (eds), *'Behind' the Text: History and Biblical Interpretation*, Carlisle/Grand Rapids: Paternoster/Zondervan, pp. 492–519.

Wright, Stephen I., 2010, 'The Future Use of the Bible in Preaching', in Stevenson, Geoffrey (ed.), *The Future of Preaching*, London: SCM, pp. 84–100.

Young, Frances, 1990, *The Art of Performance: Towards a Theology of Holy Scripture*, London: Darton, Longman & Todd.

Zink-Sawyer, Beverly, 2008, 'A Match Made in Heaven: The Intersection of Gender and Narrative Preaching', in Graves, Mike and Schlafer, David J. (eds), *What's the Shape of Narrative Preaching?*, St Louis: Chalice Press, pp. 41–53.

Webliography

http://www.anabaptistnetwork.com
http://www.anlp.org/
http://www.businessballs.com/transact.htm

Index of Names and Subjects

Index of Biblical References

OLD TESTAMENT

APOCRYPHA

NEW TESTAMENT